"AND CROWN THY GOOD WITH BROTHERHOOD":

On the Imagination of Fraternity

Paul Hamill

For Kristin
and the brothers and sisters
Paul, Stephen, Rachel,
Matt, Kate and Brendan

TABLE OF CONTENTS

4 Introduction: A Window on MLK Street

I: The Varieties of Fraternal Experience
17. Chapter 1. "Brotherhood" vs "Fraternity"
43. Chapter 2. Brotherhood Despite History
64. Chapter 3. The *Eros* of Common Pursuit
90. Chapter 4. Two Ancient Models
108. Chapter 5. The Crowd and the Vigil

II: The Poetry and Paradoxes of Fraternity
127. Chapter 6. The Mutual Dynamic of Rights and Fraternity
157. Chapter 7. Sentimental Tactics: Shaftesbury's Chapter Headings
177. Chapter 8. Poetic Nightmares and the Paradoxes of Fraternity
189. Chapter 9. The Light of American Firesides
224. Chapter 10. Walt Whitman Re-starts Himself
244. Chapter 11. *Non decor*: Notes on Modern American Poets

III: The Twin Themes of the American Third Sector
257. Chapter 12. *Bowling Alone* in Romania
271. Chapter 13. Forming "Capacity to Act"
315. Chapter 14. Networks and Partnerships
335. Chapter 15. The Grand Bazaar and the Public of Many Publics
348. Footnotes
364. List of Works Cited

Introduction: A Window on MLK Boulevard

I was walking down Martin Luther King Street in the college town I worked in—the street that used to be State Street, a change I thought a good omen for my topic—when I passed the county historical society. I saw in the window an excerpt from the United Nation's Universal Declaration of Human Rights, which said:

All human beings are born free and equal in dignity and rights. They are endowed with reason and should act towards one another in a spirit of brotherhood.

I had long been interested in ideas of human brotherhood, and in experiences that participants call brother- or sisterhood in movements and organizations. Brotherhood (including sisterhood) is almost beaten to death in sermons and social advice. yet the history of the idea is largely unwritten—perhaps because the topic seems simple, requiring not so much explanation as persuasions to avoid selfishness and conflict. My interest started with youthful participation in church groups and then social movements, sharing the generous emotions which sometimes alternated with anger, frustration, jealousies and doubts. In these societies, a "spirit of brotherhood" flowered and sometimes a surging confidence. Patient stubborn loyalty sustained the committees and splinter movements until, if successful, the spirit of their organizations expanded to wider populations.

A few of the flowerings I saw, e.g. in the U.S. civil rights era, cast light on other outbreaks of fraternal passion in history. These outbreaks marked the beginnings or ends of wars, revolutions, and other great social commotions. We often fail to see them as part of the continuum of experiences observable in smaller or quieter communities, but an assumption behind this book is that small and large fraternities illuminate each other. When we do see the continuities of small to large (and from routine brotherhoods to more frantic experiences) we discern as well that the commanding ideas sometimes change in those translations, posing new problems in the realm of meaning as well as in the realms of action, for fraternities small and large constantly interpret themselves.

Over time, the question of fraternity—"what kind of brother- or sisterhood do we have here?"—became my kaleidoscope. The same vivid geometries of relationship shone through groups as varied as sports teams, bureaucratic committees, fund raising campaigns, arts workshops, and sometimes classrooms. This was merely my way of organizing the myriad social relations that any adult may observe over time: my special interest was less in the structures of power or status in groups than in the passionate imagination of self and mutual bonds that sometimes emerged. Taking the humble and grand cases of fraternity together, it became clear that "brotherhood" can be an ethical or religious principle, a deep yearning, an exhilarating (or frightening) discovery, a steady relationship within a community—or all of these at once, for different individuals. Each of these dimensions involves an imaginative extension from a principle or experience encountered in a small group—say, a family or a platoon—to a general ideal involving a vision of a much larger human group, a tribe or sect or nation or perhaps all humankind.

As I say, the window on a street named MLK set me on the trail again. *Spirit of brotherhood!* What a set of questions the little museum window display raised! To start with, the most basic question: why are human rights connected with the idea—more exactly, with the *spirit*—of brotherhood? We touch on that issue in several chapters below but must grapple from the first with the fact that most of our conflicts are also based on loyalties that participants may call fraternal. We might distinguish good and bad fraternities but that does not take us far in understanding the desire nor the experiences involved. That is why the question of how communities, movements, and cultures have *imagined* fraternity is a useful one. Imagination—in this case, the great metaphor of brotherhood, overlaid onto many different relationships, is how humans organize those relationships as embodying of one desire, one principle, one kind of commitment.

"Fraternity" became central to modern political history in the revolutionary period initiated by the French Revolution, which seared into historical memory the two faces, which sometimes have been two stages, of fraternal outbursts in history: on one hand, the festival air of liberation, of hearts and hands joined across the barriers of social class; on the other hand, the same loosed energies erupting into mob savagery, terror, and eventual tyranny. Even amidst exhilaration, the idea encompassed a range of different understandings: national solidarity based on a new hope for equality was certainly primary, but it was affirmed in connection with universal rights and implied both national and international community based on universal rights. The grand combined vision of a fraternal nation and universal brotherhood, an offspring of the utopian rationality of the Enlightenment, was mixed from the first with conflicting regional and class loyalties and savage factions, lesser brotherhoods.

The fraternity theme has rippled through the politics of the centuries since, appealing to workers oppressed by capital, to colonies oppressed by empires. It is an inherent dimension of nationalism, often the heart of appeals for mutual tolerance among citizens but just as often central to nativist rhetoric against international forces, foreign immigrants, or domestic minorities. Over more than two centuries since the French declared their slogan, experiments with new means of fraternity were at the center of utopian dreams but also part of slowly realized national and international mechanisms for cooperation, mutual aid, and dispute resolution. The modern centuries have seen, and sometimes warred over, different versions of the ideal

Even before pursuing the twists and colors of our topic, it might be well to begin by recognizing the surprising power of the ideal of universal brotherhood over several centuries, for the evidence of feasibility has never been encouraging. Over the decades when I stopped for my newspaper at the news stand down MLK Street the headlines announced the bitter ethnic fracturing of the former Russian empire, warfare in the Balkans, genocide in several parts of Africa, numerous wars. involving Americans, and numerous appalling acts of terrorism. The press has also described the U.S. as a nation of increasingly sharp differences in wealth among citizens, where jails house disproportionate numbers of black men, and immigration—historically a human flow of millions each year, legal and illegal, entering the ambiguities of American national fraternity—is at the center of bitter political turmoil. Yet neither the UN nor the little historical society is a church, holding out ideals that we don't expect to see realized in this life. Their supporters would claim that the goal of acting in a spirit of brotherhood, while certainly an ideal, is also a mandate born of long historical experience in which war and injustices that affect distant neighbors affect the rest of us sooner or later. That is one of the simple lessons of modern history, although what follows from it is complicated.

The fraternity theme in political history from the Enlightenment onward was driven has two interrelated subthemes: discovery of the full humanity of the commons, including the poorest, and discovery of their capacity for full participation in government. These are extremely broad concepts (and hardly new to point out), but they implied new images of human social bonds in general as well as new ideas about the bonds and implicit contracts underlying social hierarchies and governments. They had and still have deep implications for fraternity, whether under the guise of rights or under the rubric of neighborliness.

Fraternities in individual experience are endlessly variable in the sense that we sustain social relationships differently at different times. However, since it is imagination that strives for coherence by bringing disparate experiences together, focusing in these pages on the *imagination* of fraternity—the underlying idea is primitively familiar—helps us to trace a few coherent strands through the multi-sided topic. From the Revolutionary era onward, passionate versions of national, ethnic, or world brotherhood have been driving motives for some political leaders but also have preoccupied great artists and social visionaries, so that literary examples, a few of which we explore in the central section of this book, tell a good deal about the power and complexity of the ideal. And finally, since daily civic life in modern democracies displays many appeals for a spirit of brotherhood, we explore that realm to highlight the underlying imagination of fraternity.

Any general idea may be used "kaleidoscopically" in the sense that it can be applied to hundreds of instances that demonstrate its reach or test its limits. But when it comes to grand human ideals like the French revolutionary triad of liberty, equality, and fraternity the interaction between idea and experience is dynamic. These grand ideas are aspirations as well as philosophical guides. Like other desires they feed on memory, on social habits, and on pictures of the ideal to be achieved, supplemented by vivid memories of failures. When individuals experiment with a grand ideal, they reveal themselves to each other and often are changed by their experience: new social relations emerge along with new understanding of the ideal itself. The flowering self-interpretation that occurs in experiments with a grand ideal is especially dramatic in the case of fraternity because it is a drawing closer rather than a distancing from others or a balancing of claims, which both liberty and equality can involve. If *action* in the spirit of brotherhood is the essential challenge, strengthening the imagination of mutual bonds across social or physical distances while organizing practically for cooperation are the two sides of that challenge.

Although thousands of sermons have addressed the theme of brotherhood, and thousands of enthralling stories of ship's crews and platoons have been told, as have innumerable accounts of political and religious movements, scholarly and historical literature on fraternity as an ideal rippling through modern history is surprisingly thin. In preparing this book, three sources—all three focused mainly on American experience—have been suggestive for my project.

The first source is a short chapter by T.V. Smith, a political scientist and popular lecturer of the post-World War II era, who described the "American Way of Life" in terms of the three great "motifs" of the French slogan:

> Perennially there arise in the dreams of men these three goals: liberty, equality, fraternity. And the greatest of these is fraternity.[1]

Smith's statement recognizes that the element of dream inherent in fraternity makes it in a sense more primitive and fiercer than the other two. He goes so far as to associate its instinctive pull with the infant's desire for return to mother's bosom in perfect acceptance and security. Smith's statement emphasizes the heroic and poetic dimension that a social scientist might acknowledge but then set aside as immeasurable. Smith's notion that fraternity, like the other grand ideals, is a *motif* is useful because many reform movements and upheavals for societal change are colored by intense comradeship that fades as the movement's purposes are embodied in the dispassion of laws or institutions. The motif of fraternity that blazed in the movement may live to a degree in memory and may be possible to awaken if those reforms need defense. At a simpler level, community ceremonies of all sorts make neighborliness and mutual respect a conventional part of their rhetoric of the moment, a reminder that colors the main purpose.

The second especially useful source for my purposes is WC McWilliams magisterial *The Idea of Fraternity in America* (1973). Written by a sociologist with a history of progressive activism and in the optimistic light of the Civil Rights movement, the book sets a sociological framework but primarily offers an intellectual history in which a wide range of thinkers are seen as contributors to a dialogue on national fraternity, a dialogue so comprehensive that Calvinist views of human sinfulness, the constitutional theories of the Founding Fathers, Melville and Hawthorne's novels, utopian dreamers, and philosophic pragmatists are engaged, up to the then current proponents of Black Power. In effect, McWilliams was trying to define an American political idealism that could be active in reforms for social justice and toleration to benefit the whole. McWilliams defines fraternity by seven criteria that constitute an ideal fraternity, e.g. "It includes a recognition of shortcomings and failure in the attainment of ultimate values...."[2] Although McWillams judges his sources as offering what he considers better and worse versions of the ideal, he explores and judges his sources without imposing a rigid standard.

The third source I have found especially useful, and to which I refer mainly in the third part of this book, is Robert Putnam's *Bowling Alone: The Collapse and Revival of American Community* (1997), which bewails declines in Americans' community associations of all sorts, from informal neighborhood barbecue to PTA and NAACP memberships. This web of interactions taken altogether is "social capital," the wealth of associations that citizens draw upon to act together. Putnam recalls the French revolutionary slogan and says that social capital is the same thing as fraternity: "Fraternity, as the French democrats intended it, was another name for what I call 'social capital'"[3] One cannot imagine the revolutionary mounting his barricade to shout *le capital sociale!* but Putnam is surely right in seeing that the mostly humdrum associations of civic life are the bedrock of fraternity in communities from year to year. What "social capital" cannot measure is the passion and occasionally heroic self-imagination of the community, nor that part of fraternity that reaches beyond the community in generous human recognition of need or in support of peace.

Over the last three decades, the neglected topic of fraternity has begun to attract increased attention in Europe and Latin America. The Focolare movement, started by a saintly Catholic lay activist, Chiara Lubich (1920-2008), is primarily active in Europe: one of its aims is to transfer wisdom about community drawn from religious experience into strategies for secular political unity for justice and peace. This movement led Antonio Baggio, an Italian philosopher, to write about fraternity as the "forgotten principle" of the French Revolution[4]. He and his collaborators sketch some immediate roots of the newly politicized idea in pre-revolutionary France, some later implications (e.g. in the Haitian Revolution and in France in 1848); and some theological, legal and international political implications. This book, unfortunately not yet translated into English, triggered an ongoing collaborative project, mainly by Latin American scholars, whose conferences and articles have involved community activists and political leaders along with the scholars, exploring theory and social initiatives together under the rubric of fraternity[5]. As we examine some typical experiences and imaginative discoveries related to fraternity in the following pages, it should also become clear why theoretic exploration and dialogue about ongoing collective challenges are a productive combination, not necessarily the case with other abstract principles.

Let me outline, briefly, the sections of this book. They approach fraternity in three different styles. I do not offer a history of the fraternity idea, except for a few glimpses of that vast topic, but for the reader who has not encountered the topic, this book might serve as a primer. Section I, "The Varieties of Fraternal Experience" explores how basic ideas of fraternity arise from familiar kinds of experience. I treat "brotherhood" as a metaphor that is extended to tribes or nations that claim a blood bond, but then also to the bonds of groups that share a limited purpose, whether in clubs or revolutions. A third source of fraternal experience is direct appreciation of others as human, which it is convenient and not inaccurate to call humanism, respect for humans as such, Chapters in this section sketch "true believers"; two dialogues by Plato and the Apostle John offer a glimpse of fraternities around an idea or doctrine; and a brief chapter considers crowds.

The great flowering of fraternity as a political theme and simultaneously as a central concern in artistic imagination occurred in the Enlightenment and especially the Romantic era. Section II offers a thumbnail history of modern fraternity as an ideal arising from the broad intellectual currents of the previous centuries and tries to explain why the theme closely tracks ideas of human rights. Chapters in this section turn to a few English and American writers who struggled with the complexity of fraternity as an ideal with new political implications. "Sentimental Tactics" sees Enlightenment sentimentalism, especially as rooted in day-to-day civic interactions, offering strategies for ethical leaders in the emerging era of democracy. A chapter on English Romantic poets describes the "paradox of fraternity," the nightmarish opening to fear of wasted life that some writers, idealists about human nature, experienced as they faced the squalor of their cities. Americans writers did not often deal with lower class misery until the later nineteenth century, but the

"Fireside Poets" highlighted modest prosperity and domestic virtues as grounds for American national bonds that could also reflect universal principles. A chapter on Walt Whitman describes him as a preacher, struggling with contradictions that preachers of universal love inevitably encounter. Finally, a brief chapter touches on American moderns who defended modernist aesthetic distance but see defense of human rights as central to their vocation. This section of the book is not a survey of the vast topic but a selection of case studies, with a largely American slant.

Section III turns to what may seem a very different realm of discourse. Recognizing that fraternity in daily interactions is expressed in civic culture and that civic culture is often expressed in voluntary associations, I reflect on a few ways in which the third (or "non-profit") sector was a factor in American history. I suggest that American experience offers models and cautions for the world "spirit of brotherhood," because Americans did not have a tribal myth to build on, and because from World War II to the present, American models shaped much of the world system.

Two competing notions of fraternity in the political dimension popped up in the news while this manuscript was being completed. At Christmas time 2018, Pope Francis 1 delivered his annual blessing, as always wishing for peace on earth to men of goodwill. He said that what he wished for the world was "fraternity," complaining that it seemed to be declining. This was one of the few times in recent years when a world figure has used the term, exactly accurate for the mixture of legal, institutional, political, and charitable relations that fraternity today implies. A *New York Times* article[6] on the blessing noted that Francis has had special concern for the world's refugees, and that his message was a rebuke to those predominantly Christian nations, many of them Catholic, that resist refugees on the grounds that they are defending their Christian heritage.

The Pope's use of "fraternity" tells us that the meaning of fraternity has broadened and become more concrete as a world ideal. In the case of refugees, now estimated to number over 180 million worldwide, desperate needs are addressed by agencies and initiatives that represent modern realization of an international "spirit of brotherhood" as far as it exists. In this process, laws and protocols declare principles and legal obligations but a complex realm of organizations must act on these. Especially in response to crises, intergovernmental agencies (IGO's), non-state actors (NGOs), and generous communities of citizens, tolerant hosts or donors, collaborate. The various world responses to refugee crises, natural disasters and epidemics represent a many-sided, always partly improvised responsiveness to human crises in many regions of the world. The mixture of actors is impressive and yet often rather invisible within each contributing society. An effort to recognize the nature of this multi-sided, responsive system and habit of brotherhood is one aim of the last section of this book, in which I describe the American Third Sector and some of the publics that the sector represents.

Illustrating an opposite pole of fraternity as a political ideal, in June 2019, Russian President Vladimir Putin gave an extensive interview to editors of the London-based *Financial Times*[7] while attending a G20 summit. In the extensive interview, he defined populism as the political wave of the future and dismissed the political tradition of liberalism. Without opening the complicated subjects of populism or liberalism in detail, it is useful for our topic to recognize that populism builds on, intensifies, and in fact identifies itself by the powerful ethnic or cultural fraternity shared by its adherents. Liberalism, in whatever form, generally appeals to a theory of universal rights, and adjusts the claims of national, racial, or cultural fraternity accordingly. However, in the ideal case this is not mere compromise among claims: mutual defense of rights is seen as the fundamental source of fraternity within and beyond the nation. As we note in chapters below, the usual history of fraternity in political conflicts is not that one powerful person stands against the brotherhood of the many, although that has happened, but that societal segments asserting the claims of their special brotherhoods are at odds. The fraternity of populists may be that of a sect or class but may support that class's claim to be the essential part of the whole nation, or to embody the spiritual unity of a people extending beyond national borders, e.g. of ethnic Russians. (Putin bewailed the plight of 20 million Russians divided from present-day Russia when the Soviet Union splintered.)

Populists resist dilution from outsiders to their group (i.e. from immigrants or forces of globalization) and are often intolerant of dissent or difference within their ranks when these undermine tradition and therefore the shared identity. Populism is often an initiative against elites or colonial remnants in national life and for that reason may work important democratic reforms, but its central instinct is to defend against the unfamiliar: religious currents, new economic challenges, or an influx of strangers. As an early example, American populism as it arose in the 1890's expressed the interests of farmers, uniting to resist exploitation in the new industrial and urbanizing society just as the rural population ceased to be the American majority. Although they eventually allied with labor unions, anti-monopolists, and urban reformers under the banner of Progressivism, Populists were typically isolationist, somewhat more racist than the times, and often anti-Catholic and anti-Semitic.

Putin's interview touches on Trump's slogan, "America First," affirming that of course Putin is for Russia first, but implying that the slogan (which in American history was a code phrase for isolationism) tells him little. For populists, the issue is not whether one's own community is to be served and valued as a paramount loyalty—which any citizen might feel and claim—but that the populist has a special intimacy with the national soul and has rushed to its defense (or to the defense of his class or region, in different versions of populism). Militantly secure in this identity, untroubled by reflection, he grows aggressive toward migrants, international neighbors, minorities, and so on. It is also true that populist movements tend to highlight heroic leaders who embody the quintessential culture and the irresistibly confident power of the people: Mr. Putin's well-advertised athleticism and physical swagger fit that pattern. Significantly, Putin passes quickly in his *London Times* interview to the desirability of international commercial structures and renewal of arms agreements that from a broad view represent the pragmatic fraternity of nations developed over the post-World War Two era; he regrets Mr. Trump's withdrawals from such agreements. In sum, he is populist in his view of national domestic politics but wants globalized commercial and arms arrangements.

It is not the task of this book to analyze current trends such as populism nor problems of refugees. It is also not the goal to analyze fraternity as a potential principle in law nor to explore its philosophic grounds. Rather, I aim to trace some ways in which experiences and ideals of fraternity have fed each other, expanding our ability to imagine the ideal and its place in our societies.

I have tried to write for the general reader, footnoting far more lightly than is fair to scholars who have examined the many issues that I touch on here. Most of the experiences and events that I discuss are widely familiar, but the context of an ultimately politically ideal of the "spirit of brotherhood" has not received the attention it deserves.

Section I: The Varieties of Fraternal Experience.

Chapter 1. "Brotherhood" vs "Fraternity"

"Brotherhood" seems instantly understandable because we grow up in families, but what it implies when extended beyond families is often a tangle. The call for a *spirit* of brotherhood that I saw on a library window seems to say that something like familial responsiveness to others should be extended far beyond our families and that the extension will feel quite natural when it occurs. The phrase stands for an aspiration to be just and helpful, for if we act in a "spirit" we affirm values of our own that others also feel on some occasion.

In family life most of us learn a very general, innately generous responsibility toward other family members. By instinct as well as by parental and societal indoctrination, we absorb ideal versions of that open-ended responsibility and intimacy even if our personal family experience is mixed. Acting on responsibilities to family members is usually a gift to them as well as obedience to an obligation, because those responsibilities are both unconditional and undefined. At the heart of that familial interdependence is the role of parents, who—again, ideally—try to provide whatever a child needs to grow into an adult who is healthy in all ways, including social behavior: their commitment is not a well-defined contract, nor is it ever perfectly carried out. A phrase I once heard an embattled Lebanese militiaman say on TV I have also heard from Italian- and Irish-descended friends in the schoolyards of my childhood: "Me against my brother, but us against the world." The claim of brotherhood here does not imply day-to-day friendship or lack of mutual conflict, although friendship makes fulfilling the obligation easier. Brotherhood here means a commitment given ahead of the occasion, a commitment like true friendship except that some of friendship's mutual delight may be lacking. The commitment is as broad as the range of the world's possible inflictions. The U.N.'s call for the "spirit" of brotherhood at first glance stands against that narrow fierce sort of loyalty to immediate kin or tribe against the rest, but it has this resemblance: it asks for a broad, volunteered recognition of mutual responsibility that is capable of rising above even the bitter rivalries that brothers and nations sometimes engage in.

Although the obvious primary source of the rich resonance of familial ideas is found in infancy and childhood, amplified by instruction and social expectation, these ideas are not nostalgias though they have that element. They are worked at, sacrificed for, and enjoyed as primary purposes of life for many adults who take responsibility for each other and for children. Both the work and the pleasures of family bonds are easily taken for granted; they are mostly private, occasionally but invisibly heroic. Maturing youths often come to recognize in their parents the models that they wish to emulate (or avoid), and the young man or woman who dreams of a family imagines and eventually works at the ideal. As a result of this endless and continually refreshed engagement, words for intimate family relations and trusting friendships are almost mythical in their richness even before we turn them into explicit myths of Mother Russia or Mary the Blessed Mother or Das Vaterland.

To inject a personal perspective, when I imagine "brotherhood" drawing on memory for my pictures, it is not abstract. I find a mixture of images and of several styles of "brotherhood." I was born into an extended family of mostly second and third generation Irish immigrants living in and south of Boston, with a few ancient aunts and grandmothers. The immigrant generations came to the area because relatives and old-world neighbors were already there; they supported each other in life's crises and often were at the heart of each others' socializing, along with close neighbors and the parish. From this network I draw vivid memories of family in general and of my actual brothers and sister as well as cousins, aunts and uncles at parties, picnics, weddings, and funerals: a rich array of connections and human types. Alongside these memories I recall the usual reality of how mobility and marriages created physical and sometimes emotional distances. I also recall the frictions that come with family life, frictions that sometimes lasted for years without breaking individuals away from the clan to which after all they belonged by right: indeed, one of my brothers described a malady he called Irish Alzheimer's, "When you forget everything except your grudges." The term "brotherhood" raises these memories as images of human variety seen close, but with a general assurance of sympathy and connection, inherited rather than contracted for or earned.

In addition to the habitual familial and clan connections, however, I have memories of brother- and sisterhood with other adults in support of causes or in professional projects of some difficulty. The causes that different family members got involved in over the years sometimes created divisions within the extended family; it was also normal for ordinary collegiate or adult career choices including the military to involve commitments and separations that made familial ties secondary for at least a while. In the realms of work- or cause-related teamwork, special friendships arose, but there was often something else, a wider bond created by shared effort and sometimes by a mutual opening of enthusiastic hearts. I have not served with a "band of brothers" in war but have read about the intensity of that version of fraternity, a commitment to one's fellows in the face of risk and strain. When I speak of these goal-focused experiences as brother- and sisterhood, the term highlights commitment to the goal as the first source of mutual commitment, which then becomes commitment to persons and the group. Although "friendship" would often be an accurate term for the group bond, it suggests individual relations while "fraternity" is the relationship pervading the group as it strives together.

If I imagine the "spirit of brotherhood" in these two contexts, family and joint action, the images are tinged with nostalgia in both cases. The best parts of those family experiences are fitfully visible in memories of weddings, funerals, and celebrations in which the eldest and the youngest generations mixed, and everyone was welcomed for the family's sake as much as for their own. The second set of images shines in recollected moments of anxiety or effort shared even more than the astonishing moments of success but includes sad or angry memories of teams disbanding and movements failing.

There is a further image of "brotherhood" that is truly universal. At certain moments, I have known joy or sorrow in encounters with other people who moved me simply because we were human. The exhilaration or misery of such moments (some are moments of pity or fear) are topics that the poets have explored, especially in the Romantic era. One can see them as an extrapolation of what we have felt at the best moments in families and friendships, but as experienced and recorded by poets and by religious thinkers like Martin Buber[8] brotherhood is a discovery, a primitive recognition of common humanity that sweeps aside barriers of status and convention. With family-like relations and purpose-driven teams, this humanism—the closest word I know—is the third broad range of experience that a fraternity ideal must rest on.

As to why brotherhood is mentioned at all in the UN declaration quoted earlier, the reason is obvious enough: the problem throughout centuries has been to spread a sufficiently strong conviction of brotherhood to make the observance of others' rights seem a pressing obligation. A theory of rights without a sense of mutual investment based partly on sympathy will motivate only philosophers. Within a society or between allied nations, a spirit of brotherhood may reflect prudence—I will protect my neighbor and hope he protects me in return—but in a class- or rank-divided community, or between communities at a great distance, defense of others' rights does usually require a "spirit," neighborly empathy as well as a recognition of prudent interests.

It is a chicken-and-egg question whether political, legal or ethical theories requiring recognition of others' rights lead slowly to a greater conviction of brotherhood or whether it is human sympathy, reaching across social barriers, that forces legal recognition of rights. One can read many episodes of history either way. In the history of racial relations in the United States, the influences have run in both directions. In the eighteenth century, the Enlightenment critique of slavery on rational grounds was influential but it was religiously motivated activists with a compassionate sense of obligation to the enslaved who would not let the issue rest. Again, the legal and political conflicts that made the American Civil War inevitable were driven in large part by the abolitionists' combined ethical and Christian principles, appealing increasingly to Northerners who held slavery to be a distant evil and were initially disinclined to act on the issue. When the American Civil Rights Movement achieved popular support in the 1960's a great foreground of organizational and legal maneuvering had preceded popular support; popular consensus on racial fairness was formed in part by appeals to sympathetic imagination represented by marches, revulsion at cruel treatment of demonstrators, images of brave black schoolchildren entering white schools, and brilliant oratory. Religious, political, legal, and sentimental forces were mutually reinforcing.

Equally common, in fact often part of the same process just described, are cases where claims to rights by an inferior class or a population of newcomers break down a previous tolerance. The new claims threaten existing bonds, hierarchies, and economic interests, sparking a resistance that in the minds of the resisters may be a defense of their communities. Immigrants to the U.S. and western Europe have sometimes found that the first newcomers, workers needed for labor shortage industries or refugees from terrible oppression, were tolerated in modest numbers. But then reaction came, that too many Irish, Chinese, Mexicans or Turks had arrived for the receiving communities to feel that they were still in control. A version of the same reaction has occurred in respect to internal classes that claim new rights: for example, when newly asserted women's rights seemed undermine men's old privileges including exclusive formal and informal associations.

An irony of the history of brotherhood is that few wars have been as cruel as civil wars, few outbreaks of savagery as mean-spirited as where former neighbors turn on each other, as occurred in Bosnia and Rwanda. It is hard for an outsider to know whether the cruelty is truly greater in these cases than it was in ancient times when (for example) enemy strangers poured over the steppes or across the sea to rape and pillage. Perhaps the cruelty of war between brothers merely seems more bitter because of the betrayal involved. Brotherhood within any group makes it potentially ferocious against enemies of the group; but when the collective ferocity turns against the "traitorous" brother or neighbor it is as if the previous intimacy had reduced inhibitions against cruelty.

From the first, we want to praise brotherhood rather than to seem cold to it in analysis; yet we know that the cluster of emotions and perceptions that we call by this term is, like all instincts, naturally good but morally indifferent. Its power can turn to good or bad, and often turns to ends that decent people disagree about. There is no reason to think that the experience of brotherhood *within* groups differs between members of a warlike tribe arming to pillage rivals and citizens at a noisy New England town meeting. The tribe and the town have different ideas concerning treatment of outsiders, but we cannot understand the somewhat rarified ideal of brotherhood across humanity without examining how specific experiences of brotherhood make the ideal imaginable. The war party will tell us at least as much as the town meeting.

If experiences of brotherhood arise instinctively, with little reference to the virtuousness of the group's purpose as judged from outside, they also can arise without much relation to the intrinsic significance of the group. I will modify this argument below, to suggest that a myth of community and depth of understood purpose deepen fraternity. But the truth is that in hobbyist clubs, volunteer service organizations, and amateur theatrical societies–all forums where one would expect that the stakes are low–heartfelt alliances and passionate rivalries are common. C.P. Snow, who had served in the British Cabinet, once quipped that anyone who has ever sat on the church committee to buy a new steeple bell has seen everything that goes on in a national cabinet. The fact that astonishingly high feelings reveal themselves in even the humblest collaborations and the driest of bureaucratic committees is so familiar that it often goes unanalyzed except when it is an extreme nuisance, as it too often is. It tells us how readily enduring instincts and self-regard become engaged.

The simple fact that the fraternal dynamic arises naturally, expressing personal needs that may be matched well or poorly to work at hand, is a key to many aspects of the history of fraternity. The passions and jealousies of brotherhood spring up constantly in organizations large and small. And yet, historic eruptions of brotherly feeling seem wonderful, terrifying, and novel. We will try to find some of the reasons for that.

It is useful to use the word "fraternity" in this chapter as if it had a slightly different meaning from "brotherhood," though it is not a distinction we can carry through the whole book. The English language has a useful ability to take in a foreign word whose basic meaning is already present in an English word and assign the newcomer a more specialized definition. "Fraternity" is of course merely latinized "brotherhood," but we use the word as a slightly specialized term in history and politics to mean, usually, the bonds of citizens in a polity that help them work together to sustain their city or state from year to year. It also is used for the overarching sense of nationhood or community identity to which citizens appeal in crises.

In addition, we use the word for almost any "brotherhood" formed for explicitly limited purposes by people who are not otherwise family members. Thus, fraternal orders are clubs developed for socializing, often with a secondary purpose of social service, such as the Lions, Elks, Moose, Knights of Columbus, Sertoma ("**Ser**vice **to ma**nkind"), etc. A few of these have been powerful, often secretive alliances within their society, like the Masons in some earlier periods and Opus Dei in modern Roman Catholicism. Fraternities and sororities on college campuses fit the definition: they are voluntary societies whose members live together, aiming to develop social bonds as part of the college experience. The words "sisterhood" and "sorority" are equivalent in most cases although in some contexts "sisterhood" currently has overtones of mutual support of women specifically, implying resistance to male domination. (In this book I use "brotherhood" for both genders.)

In some cases, (e.g. in the college versions) members of fraternities may pledge to support each other in later life or beyond the scope of their organizational mission: there are adult organizations of college alumni, co-religionists in various churches, and exclusive clubs that pledge mutual support in politics or business, just as secret societies do: "fraternity" in these cases is sociability combined with tacit alliances by which the "good ol' boys" (or sometimes, "the girls of the club") retain control in their locales. To sum up our distinction, "brotherhood" is open-ended and may have no bottom to its depth but also no specific expectations while "fraternity" arises from a common mission or ruling principle. It is quite possible for "fraternity" to require heroic sacrifice and profound unity, leading often to a deep sense of "brotherhood" arising from respect for the virtues and generous efforts of one's fellows in the mission. Thus, the Declaration of Independence pledges loyalty to the joint cause but like other American revolutionary documents says nothing about family-like bonds nor the shared character of the "people" who will separate from mother England:

> *And for the support of this Declaration...we mutually pledge to each other our Lives, our Fortunes, and our sacred Honor.*

As we distinguish "brotherhood" from "fraternity" we immediately encounter one of many paradoxes of our topic: in day-to-day experience there is an instinctive pressure in most organizations to turn each kind into the other. Expressions of general respect or affection in a purpose-driven organization—habits of courtesy, play or relaxation together after hours, or help in illness—are typical ways in which members express affection beyond the requirements of the work: they thereby characterize their organization and themselves as more than merely functionaries serving the goal. Even in groups or teams where the members are fiercely competitive with each other for personal advancement or reward, mature participants may be able to restrict their competitiveness to the functions by which they will be judged while respecting and perhaps fraternizing with peers: this is a common situation at management levels of some business organizations and in sports teams, and in fact teaching the ability to combine comradeship with mutual competition is part of what youth is expected to learn from athletics.

If what we mean by "brotherhood" or the "spirit of brotherhood" is general recognition of others as humans like ourselves, one of the distinctive aspects of "fraternity" experiences is that individual qualities are unveiled and new bonds defined as individuals reveal themselves to comrades in working together. Over time, obviously, deepening mutual recognition and new senses of the shared bonds arise in families, among siblings, parents and children, and other relatives, but the mutual commitment and the sense of closeness to the others precedes the testing through collaboration. Mutual recognition and self-revelation occur through action in purpose-focused "fraternity" because one participant shows his steadiness, another her courage, another prudence in making decisions, deepening respect and creating greater intimacy.

A further aspect of "fraternity" in our special sense, as distinct from familial "brotherhood," is that if the purpose of the organization is complicated and the work takes time, the controlling idea evolves as well. This is a process of great interest and importance in the history of religions, political movements, and revolutions because the group not only shares the idea of the common purpose but must share reinterpretations. Organizational unity becomes an experiment in the power of the key principle to support cohesion: a common narrative defines it and in time members may divide over that narrative. In enduring organizations, moments arise when the members' shared understanding as well as their sense of mutual bonds must be refreshed and renewed to prevent disaffection or schisms, and to adjust to the fact that roles and mutual connections among the brothers have changed as action went forward. The mixtures of "brotherhood" and "fraternity" that mark the organization become visible at these moments of renewal, which are often moments of crisis. At these moments, leaders will appeal to the sense of friendship or identification with others that has developed, but the main emphasis is usually either the primal, family-like bond of a tribe or city called to defend itself, or on the other hand a reaffirmation of a central ideal. Combination of familial bond and guiding principle is often the most powerful appeal possible. Both are found in the famous phraseology of the Gettysburg Address: the new nation was created by "forefathers" (a familial appeal) but dedicated to a "proposition," that of equality. At the founding of the nation's first military cemetery the terrible brotherhood of fallen soldiers did not need to be described, but the pious, i.e. familial, unity of the living and dead is affirmed: "from these honored dead we take increased devotion." Lincoln describes the war as a dire experiment: can nations based on equality "long endure?" and then rises to renewed determination to carry the common purpose through for the sake of the nation but also for mankind, lest government on that principle "perish from the earth."

Many limited-purpose fraternities in the school and civic sectors encourage service or support of some broad value (the "fraternity" nuance) but really exist to foster sociability among the members, By the same token, even in family or community settings where solidarity is an accustomed and open-ended inheritance there are common tasks to be done and the "fraternity" dynamic takes over for a while. And there are many cases where conflict over tasks, such as work and profit in a family business, have destroyed the familial bond.

There are instances and professions in which "professionalism" means that an individual can act according to appropriate collaborative standards whether he likes his colleagues or not, or they him. In these cases a team may be effective because the members share a goal but also because they would not seem weak before the others: military officers have often cooperated on that footing and professional athletes clearly do so. In the great historic outbreaks of fraternal emotion, brotherhood often gleams in a new simplicity, yet in most of life, as the examples given are meant to suggest, the individual ability to modulate fraternal relations is complex and plastic.

This discussion of terms for brotherhood should also point up the familiar fact that words for social relations are rarely just descriptive. They may be conventional names for types of groups or interactions, but they often take on an active power. By shaping the conceptions that members of a group have of their common purpose, they affect the substance of their relations. Words channel feelings that might have been left indistinct and suggest actions that might not have been taken without the catalyst of expression. "Brotherhood" is one of a class of words that always hints of an ideal, the way things ought to be rather than the way they simply are. If I speak of brotherhoods of gangsters or fraternities of college students, the context makes clear that I am simply using a standard term for a self-recognized group without suggesting that it expresses admiration, but if I speak of brotherhood in its essence—opening to the depths of the metaphor—an expectation may creep in that I should speak in tones of reverence for the moral aspiration of brotherliness. Depending on audience and context, other words with the same ambivalent but nascent power include democracy, justice, patriot, motherhood, warrior, birthright—the list is long. In these pages, I cannot avoid the normal idiom that says, for example, that Cain was not brotherly when he slew Abel (i.e., not what a brother *should* be) when, unfortunately, he showed the vicious resentments that can arise between siblings.

Although I have described "brotherhood" as a metaphor that groups a wide range of relationships under a familiar heading, there are two large classes of instances where the familial term as applied to large groups is seen as expressing either literal historical or literal spiritual truths.

Numerous peoples, from indigenous tribes to some modern nations, have claimed inextricable bonds to each other rooted in an original family, usually the extended family of a tribe or migrant clan. The loyalty among the original people is seen as continued in the succeeding nation, defining the loyalty and usually the cultural identity of citizens. The implications of a common familial origin and sustained family-like connection are extraordinarily powerful elements in explanation of community mores; the family connection also defines who belongs to the community and who is excluded. That shared imagination of the blood bond, embellished with heroic stories, has often been divisive between communities but is culturally rich within the tribal family. It has often been turned to support patriotic tyrants in nation-states, but also has driven national revolutions against empires. In the case of many aboriginal peoples the last acts in the story have been tragic: the familial connection defines the people and the culture in its own eyes so that dilution by new traditions, new technologies, or assimilation with other groups has meant the loss of the defining values of their lives and usually of the cohesion necessary to let the people survive as distinct.

In familial myths of national fraternity, bonds of blood underlie the historical continuity of a people that became a modern nation-state while language, usually religion, shared heroes and (above all) the traditional territory became complementary elements of national self-definition. This sense of "blood and soil" is hardly obsolete: most modern nations award citizenship by citizenship of parents (*jus sanguinis*), i.e. as family heritage, though modern awareness of rights of movement, stateless peoples, and openness to immigration have loosened the restrictiveness of the standard. The American standard for citizenship, embodied in the Constitution, is relatively unusual among nations: citizenship derives from birth within the United States. This standard, which recognized the streams of recent populations that made up the new nation, has its own difficulties including, currently, controversy over how to deal with young native-born children of illegal immigrants. For most nations with a familial standard of citizenship, including the nations of Europe that created our sense of what a "nation" is, the sense of distinctive inherited national bonds runs so deeply that it is easy to understand why they may feel the national identity threatened by immigrant populations as, in past generations, new political ideas were threatening. As we note in a later chapter, American efforts to imagine nationhood flowered in literature about common historical models, character traits and continental destiny but not about familial continuities, which were obviously absent for the nation taken as a whole even when cities or regions might claim them.

Whether loyalty to the state must be family-like became central to the long debate led by early defenders of republican politics and inherent human rights. For them, states had essential differences from families, shaping the loyalties involved. The distinction goes at least as far back as the ancient Greeks. Socrates, explaining why he will not abandon Athens when it has condemned him to death, personifies the "laws," whose role is absolute and parental because they protected and taught him: "...you are our child and slave, as your fathers were before you...."[9] This formulation can be read as an expression of individual gratitude resulting in loyalty, so that it is not appropriate to simplify them as a simple familial appeal, but that is part of the argument. On the other hand, Aristotle, who starts the *Politics* by describing the evolution of the state from families expanding to tribes and tribes to city-states, says that "*justice* is the bond of men in states"[10] (my italics). Aristotle's phrase clearly indicates that fraternity with fellow citizens is not unconditional like family bonds. Jumping far forward, early libertarian writers like Locke[11] and Rousseau[12], proposed social contract theories of the origin of governments and resisted familial theories of the state partly because they were used to imply the power of the King as father of the nation, inheriting a version of Adam's divinely sanctioned paternal authority. Although the entire human race was entailed in biblical history, both the republican theorists and their opponents were focusing their arguments on state obligations, not universal brotherhood. Universal human might involve the notion of a common original creation but did not explain the rights and duties of the state, except for the assumption that human life was impossibly savage and dangerous without that institution.

Both Locke, who was profoundly influential on American thinkers, and Rousseau, whose thought shaped so much of French revolutionary and later romantic sentiment, offer perspectives on experiences of fraternity as well as theory: thus, in the *Letter on Toleration* (1689), Locke takes up the question of the state's identification with the church (the sacred family), which especially in England, implied a level of sacredness that the kingship, now under Parliament, could not easily claim. Locke argues for toleration of all sects and insists on the wholly secular nature of the civic authority, making clear that the fraternal bonds and authority of churches among believers are quite different from civic society. However, civic society should not reflect not bare indifference to others, but

> charity, bounty, and liberality.... This the Gospel enjoins, this reason directs, and this that natural fellowship we are born into requires....[13]

The generous values taught by religions, in a word, do not require the creedal base or church organization to be valid for society. Further, the state's proper stance is that churches are merely voluntary associations in a society full of voluntary associations.

> Some enter into company for trade or profit: others, for want of business, have their clubs for claret. Neighborhood joins some, religion others.[14]

This startlingly matter-of-fact dismissal of sacredness attached to membership in the kingdom, as distinct from membership in a chosen sect, is one of the first glimpses we have of the centrality of independent "associations" to liberal civic culture, a topic to which we return repeatedly later in this book. As for Rousseau's even wider influence, what is crucial for his fraternity ideal is not the contract, which might be conceived as practical accommodation to the problem of living in community, but the idea of a general will, a national essence embodying the will of all citizens. The patriot is a citizen who serves and in effect embodies that national spirit, raising his relation to fellow citizens to a transcendent communion that would soon be called Romantic. Fraternity becomes participation in the spiritual essence of the nation, an ennobling vision but one that arguably encourages absolutism in those who are sure they represent that will.

Regardless of theories of origin, there are natural connections between kinship loyalties and national fraternity. Families teach love and loyalty, and kinship networks teach and sustain the practices of fraternal cooperation at local and regional levels in many societies. Extended families and mutually helpful small towns and villages (which often house extended families) are settings where citizens practice collaboration and mutual decision-making, for instance in rural harvesting or in the shared tasks of a fishing village. European writers from the nineteenth century onward who were alarmed at the loss of tradition and hierarchy, with Burke among the earliest, began to imagine mass societies as rootless and turbulent by contrast with the denizens of an historical landscape in which stable subordinate orders and kinship groups defined meaningful life in society. The process and argument run to the present, for the issue of lost traditions, which is of course real, became universal. Among great literary exemplars the novels of Chinua Achebe (e.g. *Things Fall Apart*) record the confusion and shifting loyalties that come to an African society with the crosscurrents of what we now call globalization. Commentators on the American civic culture have had fewer lost traditions to lament but have regretted the decline of the neighborly small town and the atomization of families through mobility and urbanization as factors undermining civic culture. The issue of how small communities and kinship networks support and offer training in civic collaboration is clearly relevant to fraternity in nations and across the world, for one of the practical characteristic expressions of the spirit of brotherhood in the present era is engagement of ordinary citizens in local gestures of charity or hospitality to strangers from afar.

Hannah Arendt has suggested that in the twentieth century the notion of the national community formed by "blood and soil," i.e. "organic theories of nationalism...[identifying] the nation and the relationships between its members with the family"[15] became permanently obsolete. In the modern world, communication among humans is that of a single community, and the "soil" effectively the whole earth. Arendt adds that the idea of "mankind" has become a reality for the present era, implying the impossibility of a historical familial basis of fraternity and a necessarily global conception to replace it. She describes

> [T]he decline of the European nation-state system; the economic and geographic shrinkage of the earth...; [and] the transformation of mankind, which until our own time was an abstract notion or a guiding principle for humanists only, into a really existing entity whose members at the most distant points of

the globe need less time to meet than the members of a nation needed a generation ago.... (232-33)[16]

Arendt's comment on "mankind" as an idea meaningful only to humanists is of course highly suggestive for our topic, and a few pages below I discuss humanism as a tradition central to imagination of the "spirit" of brotherhood. Encounters with individuals and cultures different from our own, whether actual or virtual through arts and media, is the third broad category of experience from which a "spirit of brotherhood" may develop.

consideredThe familial or contract theories mentioned above as theories of the state generally related to distinct peoples who had created states. The vision of peace attached to these theories was one in which nation-families were at peace internally, with little further exploration of brotherhood across boundaries except as the issue came up in relation to colonialized peoples: colonies and empires posed major intellectual as well as ethical and political issues. By the end of the eighteenth century, when Kant wrote his *Universal Peace: A Philosophical Sketch* (1793), the relation of nations was paramount, and the center of his scheme was fair treaties made in good faith without secret alliances. In the nineteenth century the rise of socialism in its various forms reflected a powerful international impulse toward *fraternite,* which various movements aimed to solidify among the proletariat internationally. At the same time, from the nineteenth century to the present, both fictional and experimental utopias including environmentally sustainable models have imagined communal life marked by combined equality and productivity. Equality among the sexes has often been part of both socialist and utopian visions along with models of peace that nations might follow, for war and imperialism were seen as results of lust for property. Nationalism has been problematic for many socialists, but even for them the general vision was that the nations and peoples would persist in happy retention of their national identities, at peace because freed of class oppression and sharing more equally the means of production. The reader must forgive this swift summary of a vast and rich topic: my purpose is to point out that one implication of Arendt's analysis, obvious in theory but a perennial challenge to both imagination and implementation, is that for a "spirit of brotherhood" to flourish among "mankind," a vision of humanity mirroring what humanists have long developed must accompany universal principles of justice. This understanding must be brought to jibe with the fraternities that unite the different peoples and their communities, a many-sided challenge.

The great problem, of course, is that no one lives in "mankind," but in cities, cultures, and nations, which support their cohesion by defining boundaries, members vs non-members. Long traditions in ethics, religion, and art and recently in biological sciences affirm that mankind is one, entailing obligations drawn by great thinkers for millennia that rarely operated across cultures until defenses of human rights were mounted in the modern era. What Arendt's comment calls for is a step beyond the familiar ethical principles to a mutual recognition that values, as humanists do, both individuality and diverse communities, with claims that require respect and mutual adjustment.

The greatest of the many paradoxes at the heart of the fraternity motif in political history is that while religious, revolutionary or utopian enthusiasms urge us to reach for brotherhood beyond our usual borders and beyond the inequalities of our societies, valued older patterns of cohesion stand in the way. The great historical conflicts that involve the fraternity motif are not cases of individual selfishness against the collective good, but alliances of one system of classes or rulers or social bonds against another. For that reason, even in a shrunken world of endless digital and other media exposures of the "other," looking beyond social divisions and legal borders takes education and generous effort.

As a matter of ordinary adult life, most people learn to mediate among the claims on their loyalty that come from different communities to which they belong. The claims of family, friendships, church, work, city, and nation are understood to involve hierarchies and vary with situations. In times of war, the national service might take primacy, at other times perhaps the family duties, and so on. A great deal of formal and informal discussion of practical ethics is devoted to clarifying the principles by which we adjust our loyalties. The child learns the weight of family bonds against friendship with playmates, honest officials set obligations of office above family or friendship, and so on. Commonplace decisions on one hand and great dramas of moral conflict mark the range of these mediations. In speaking of fraternity with "mankind" we imagine the same process of mediation among values of world fraternity that we see in daily life in our communities: a mediation that values community but lies under a more universal rubric than seemed relevant long ago.

The simple but universal fact that we mediate among many loyalties tempers the fraternity motif for good and ill. At any given moment, one among the variety of mutual loyalties that adults feel may be paramount because action in common is urgently necessary. In these periods, often crises, the half-hidden fraternity motif takes on sweeping power. The patriotic citizen, having swelled with pride in yearly ceremonies and marches, is swept up more passionately with his fellow citizens as looming war calls for resolution. Or, it may happen that the devout brothers and sisters of a sect who have praised their blessed unity at every prayer meeting feel it rise to desperate levels as a new revelation or a schism occurs. So, too, the family under a sudden new stress reaches out to each other for unity, and so does the revolutionary party at a climactic moment. Fraternity is both felt and called for, and for the moment the specific fraternity—nation, sect, family or cause—casts the other kinds into the shade. Often, the sign that the emotions of fraternity are nearing as absolute level is that tepid members of the group seem betrayers, in effect aiding the enemy—and at these moments the believers see friends and enemies fiercely. Depending on the crisis, fraternity without that edge of suspicion is often a wise and tempered version, a collective remembrance that after the crisis passes, we may turn our enthusiasms again to civic cooperation, church, family, and ordinary routines of work together.

These considerations illuminate why fraternity as a political ideal is rather difficult to formulate except as a general, overarching commitment. To be dependable, it must be rooted in ethical principles, laws, and habitual cooperation, but will rise to different expressions with different values at stake as occasions demand. This helps to explain, too, why laws, alliances, and public and private bureaucracies combined have developed as instruments of the "spirit of brotherhood." They allow societies to act through prepared modes without inventing fervent response for each new challenge.

One might imagine that feeling for "mankind" is so austere and general that it could never compete with stubborn local allegiances, cultural prejudices, or the soaring themes of patriotism. Yet part of the modern history of fraternity is that movements and reformers have at times been moved to give aid or defend justice across borders, successfully pulling the nations behind them so that (among other examples) anti-slavery laws, protocols for war prisoners, world health cooperation, and alliances for arms reduction have enlisted national passions to defend common interests of mankind as well as those of the nations.

As noted earlier, T.V. Smith[17] explained the intensity of what he called the fraternity motif by arguing its root in infancy. The historical outbursts—wholehearted, often fantastical—can seem infantile, marked as well by sudden rages, like the ecstatic security of the infant with its mother. Although there is clearly a dimension of ecstatic delight in historic outbreaks of fraternal enthusiasm, I suggest that the primitive aspects of fraternity are less those of the infant than of early youth, delighting both in discovery of others to play or perform tasks with, and delight in one's expanding power of action in the fascinating buzz that is the world. We see this early in childhood by the third year, when children have begun seriously noticing each other and playing together, but it is not a "phase" that humans leave behind. Instead, like that primal intimacy with mother (which persists), the youngster's entrance to the active world transforms as discoveries, sociability and new competencies enlarge. In the progressing lifespan the next dramatic blossoming of intense fraternities and sometimes of raging enthusiasms (for the latest music, romance, or a cause) occurs in adolescence, but again the instincts involved do not fade away as years pass: however, adult years typically involve more longstanding ties and more experience with mediations among loyalties. Throughout life, the desire for fraternity and the exhilaration shared in fraternities arise out of the same basic instincts: assurance of belonging, delight in others, and among the other brothers and sisters exerting some mastery of one's world.

Arendt's dismissal of the familial concept of national bonds as insufficient for the present and future of mankind offers a convenient segue to the second great class of thinkers for whom brotherhood is a literal and factual current relation, needing only to be actualized in our behavior. In the West the usual source of this conviction is faith that we are all children of a father god, each of us in a direct personal relation to Him/Her. (This class overlaps in rare cases with that mentioned earlier, for a god may be creator or special guardian of a tribe but not its neighbors (as in some Native American stories in which a particular divinity creates the people but other tribes are not part of the story). In other special cases, the Father may designate lower and higher status to some humans, as in the American Old South where the dark-skinned children of Ham were said to be destined for subservience.

The first crucial instance for the Mosaic religions, which ultimately shaped the fraternity theme for the West, is the story of Abraham: he has a direct relationship with God, who gives him direct instructions at times and establishes a special relationship with his family, an ongoing covenant that gradually implied individual devotional relation to God for all the Jews and a duty of brotherhood within the covenant. Over time, as we note below, personal rather than purely tribal relation to the Father began to imply immediate spiritual brotherhood with his other children, even those outside the tribe: the equality of all Jews in God's eye came to imply obligations of justice among the classes of Israel, and by a century before Christ the notion that all individuals are equal before God and due equally ethical treatment is familiar doctrine.

To leap forward to the impact of divine fatherhood on the political idea of fraternity, Adam Smith was a philosopher of ethics as well as of economics; his *Theory of Moral Sentiments* (1759), an important work in his era, in some ways reflects the issue raised in this book: for it considers the basis of ethical motivations in imaginative empathy. To oversimplify, if our neighbor is in need we are moved to act fairly to him or her because we imagine instinctively how we would feel in the same situation. (The theory highlights the "as thyself" side of the scriptural version of the Golden Rule.) A surprisingly brief chapter in his work is entitled "On Universal Benevolence." Smith jumps to the importance of belief in an all-wise God who assures happiness for all. The passage is worth quoting at length because it admits, as alternative, the nightmare of vast human misery in a cruel universe that we explore later in these pages as the romantic problem of fraternity laid bare by the French Revolution. Smith assures readers that "good-will is circumscribed by no boundary, but may embrace the immensity of the universe...." However,

> This universal benevolence ...can be the source of no solid happiness to any man who is not thoroughly convinced that all the inhabitants of the universe, the meanest as well as the greatest, are under the immediate care and protection of that great, benevolent, and all-wise Being.... The very suspicion of a fatherless world, must be the most melancholy of all reflections, from the thought that all ...space may be filled with...endless misery and wretchedness.[18] (p. 213)

In other words, in the absence of optimism rooted in the all-wise fatherhood of God, humanity would offer a scene of endless wretchedness. This gives us a foretaste of what was at stake when the French Revolution opened the fraternity theme in political rather than philosophic optimism. We associate the Enlightenment and its widened view of human nature across world as one of intellectual confidence, the confidence in humankind with which many entered the first revolutions. However, as we see later, recognition of severe poverty and wasted lives darkened the first optimism about human potential, and sentimental identification with the most degraded souls became nightmarish.

One challenge for a modern "spirit of brotherhood" is that of broadening and secularizing concern for "mankind" as a sympathetic common possession of communities worldwide without appeal to a specific credal base. Historically, the creeds did not prevent horrible oppressions of those whose creed differed—quite the opposite—but by the revolutionary era, originally religious perceptions of human worth had been generalized as ethical universals separable from the doctrines and heroic examples that so often had unveiled them. Although it might be hard to find a professed devotee of any world religion who would not recognize some version of brotherhood as a principle, we are astonished and full of admiration when we encounter individuals and movements that insist on acting on the principle. In rare individuals and specially dedicated communities such as charitable religious orders, expression of brotherhood with non-related persons may operate as a fervent and systematic rationale, but ordinarily, even in societies whose landscape is dotted by churches, synagogues, or temples, brotherhood is treated as one good idea among many, temperately enacted in organized or personal charities but hardly a guiding beacon in most minds. Yet it is repeatedly imbedded—it is hard to find a proper term for what is abstractly agreed to by so many and partly alive in many institutions, yet rarely the top priority of that multitude. When a rare soul acts with persistence and fervor to realize brotherhood, e.g. insisting on reforms to benefit the downtrodden, we see that individual as having a special character, a moral hero who awakens the shared principle from its somnolence in most of us. In the face of such a character society reacts as individuals do when matters guiltily buried in the psyche are forced into view: some admire, and a few become disciples, while others grow angry and try to punish the troublemaker.

Admiration for moral heroism in saints, reformers and even some fictional characters is often an ingredient in intense fraternity experiences. The awakened participants enlist in the deeper fraternity of the movement and battle to keep the vision from falling asleep again in their society. Even within the brotherhood of the movement the character who acts on fraternity to a radical degree is a special case, a hero or fanatic herding his comrades forward.

In the famous parable of the good Samaritan a "lawyer" asks "who is my neighbor?" and is answered by a fictional tale. The basic principle under discussion is clearly common doctrine ("love thy neighbor as thyself") but the lawyer is leading up to the great difficulty, the relation of brotherly love to relations among sects and nations. If allowed to follow his track, he might have asked explicitly whether he and the Jewish theocracy must love the Romans as well as Jewish heretics like the Samaritans: what would Jesus propose as state policy? Jesus short-circuits the inquiry with his story of a man who might have been reaching across a social divide but certainly was reacting to a dire immediacy of a need that he had the capacity to try to deal with.

As noted earlier in this essay, "fraternity" may be variously a principle, a desire, a discovery, or an active virtue. If we think of it as a virtue it is, like equality and liberty, a collective trait of communities as well as an individual stance. This means that "brotherhood" as a universal relation is enhanced when a community is in the habit of acting charitably or defends justice beyond its borders, but this extension is always complicated by the community's social borders. It is not a mysterious matter and is admirable when, for example, a community whose churches and synagogues offer food to their homeless neighbors each week mounts a fund drive to help victims of a hurricane in the Philippines as well. There *is* mystery—what we have called an "eruption"-- in the waves of great enthusiasm that saints, heroes, revolutions and great movements create: they touch the imagination differently and shake their communities to the foundation.

The imagination of brotherhood and fraternity traced in chapters that follow is mostly secular, but the discussion above seemed necessary to acknowledge that secular ideals of fraternity have been informed again and again by religious notions exemplified by religiously motivated heroes who almost invariably learned to make a sympathetic ethical argument far beyond the narrower beliefs of their home church or temple. When fraternity is intensely imagined, whether in political eruptions and in art, the power of the experience is new; the discovery of the other involved includes new recognition of an old idea as a newly powerful force in life. These experiences can be illuminations of oneself and of human nature at the same time. Intellectual ideals of human rights, an expanded imagination of "mankind," and unexpected heroisms, victorious or tragic, combine to enlarge that intuitively simple idea that we should treat each other as good brothers.

Chapter 2. Brotherhood Despite History

The cannibals and the Anthropophagi,
Which have their eyes below their shoulders....
Shakespeare, *Othello*

We can simply define away the intrinsic complexities of the
brotherhood theme by saying something like this: "True brotherhood is the active, deeply emotional recognition that others are like ourselves—brothers and sisters, in fact—despite all geographic, cultural, political, and religious differences." In that case, the only real issue of brotherhood is how to further it in the face of obstacles. But defining "brotherhood" in this way as good connection while defining violent fanaticism, chauvinism, mob spirit, and parochialism as if they were wholly different is not helpful for very long. Outside the immediate family, experiences of brotherhood are rarely universal world-friendly revelations, but often experiences in specific groups under some pressure of work or opposition. To miss the double-edged sword that fraternal experience can be would be to mistake its power. Alas, if a Serb or Croat Christian in the wars of the 1990's raped his Muslim neighbor's wife, he was not brotherly to the victim (of course, nor "Christian" either) but he may have been started on his course by some appeal to unite with fellow Serbs, Croats, etc. People do terrible things when insulated from punishment and eager to show how fiercely they belong.

What is true of the instinct of brotherhood, that it can turn to friendship with outsiders or to their destruction, is equally true of cultural constructions of brotherhood. The myth of Babel tells that languages, which are at the center of culture, divide us. Yet reaching out to other peoples, indeed reaching across divisions within one's own culture, involves the most skillful use of one's cultural tools. The international ideal of brotherly "spirit" requires either a child's innocence or urbanity. The double-edged sword of brotherhood is apparent when we think of the uses of history involved, for histories divide us as well as unite us. Students of this fact as it has been displayed across the globe (South Africa, Mississippi, Crimea, Palestine, Iraq ...a long list) speak of the always tangled "politics of memory."

We might ask, coming back to my moment of window-reading on Martin Luther King Street: Why did the officers of a *local* history society think that its mission should include reminding us about *international* brotherhood? Looking beyond our peaceful streets, we see militants raging for and against different claims of brotherhood, whether of sect, party or nation. Groups affirm or sustain their coherence by opposing others and refusing basic identification with others, setting their religion firmly against a rival creed, their tribe against the state, and so on. In a world of diversity, recognizing the humanity of others—seeing them as somehow like siblings, acting "brotherly" toward them—must imply recognizing how they, with communal histories so different from ours, may have hopeful links to our own needs and experiences.

Affirming our own special histories and universal brotherhood in the same breath is difficult in practice. It requires art in both the understanding and the telling of the tribal stories. The difficulty is that we hold to our communal identities by holding on to the embattled history that makes us different. Often, as with the Palestinians and the Israelis or the Irish and the English, retelling history is inflammatory, worse when the leadership on either side is invested in keeping the injuries inflamed. History brings up the uneven score of losses, restates our reasons for hating. Common sense would say *Let's not bring this up, it tears our friendship to pieces.*

However, in a world that saw the Holocaust, the eradication of native tribes in the Americas, and a host of other group-to-group and tribe-to-tribe cruelties, we find that accurate history is one of the first things that warring sides must agree to face in common if there is to be peace. This is especially true if there is to be a democratic peace with free expression of opinions and open airing of disagreements. Common willingness to try to speak the truth is a ground for peace even if the truth is full of pain and calls for some sort of redress.

Moreover, the cruelest public acts we have seen over the last century, including the Holocaust, Stalin's purges, and horrors such as the Serbian massacres of Muslims in Bosnia, have required viciously distorted histories to sharpen the division within the societies that undertook or tolerated them. I have not read that raiding nomadic tribes needed phony histories to attack their neighbors, but civil societies seem to need false histories as the prelude to injustice. Those distorted histories are always about group action and group affiliations, rarely about individual experiences that might seem so familiar that they trigger sympathy. There is a long experience of resisting *misuse* of history behind the conviction that reverence for accurate histories contributes to the "spirit of brotherhood."

To serve the spirit of brotherhood, tribal and sectional memories must be transformed into a story of that group's unique avenue to a common body of human experience. This simple fact alerts us to one of the ways in which brotherhoods have been shaped by art and literature, and more recently by modern media. Often, it is the common willingness to confront the truth, not the particular version, which serves as a common ground. The dialogue that seeks greater truthfulness must usually be accompanied by a commitment to deal with implications of the truth, perhaps with injustices revealed when it is told. Acquiring a broad sense of individual and group histories across the world will not erase a justified sense of injury, but truth-telling suggests that the motives of the neighbor who wants to acknowledge and collaborate are different from those that harmed my group. And perhaps there were injuries given as well as received. The truth-tellers become a fraternity with a shared task, that of recognizing a divisive history as a tragic part of a common past, a heritage both sides must wrestle.

It is by no means easy to use a divisive history as a communal asset. After World War II Tito, to hold his power over Yugoslavia, forbade the retelling of the histories of his various people's ancient grievances against each other's nations. It is almost miraculous—a testament to the religious sincerity of figures like Desmond Tutu—that the "Truth Tribunals" in South Africa were critical steps in justice when apartheid ended. In something like the same spirit, the Mothers of the Lost in Argentina and Brazil, whose sons and husbands were kidnapped and killed by government forces, refused the offer of return of bodies for burial: they wanted truth, the crimes to be acknowledged. In Northern Ireland, official British acknowledgement that British troops reacted to a non-existent threat with fatal gunfire on "Bloody Sunday" has made the gradual development of a civil peace more feasible. The defense we would give for accurate histories of our divisions is rather like that which Aristotle gives of tragedies: they are a source of sorrow and fear but also an occasion for pity, and at last for purgation, which leads to temperance.

All of this may be merely acknowledging that history-telling, like other forms of truth-telling, is risky: but it seems important here to say that it is especially problematic for brotherhood, which is often brotherhood against the foe. Over the centuries, one source of hopes for brotherhood among nations has been the reading and playing of tragedies and other personal stories, transported from culture to culture in the works of great literary artists, and making humanity

47

recognizable in its many guises. In public history and great tragedy alike, telling the story to admit and yet tame t divisive and anarchic implications requires skill and tact. One reason why literature is an important tool for understanding the historic theme of brotherhood is simply that if we would understand how connections and conflicts are interpreted by those who feel them, sympathetic imagination is crucial. Even if we focus on abstract ethical and legal principles, our specific actions are guided by what one philosopher, Kekes, calls moral imagination[1]: to act ethically we must imagine what various courses of action are open to us and how our choices affect others. Especially when obligations stretch across cultural or ideological rifts, the sources of moral imagination are important to understand; and to the degree that the "spirit of brotherhood" is a desire as well as a principle, like other desires it feed upon imagery.

The "spirit of brotherhood" includes two elements, recognizing the humanity of others and agreeing that a bond, an implicit community, is created by that recognition. "Recognizing the humanity of others" is perhaps begging the question. For if we "see someone as human" we presumably admit that ethical or moral imperatives do govern our relationship. The phrase has a sentimental connotation indicating reaction to a presumed human *essence*, which affects us because it is a mirror of ourselves. It is what we call up when we say, "I'm only human" (meaning, "forgive me for my fallibility, which is like yours"); or "he is inhuman to her," (meaning, cruel in a way that seems to deny his personhood, acting below the moral dignity of the rest of us). We may say of a friend that he is a "mensch," Yiddish for the down-to-earth good-heartedness that we like to think is the truest human nature. The soft connotation of "recognizing the humanity of others" is not truly soft: international conventions against genocide and in favor of human rights across the world assert that humans are recognizable to each other as such, and that legal obligations follow. At the same time, it appears that it is perfectly possible, in fact customary in many societies, to recognize humanity in some classes of people without treating them as fully "human" if that means equally. There have been societies where slaveholding or serfdom sometimes wore a relatively mild face, and there are still many societies where the subjugation of women implies much less than full humanity. In these cases, as when Greek slaves were used to educate young Roman aristocrats, some masters could recognize the human nature of the slave without rescinding claims of ownership, just as many individual men in societies that oppress women love and respect their mothers and wives but hold them to their fixed roles.

As a very different example of recognition of the human, one of the ironies of extended wars has often been that actual combatants cease to demonize the enemy: they come respect his virtues and acknowledge sufferings common to both sides. After a war, opposing warriors may be among the first to abandon resentment. [2] In the veteran soldier's mind, the fact that the two sides must kill each other may seem no more than their unlucky draw in life's lottery, a sad fact of the way the world works when comradeship would have been his preference.

It seems true—an old observation—that mutual recognition of humanness is instinctive until cultural distinctions or competition for power intervene. After brief hesitation, children and amorous teenagers fall in naturally with others who come from different cultures, accepting that there are differences of tongue or manners to explore. Very young children are helped, perhaps, by the fact that their interaction is pre-verbal, and the mutual attraction of older youth across cultures is more about flesh than culture. When an opportunity to connect across familiar divisions occurs, it often awakens the insatiable urge toward new experiences and new social ties that marks youth, who are not wed to elders' loyalties. In adults, as we said earlier, culture can either divide or reunites us: the ability to reach across lines of difference, to see a human whether beneath a bowler or war paint, is a sign of urbanity, shrugging off the curse of Babel. In many ancient societies and some traditional modern ones, a special sacredness is assigned to rules of hospitality, protecting the stranger who arrives in apparent good will. In the Old Testament, Lot sacrifices his daughter rather than violate his duty to guests under his roof; in Greek myth, the god Dionysus sometimes arrives at one's door as a stranger, and woe to the host who violates the laws of hospitality!

"Humanism" and "humanities," the study of arts and history, have shaped and endlessly reflect our shared perceptions of the human. They supply a crucial part of what we see when we "recognize the human" across physical and spiritual borders. The humanities mostly deal with recording and interpreting images and stories, using them to reason about human issues. The reasoning and interpretations, intellectual and non-parochial, are passed from generation to generation, deepened, and (in such forms as drama) renewed by fresh performance.

Several early sources are worth mentioning as setting the stage for explicit recognition of human connection across cultural lines, influencing Western cultural strategies permanently. In the Old Testament *Book of Isaiah,* the so-called Second Isaiah, author or authors of the latter parts of the book, faced a delicate issue relevant to the tension between universal and sectarian versions of history-telling. *Isaiah* tells a story of two episodes of deliverance that occurred over more than two generations' time. In the first episode, Israel had taken the extreme risk of resisting the Assyrian army, urged on by prophets who believed their god would rescue His people. The Assyrians mocked the notion that the gods of lesser peoples could withstand their power; *Isaiah* agrees that other nations' gods are indeed mere objects of stone or wood, satirizing their idolatry: he preaches a profound conception of the Lord as a spiritual being who had created the universe, but has faith in Jerusalem's rescue. When plague drives the Assyrians off, Isaiah exults: *the Lord has done this for Israel!*

Being part of an empire creates cosmopolitanism, and at the second great act of the story, when Cyrus the Persian conquers Babylon and returns Jewish exiles to their homeland, *Isaiah* is conscious of the variety of peoples affected. Did the Lord change the face of Asia merely to help little Israel? He is, after all, the Creator, not a parochial giver of favors. The answer is that the Lord is creator of *history* as well as of earth and the things upon it: He wishes to be recognized by all the world through the agency of Israel's faithfulness, "So that [the nations] may know, from the rising of the sun/ And from the West..."[3] Isaiah's answer affirms Israel's specialness, but only by setting a context where the Lord intends a somewhat comparable relation of respect from all peoples: "....a teaching will go out from me,/ And my justice for a light to the peoples." It is implicitly a vision of human brotherhood under the Lord—a shrewd solution to the problem of the Creator's special response to Israel's need. Tribal and world history intersect to further a regime of universal justice. Later prophets, insisting on the equality of all Jews before the covenant, went on further to an ethic encompassing all humans. Biblical scholar Harry Orlinsky writes:

> When the Jewish descendants of the prophets, during the hellenistic and especially the roman periods, became more fully aware of living in a single great unified society that encompassed all of the known world, they drew upon and expanded the universalism of the prophets. The prophetic concept of the Covenant had aimed at making all men—of the

Israelite society, to be sure—equal in their essential human dignity. This concept, in turn, led to one much broader in scope, of the universality and inevitability of individual moral responsibility toward all men.... [4]

If we try to imagine a history of the fraternity idea and its entanglements with experience, the great empires will be central to the story, as Isaiah's case shows. Founded on violence, they destroyed cities and peoples, and were chronically engaged in frontier wars; yet when stabilized internally they provide security for trade and travel, causing peoples to mingle. They almost always involved a bureaucratization that set down the rights and status of various populations vis-à-vis each other, often the first time that the rules of relationship among peoples became explicit. The networks of trade often meant that cities became multicultural, containing neighborhoods of minorities from varied regions; empires often encouraged settlement or resettlement of strategic regions by loyal populations, perhaps starting with families of garrisoned soldiers. In other cases, like that of Germanic tribes that attacked the Roman Empire, invaders settled and guarded borders they had attacked. When empires collapsed or borders shifted, trade routes were often sustained, and the peoples recalled far-off regions as parts of the world.

For Western ideas of brotherhood, a crucial next step in the unfolding of Isaiah's argument is recorded in the *Acts of the Apostles* in the New Testament. Again, the event occurs within a vast empire, that of Rome. Paul, the central actor, fits Orlinsky's description of "descendants of the prophets" exactly. Jews were widely disbursed around the Mediterranean and, as we might say, multicultural, and Roman citizenship could be possessed by them and by other peoples: citizenship was portable around the empire. Paul, a member of the rigorous pharisee sect but also a Roman citizen, started as a fierce defender of orthodoxy in outlying communities like his home city of Tarsus, but after conversion to the Christian sect argued successfully for admission of non-Jews and freedom from old rituals. The new sect's messianic message to the Jews became a mission to all humankind, a community of equals without respect to birth origins.

Despite the universalism of the Jewish spiritual understanding of human nature that Christianity inherited, the institutional histories of the three great Mosaic religions offered a different spectacle: Judaism, Christianity, and Islam were or became exceptionalist, often persecuting both unbelievers and the unorthodox. The story of democratic political principles from the Enlightenment onward has involved, at the intellectual level, affirmation of equal human creation without the theologies that made that view widespread.

The second bedrock of Western recognition of the "human" is Greek tragedies and comedies, first source of the long tradition we call humanism. The term nowadays means a group of disciplines of study, but it also names a view of human nature that unfolded from the Athens of Sophocles' time to the late Roman empire, was valued in fragments across the western Christian and Islamic middle ages and became the dominant shaper of high culture for the West in the Renaissance. It is a deepening tradition of art and argument about the universal aspects of human nature, and for that reason, despite the academic overtones, it is hard to find a better word for the imagination that underlies mutual human recognition.

Satiric examples of democratic freedom of speech are combined with witty, often ribald judgment of common human nature in Greek comedy, while the tragedies offer deep questioning of suffering and the gods' justice, and thus of the deepest values of life. They have been touchstones of depth for western culture ever since. Arising from celebrations of

Dionysus, the half-human god of wine who suffered death and was reborn (thus especially significant for Christian civilization), early Attic comedies capture the freedom of feast days when wine flowed and even the most powerful members of the community could be mocked, asserting community and partial equality. Tragedies enacted the horrific deaths of deliberate or accidental enemies of a god: King Pentheus in *Bacchae* jails the god Bacchus and suffers for it, while Oedipus sins accidentally. When Athenians dismissed a poor play as "having nothing of Dionysus," they were likely speaking not just of the playwright's skill but of a failure to capture the drunken god's hilarity and wit on one hand or, on the other, the horror of sufferings that temper any human hope. For our purpose, the great fact about the tragedies especially is that they were culturally portable. Rooted in specific city-states myths they became universal art for the Greeks and then for the Hellenistic world, presenting Oedipus or Jason as sympathetic figures to audiences unconcerned with the specific histories of Thebes or Argos. Even the characters of Homer, figures of the more primitive genre of epic, came to be understood by later Greeks and then by the Hellenistic world as actors in dramas of universal passion.

In humanism as we invoke it here, the tradition of philosophically inquisitive learning itself is the crucial thing: not specific texts or ideas (though these are of intrinsic importance) but an insistent discourse revisiting great themes that was already a thousand years old when the western Roman empire was disintegrating, It was and is an international and cross-cultural legacy imbedded in masterpieces but refreshed in a flow of probing responses to new as well as old works. A student who is led to immerse him- or herself in Goethe or Dickinson, Ibsen or Kafka, Heaney or Morrison, with even a little exposure to the reflective commentary that surround such writers, has immersed in the central current of "humanism."

Among so many profound voices there are many examples of how humans mediate among historic loyalties: one especially useful early exemplary is Plutarch (d.119 CE). His *Moralia*, a collection of treatises and dialogues about miscellaneous topics, is not only cosmopolitan itself but a lode from which Montaigne and others in the early modern flowering of humanism fashioned a world view of universal toleration. Plutarch represents particularly well the balance between affirmation of one culture and urbane respect for the gifts of other cultures: he was a priest of Delphi, proud of Greece, but his learning welcomes the whole classical world. His historical masterpiece *The Parallel Lives* is a model solution to the problem of broad and local historical perspectives that we posed earlier as an issue for brotherhood: an individual's greatness, for Plutarch, did not lie in the breadth of the historical stage on which he acted but on qualities displayed in whatever sphere had called them forth. Some of the most admirable Grecians he portrays commanded states or armies that were minuscule by the standards of the great Romans who were their contemporaries, yet they were not less heroic nor were their histories less instructive in Plutarch's eyes.

The English poet Shelley, writing to defend the art of poetry and by implication all play of imagination, argued that the Greek tragedies in ancient times and the plays of Shakespeare for the modern era had a secret but powerful civilizing effect. Lumping together such creative writers with the great lawmakers, scientific discoverers, and social visionaries, he claimed that they were all the "unacknowledged legislators of mankind." James Joyce's Stephen Daedalus, heading off to self-exile from Ireland, repeats the notion as his vocation: he will "forge the uncreated conscience of his race." It would be hard to prove by plain statistics or long stretches of civic virtuousness that such arts as interpret individual lives with compassion make societies more compassionate, for the arts have often been ornaments of arrogant and warlike states. Moreover, few states have ever been so wholly good or evil that some arts could not be vibrant in them. Yet it is certainly true that what we mean when we attempt to imagine the "spirit of brotherhood" or to protect human rights or in any other way to act as just citizens of the world, rests on a sense of the human that was long shaped by humanism and its masterpieces.

It may be helpful to clarify the claim just made a little further. Literary and philosophic humanism have enlarged and refreshed the "spirit of brotherhood" in the West and later across the world by adding elements of comprehension— deeper human recognition—to the principle of justice.

Modern humanistic enrichment of the "human" in cultural models occurred in parallel with the development of political ideals of liberty and equality. An example is that in the eighteenth century the rise of the novel offered the growing audience of literate middle and lower-class readers the dramas of their own lives: the heroes and heroines were girls who worked as maids or governesses, men in commerce or farming, gentlemen or ladies of limited means. These characters, recognizable to readers as like themselves, were given the same essential dignity as tragic or epic heroes. That democratization of the world of fiction, increasingly realistic, eventually pictured empathetically the whole range of human nobility or misery in many societies, a range of recognition augmented in the nineteenth century by the growth of social sciences and the shrinking of the world by improved transportation. To add to the vastly expanded media of traditional humanism, starting two centuries ago photographic media and then centuries of expanding electronic media have offered images as well as news from all over the globe. These developments are so familiar, and so often celebrated as aspects of the modern interconnected world, that to point to them seems banal. Yet they mean that there is a treasury of ways to imagine others, including the humblest—whether foreigners, lower classes or even enemies—that did not exist a few centuries ago.

The ethical and religious traditions affirming brotherhood in principle have been enriched by modern humanism: from eighteenth century rationalist scorn of slavery to reforms of child and women's labor, expanding suffrage, and exposures of urban poverty, often in appeals by labor and socialist movements starting in the nineteenth century, and in twentieth century actions for international aid, strengthened by pictures of damages done to more than the bodies of the poor and oppressed. Even rather traditional religious vision has been enlarged in this respect: Thus, a passage from a recent sermon by Pope Francis I promotes an enriched understanding of "human" in the old precincts of religion: in "A Church that is Poor and for the Poor," he says:

> We are not simply talking about ensuring nourishment or a "dignified sustenance" for all people, but also their "general temporal welfare and prosperity." This means education, access to health care, and above all employment, for it is through free, creative, participatory, and mutually supportive labor that human beings express and enhance the dignity of their lives.[5]

What strikes here is not the call for economic justice, which is hardly surprising, but the implied image of fullness of human nature in a productive society, seen as a spiritual as well as temporal good.

Although the humanistic tradition does not work its effects surely nor automatically, there have been many instances when a book or a poem, opera or picture opened human truths that a regime wished to deny, one of the reasons why we defend with special fierceness the rights of free expression by journalists, artists and scholars. The writers who have suffered exile or worse for ethical principles and truth-telling, from Voltaire onward, were persecuted by those who wished to hide crimes or follies: open revelations had impact, either swiftly or over time. That preservation of truthful voices through time is part of what we mean by humanism, which always involves resuscitation and recovery of the accurate past and its deepest imaginative resources as well as interpretation of the present. Among a hundred instances, one that jumps to mind from American history was the publication of *Uncle Tom's Cabin,* which undercut slaveholders' claim to Christian virtue in religious conversion and humane treatment of slaves in the southern U.S.

The preservation and elaboration of great themes in the contemporary world that I am trying to describe deserves the name "humanism" because that term always has implied a focus on the universal human. For our current purpose we might add "modern" or "critical" to our term, to insist on the modernity, the living tradition of universalizing interpretation m high art literature, movies or daily news, relating them to large notions of who or what is human. Calling it a *living* tradition means that it does not reference a static body of texts but that insistent voices raise the old questions of value, sometimes affirming the importance of the old wisdom but finding depth in new voices. Neither the great old voices without that amplifying dialogue, nor cultural chatter without a sense of the enduring magnitude of some minds and ideas, would have the same power. Sometimes it is the declarations and works of the artists themselves, but equally often the context that critics and commentators give rather than explicit messages in the works makes them central. In the nineteenth century, sentimental and romantic idealism in literature often supported fraternal or moral values directly, but that explicit didacticism was displaced in critical prestige by stories that highlighted authenticity of experience, often exploring ugly and degraded conditions of humanity. In fiction, the transformation involved the nineteenth century's progression into realism and then to naturalism. Stories of economically doomed sufferers like Zola's *L'Assomoir* (about washerwomen and other workers declining into alcoholism) or Crane's *Maggie, Girl of the Streets,* were distasteful to conservative tastes and the plots represented economic and political protest more than an uplifting pleasure for the reader. However, the characters and stories have outlived their immediate economic moment and remain valuable as portraits of humanity under stress. In the twentieth century many great modernist works, anti-idealist, were ironic and often contemptuous of genteel classes and social institutions. But as contributions to the ongoing dialogue and as sources of insight they take on a different importance, sustained by genteel readers and educational systems. Thus, a Dublin pub-crawl becomes a monument to human resilience and dignity in *Ulysses*; a sweeping indictment of western spiritual exhaustion becomes perennially prophetic vision in Eliot's *Wasteland.*

The allusion to Arendt above brings up an argument made by her that in our context underscores the profound intertwining of the elements of the humanistic and Judaeo-Christian tradition. The current humanistic tradition is secular yet deeply informed by religious values that are taken to represent some of the deepest human impulses, including those that involve compassion and longing for fellowship. Arendt, trying to distinguish the elements of the *vita contemplativa,* the inner life that traditionally pursued wisdom, found a new historical category identified with Jesus: goodness, essentially a private trait, slowly becoming a touchstone of public values, helpful to the polity as good works but destructive whenever good people retreated from politics.[6] Her argument is implies that the dimension of inwardness that she calls goodness has become a part of what we understand as the universal political potential of humans:

it is regularly explored in the democratized dialogue about life that in its more artistic expressions we call humanistic. Part of the broad story of Renaissance humanism's transition to Enlightenment sentimentalism and rational benevolence, and of these to romanticism, which we briefly sketch later, is the universalizing and secularizing of visions of inner and public goodness combining in service of the just society.

Ceremonial moments often remind us that the humanist meta-dialogue is habitual and so widespread that almost any insightful story is capable of interpretation that reminds the audience of human solidarity. Whether in a Nobel literary prize winner's speech or the annual televised Oscar awards, we are likely to be told that the most celebrated works present models of courage or awaken our compassion or penetrate valuably into the human psyche. A glance at the history of Nobel Prize awards in literature illustrates an evolution along this line. Alfred Nobel's instructions had directed that winners' works show "something of the ideal," i.e. explicitly uplifting moral instruction. In early years chosen writers were mostly outstanding exemplars of their national literatures, which has usually continued to be the case, but by the 1920's the idealistic requirement was uncomfortably abandoned. By the time of Faulkner's 1949 Nobel speech, the ennobling is rooted in the interpreters' broad understanding of the range of human experience: among the ferocious slaveholders, rural con men, gangsters and neurotics whom he drew in his fiction there are only a few admirable characters, but the artist rejoices that his life was spent exploring "the agony... of the human spirit," the "problems of the human heart in conflict with itself which alone can make good writing." [7] Over the last half century, the Nobel choices, originally heavily western, have been extended to include more figures of the "third world" and the overlapping category of voices of resistance, opposing tyranny in the native land.

It would not be accurate to call the humanism of constant free critique and interpretation a tradition in the strictest sense of a body of beliefs or principles that must be sustained, although academic humanism is certainly that. Rather, the constant and habitual sharing and analysis of all aspects of human experiences is more a living, self-refreshing tradition, the present in curious dialogue with itself and with the past as well. At its best, it translates news, arguments, and data to gauge their relation to what is "important to man" (the phrase is Wordsworth's).

Societies are more humane if something of that common awareness can be awakened in the collective conscience. When the state or a creed in power decides that there are fixed official truths, suppressing new voices, whatever greatness lay in that controlling political or religious creed is devitalized. In some of these cases, tradition opposes tradition: the rigid doctrine of the sect resists the humanistic tradition as I have described it, because of the latter's inquisitiveness, which unearths profitable falsehoods and corruption. In these instances, modernist humanism creates the tacit fraternity of a new, more critical public.

Almost as important as the works themselves of a Rushdie, a Bao Dai, or a Baraheni[8] is the seriousness with which readers and critics amplify their wrestling with life. That is the living tradition, widening the audience and elaborating the key issues precisely because they and the readers' dialogue sustain a common desire for authenticity and truth. From the early twentieth century but especially in recent decades, increasing numbers of national and international organizations have arisen to protect writers, journalists, or scholars who cross their governments. Their first priority is protection of the writer, but a close second priority is preserving and publicizing free expression, The organizations try to enhance international dialogue about threatened writers but also about the importance of universal freedom to speak and write, a freedom that is participatory for readers and for engaged commentators.

When the revolutionary French announced that their motto was *fraternite* it implied above all that Frenchmen (and for a few, French women!) had superseded divisions of class and religion; however, in the heady early days it was further proclaimed that the newly affirmed brotherhood among the national classes (in some respects both a discovery and an invention) also represented the brotherhood of humankind. A figure of the First Assembly who fascinated later writers like Carlyle and Melville was a fitting symbol of the quixotic idealism of the moment: Anacharsis Cloots, a Dutchman, was admitted as a delegate after he paraded a group of representatives from different parts of the world and announced that he would represent the non-French portion of the human race! This liberating moment was both significant and surprising because a powerful brotherhood is not only *for* itself, but usually *against* some part of the world, an opposition which it claims to see with special clarity. The group may feel what the Evangelist John calls the hatred of the World, or it may feel that it represents the surging power of a new wave that is sweeping the world—in France, sweeping off the injustices of aristocracy. The presence of the world, whether opposing or acclaiming or both, is an intense and defining relationship in revolution and movements: it shapes how members interpret their moment in history and their relation to each other. In movements and revolutions, a sort of public identity, stature as an actor on an enlarged stage, is conveyed by group membership when it is taken up against the pressure of the world, the majority, or the social norm. Narrow as he or she may be, even the most fanatic sectarian has a world-view, an outlook on history and a typology for its peoples and movements that arises from his membership and in its way is more cosmopolitan than the view of one who does not reflect on such things and has always merely tended his own garden. Critical humanism as I have described it brings the world, its variety and tragicomedies, even to the gardens of the unengaged.

Although groups and sects that set themselves against the world (or against the current majority) offer illuminating extremes of groups that choose exclusiveness for the sake of their own system, one of the timeless pleasures of comradeship is setting out together to share an encounter with the world. One rather quiet ancient model of that pleasure is the classical symposium, which will be discussed as a model of fraternity in a later chapter but is convenient to introduce here. *Syn posein* means to drink together; the ancient Greeks enjoyed drinking-parties where small groups of friends came together to argue and share views on a chosen general topic. As recorded in literary examples, the symposium is the ultimate image of cultured dialogue about ideas and the observed world, but in practice could also erupt in drunkenness, brawling, and lechery. The patron god of the symposium was Dionysus, god of wine, who is also the god of the drama: a god of dark mysteries, whose effect on crowds and cities can be terrifying (as in Euripides' *Bacchae*). He is an international god—he came to Greece from Asia Minor, and as noted earlier was associated with hospitality to strangers. He was not only a god of frantic passions but also the god who stood for their tempering. One of his sacred titles, originally priapic, was "the Upright One": in later centuries, moralists claimed that it was given because he had taught mankind to mix wine with water, thereby remaining sober and able to stay upright. In Plato's dialogue *The Laws*, which is largely about the structures and disciplines that hold societies together, one character, the Athenian Stranger, argues that children and youths must be trained to act together as citizens by taking part in choruses: dancing and singing together become both the means and the symbol of harmonious collaboration. For the youngest children, singing and dancing the delightful and beautiful music whose divine patron is Apollo, god of light, trains the youngsters to act in instinctive harmony with their fellows. The choruses of older youths include martial music and gymnastic activity: they learn courage and mutual dependence under the patronage of Ares, god of war. But the third kind of chorus, suitable for young adults and ideally steered by wise old men, is Dionysian—well-ordered drinking parties in which the young citizens see human passions, including their own, at play with loosened bridles[9]. Dionysus is thus at once the god of sociability and social excess, the god of pathos and the god of hilarity, an embodiment of society in its whole fraternal and erotic potential.

I take this passage to be a useful fable about the communal value that we are treating in this book. The children's chorus involves producing and enjoying beauty pleasure for self and the community, with unconscious assurance of belonging: basics of culture and social development. The chorus of adolescence forms heroic ideas of loyalty, bravery, and collective strength for protection of all. The third stage, which introduces a mature fraternity, involves hearing conflicting arguments, observing personal agendas and intoxications, and judgment and discipline of oneself and one's fellows.

In the Dionysian view of communities and passion, it is not only delight in belonging and acting together but experience at controlling the needs and pleasures involved, with some compromise towards the force of impulse, that results in temperance. Untempted virtue is not virtue in the Dionysian world, for it is not proof against the intoxicating emotions that sweep individuals but also cities, sects and nations. By the same token—and this is what we would import to an understanding of fraternity as a serious political ideal— citizens may enter into celebratory and even ecstatic moments of unity, but neither the divisions among the brethren that always arise nor their own potential for excesses are denied. A

Dionysian community is like Mark Twain's Hadleyburg, which after being exposed as hypocritically self-righteous struck a medal for its citizens, saying "Lead us Into Temptation."[10]

Chapter 3. The *Eros* of Common Pursuit

1. Transformations

Just as there are political ideologies that implicitly celebrate or damn the great surges of shared emotion, there is a literature—in fact, there are many literatures—about the transformation of individuals in moments of intense fraternity, whether in war, politics, sports, sailing vessels or exploring parties. Some of these moments, and some of the groups have also displayed a long term process of interpreting and refining themselves, adjusting the central ideas that participants committed to. Both the personal transformations and the development of the shared myth are inseparable aspects of fraternity experiences. In this chapter, we consider the personal aspect and then the development of ideas (or truths) as a sustaining purpose; a following chapter uses two ancient symposia to illustrate fraternity around an idea.

First, as to what may happen to the individual amidst the revolutionary crisis or battle: filled with the moment's power, individuals may reach the most intense competence, the deepest sense of connection, the clearest confidence of their lives. The moment may be the first in which they can fully express latent gifts for persuasive speech or action: it is one of the repeated mysteries of history that unexpected actors arise who have brilliant charisma at such moments and shrink to ordinariness when the spotlight passes to others. To return for a moment to an analogy drawn earlier, the moment of individual brilliance enacted before a crowd is what we see modeled in heroic athletic performances. It may be that these sports events prepare the participants for leadership: that is one classic justification for idealizing sports, although athletic competitions are just as often a popular opiate, diverting attention from social or political issues dangerous to those in power. Regardless, for players and their fans ("fanatics") something like the same coalescence of brilliant collective action with all-out commitment of self that marks the eruptive fraternity of revolutionary moments is mimicked in high moments of sport. For onlookers, participation is brief but charismatic drama, when even the couch potato by his TV leaps from his recliner to cheer in unison with others in the stadium or sports bar.

The opposite picture of individuals swept up into brotherhood distrusts the "enthusiasm" that fills them, to use the eighteenth century's word for visionary excess. This model pictures the neediness, the inner emptiness and indiscipline of characters who come alive only in the fire of the collective passion. They are the fodder of the great popular "isms" of the last two centuries, monads in Ortega Y Gasset's masses. Eric Hoffer's classic analysis of this type[1] saw them as "True Believers," closely akin to religious zealots, fleeing the mediocrity of their lives and the emptiness of their private souls.

Like other useful stereotypes, "true believer" takes on the color that the user of the phrase imparts. Within the circle of belief, it designates an individual of deep authentic belief and unquestioning loyalty to the group and current leaders. In less sophisticated communities, the true believer may be part of the large class that the Catholic Church used to call the "simple faithful," fully accepting of doctrines and authority but essentially childlike, so that protection of the believers' innocence justified lists of forbidden books and in recent years the covering up of sexual molestation by priests. When leaders at odds divide true believers into the two parties of a schism, each side tends to assert the old rigid authority through pressure or violence toward opponents. When the division is one that sets a tolerant middle against the extreme, the fury on the zealous side is especially ferocious, because (as Hoffer points out) true believers loathe above all those who don't care about their issue as they do. As a result, extremisms combine to destroy the middle ground.

Hoffer's sardonic version of the true believer reflected his observation of adherents to communism and fascism, including those whom he saw at close distance in their American versions. Hoffer had worked for much of his life as an itinerant laborer in California, viewing many human types and coming to respect the average American's good sense in resisting ideologies. He became a longshoreman in San Francisco, where the union was long associated with the American Communist Party, and he developed the veteran working man's disdain for overblown leaders and hysterical followers. Hoffer's contempt extended not only to local examples but to many of the characters who rose in leadership of the century's totalitarian movements: Hitler, for instance, whose party leaders were criminals and utter mediocrities during his rise to power, so that he abandoned many of the most thuggish, the S.A. leaders, when in full power.

The topic of extremist adherents became a matter of wide interest in the nineteenth century as increased awareness of world religions and the psychology of revolutions and other mass moments came under examination. In the twentieth century and up to the present, investigators have often tackled the issue of why people join ideological or prophetic movements and also—especially after the Holocaust—how these loyalties move otherwise conventional people to cruelty or heroism. On another side of the same issue, the question arose during the Cold War as to how people can be "brainwashed" to betray old loyalties. One stream of the twentieth century analyses can be traced, I believe, to writers propagandizing against German militarism before and during the First World War; after that war the same streams of argument used intellectual ammunition supplied by psychoanalytic studies of guilt and neurosis as national traits.

An example is found in W. H. Auden's "September 1939," which echoed the notion that something was psychologically wrong with the Germans, from Luther on:

> Accurate scholarship can
> Unearth the whole offense
> From Luther until now
> That has driven a culture mad....

"Accurate scholarship" probably never can explain such moments so confidently, though profoundly instilled respect for law and authority may explain some portion of German obedience when crimes were turned to legal obligations. The great psychologist of identity, Erik Erikson, developed a parallel psychological analysis of German culture in post-World War II studies and in *Young Man Luther* (1958), while other postwar social scientists speculated that there might be fascist personality types and experimented, sometimes unethically, on how ordinary people can be persuaded to act cruelly. The brainwashing of American prisoners of war in Korea and Cold War concern about communist cells and sympathizers in the 1950s added to the flow of studies and commentary about how movements attract and hold adherents. Even believers in space alien visits were examined in that context (*When Prophecy Fails*, 1956). In later years analyses along the same line have sketched the attractions of guerilla movements, urban gangs, and most recently the psychology of suicide bombers and other jihadists. With respect to this last group, some leaders have been ruthless and presumably highly confident personalities waging war for their cause; we do not feel obliged to explain a Bin Laden or a Zawahiri in terms of psychic neediness but many of the recruits, including some who have carried out lone acts of terrorism, fit the picture of the drifting or despairing soul who joins to give meaning to an empty life. For a few individuals, especially in areas of extreme unemployment such as the Gaza Strip where marriage is financially impossible for many young men and some married individuals cannot support the family, the decision for martyrdom has reflected an extreme reaction to an actually desperate situation: some Palestinian suicide bombers knew they would receive fiscal support for their families. Video testaments before the fatal act have been standard and have been received with reverence by the martyr's community. Thus, although the leadership does not seem to need explanation in terms of susceptibility, the lower level recruit and even the bomber or lone attacker often is so explained. A 2015 report in *The New Yorker* analyzed the growth of jihadism and antisemitism in France, along the way noting patterns that demonstrate the complexity even of the "true believer" profile. On one hand, recruitment to radical Islam in prisons is said to aim at the "weakest" of prisoners; on the other hand, the few who commit to violence fit something like a contagious disease model, i.e. random individuals catch a severe case of the anger and antisemitism endemic in their population. British scholar Andrew Hussey is quoted: "This is not about…improving people's conditions…. It's about hatred, to some extent, Purification."[2] The few who commit to violence often isolate themselves from the community they mean to represent, connecting with at most a few fellow extremists to keep their secret.

As these examples suggest, the picture of the psychologically needy "true believer" serves to illuminate the sheep but not so well the shepherds, the hardiest and most self-driven. Seen from within the circle of belief there are circles within circles, with "true belief" a common trait but the nature of decisions that follow, and the abandonment of restraint, highly variable. Seen from close in, the picture of the fragile enlistee and the opposite picture, that of an inherently powerful character who drifts until given focus by brotherhood and a cause, are nearly the same picture: points along a spectrum. Nothing says *a priori* that a powerful character does not need fellowship and purpose to be unleashed; quite the opposite may be the case, while on the other hand apparently unremarkable people once set in action show unexpected powers. Moreover, the great movements and religions do not admit to valuing passivity of belief and simple acceptance as they actually do for the mass of adherents, but just the opposite: they offer emulation of heroic individuals and aspiration to grow in personal qualities, to shine in God's or history's eyes. That is attractive to the inherently weak and to the potentially strong. Movements that enroll true believers propagandize both before and after conversion to assure them that they have no worth outside the movement, but inside the movement have the power of the collective. It becomes not only doctrine but a psychological truth that there is "no salvation outside the Church," no meaningful place in history outside the Party.

It is not surprising, then, that while the prison-based recruiters to Islamism just mentioned are said to seek out the "weakest" to enlist, the article cited records observers who are puzzled to explain patterns of actual conversion that do not fit expectations. The misery of a great many Muslim immigrants is an obvious factor, as are both French and Islamist antisemitism, but the specific actors who become radicalized can be well-educated persons, sometimes middle class youths filled with sympathy for fellow Muslims in Syria and recruited by social media to join ISIS there.

As I write this, several recent mass shootings and assassination attempts by lone gunmen in the U.S. have been designated "terrorist" attacks while other massacres have not. Almost all the cases have been solitary attackers who appear to have carried deep rage and/or delusions of persecution to which their cause gave a name: they might have found that alliance through reading or social media rather than any extended bonding with peers of the same persuasion. In this pattern they resemble delusional assassins of earlier history rather than extremist plotters with an organizational history, differing from the plotters who attacked the World Trade Center and from the coordinated teams that carried out several French atrocities.

A pattern in which individuals take on personally, perhaps in lonely fashion, the supposed obligations of a group or brotherhood is part of the universal spectrum of fraternal behavior, with mass conversions on the other end. It is not the case that an individual's neediness would be readily observable beforehand: some of the great religious conversion stories, for example, involve a saint or founder who seeks out the gifted people whom his or her cause will need—potential leaders whom the *recruiter* sees as adrift, whom he can awaken to their emptiness and lead to greater ideals. Thus, in the Spain of the conquistadors, former soldier Ignatius Loyola (founder of the Jesuit order) picks out the brilliant student Francis Xavier and confronts him: "What does it profit a man to win the whole world and lose his soul?" Once inside the order or the church or the party, the empowerment of the believer—the self-realization, as we say now—may be self-congratulatory ("I am powerful!"[3]) or it may be humble, but in either case the true convert affirms complete dependence, with gratitude for the vision of his humiliation and worthlessness that preceded conversion: "Amazing grace! To save a wretch like me!"

As the popularity of hymns like "Amazing Grace" among believers of so many different Christian sects suggests, we tend not to take seriously the yin and yang of need and self-realization among members of sects or parties that exist familiarly around us. We are not surprised when a robustly confident preacher says that he is "nothing without God" (he has taken on the role of enacting and thus heightening the desperate need met by faith). We are amused if a neighbor takes the regalia and secret ceremonies of his lodge too seriously; we may joke about a "lunatic fringe" when extreme political sects emerge but are not surprised when a few of our neighbors become stridently passionate about the usual parties every two or four years. Affiliations that in theory are intense life commitments, and that have been so in other times and places, may be loose and flexible affiliations for adults precisely because they have become conventional associations rather than the shared passions of a tight circle strengthened by resistance of non-believers. In religious communities, children or teenagers will be guided to hold their beliefs more naively, and more intensely, than many of the adults around them seem to do. Indeed, it is not uncommon to find adults who feel a little guilty or even bereft because they have lost a youthful faith in their church or youthful political causes. The conventionality of belonging to a church or a familiar party or well-established movement makes it easier for participants to scale up or down in intensity, so that switching political loyalties or (in American religious life) denominations is often a fairly casual decision. The same is probably true of decisions to join the single legally permitted party in a Baathist or communist state: it is a necessity for certain careers and private ambitions. If I can judge by the flow of social media I have received in recent years for various political causes (both left and right), the intense adherents of different movements are typically near hysterical in tone—or at least darkly prophetic—when they ask for support *before it's too late!* —crying into the wilderness of my apathy. In most cases this is a rhetorical ploy similar to the near-hysterical huckstering of car dealers on TV, whose latest offer of discounts will not last and may even mean that the dealer is "crazy," positively giving away his cars to those who act *now*. The car dealers' ads reflect the fact that buying a car can be a panicky (and very expensive) moment, so that a tone of crazed urgency pushes the buyer along. The political huckstering takes on the half-panicked urgency of those who see the direness of the immediate moment and are frustrated because the cause is not understood by most others: surely, *I* understand the urgency and will join and donate!

Unlike the relaxed conventional adherent to a conventional ideology or party, the passionate convert, whether weak or powerful in his native strengths of mind as others have previously observed him, is not content to study and meditate on the truths that move the fellowship, but typically must convert others, or in the extreme case force his truth into the public spotlight by a drastic action. Proselytizing or demonstrating, he derives new energy, becomes even more fully the embodiment of the group's vision of truth and collective energy. If he belongs to a church or a well institutionalized movement that fellow citizens take calmly, he seeks out the cell that shares his missionary intensity and scorns the dishwater passion of most of his fellow adherents. The passion of the new convert to enroll others is such that creeds, parties and movements try to engage new recruits very quickly in action, for the typical curve of a participant's commitment is not to rise from study and reflection to the experiment of acting but from a first action, however mild, to deeper immersion in the group ideology and more extensive actions. In a society where conversion is hard to carry out because the convert's creed is familiar, as is the case with the Mosaic religions in the United States, a believer with missionary zeal may be seen by neighbors as a nuisance whom we avoid because we do not need his company in belief as he wants ours.

In these examples, to sum up, the varying stories of need to belong, of desire to serve, and of realization amidst fellowship offer universal themes. Incidents in which a heroic action on behalf of the group occurs, or when a terrible crime is committed out of loyalty to a creed, are often cases where an ideology is common to many but willingness to violate ordinary limits of behavior or morality characterizes only a special few. Thus, in the 2001 terrorist attack on the Twin Towers, one of the mysteries of the brotherhood among the attackers is not posed by the main ringleaders, who were part of an enduring long-seasoned movement with experience in war and previous terrorism. The surprising partners were the "sleeper cell" members among the attackers who had previously made religiously motivated vows to help but lived quietly in various American communities until called upon, having no advance details on what the plot involved specifically and no previous evidence of murderous character. The psychology of such a situation strikes us as tribal or perhaps medieval, undiluted by civic life and unconsciously abetted by daily religious practice, a private secret and yet an obligation to follow at the great call, ironically made more possible by the "sleep" of the cell, since neither dilution nor discourse entered in. Like the problem of the "good German" during the Holocaust, or that of massacres like Mi Lai in the Vietnam War, the recruitment of persons of apparently normal morality to deeply criminal acts is the most puzzling and in its way most terrible aspect of fraternity. On other side of the same event (my personal image of brotherhood in courage) New York's "first responders" entered burning towers together hoping not for climactic martyrdom but simply to fulfill, as they did each day, a constant promise of service.

The themes just mentioned are universal because flowering in shared action is an experience that everyone has the capacity for. Even the most vivid and apparently independent souls may become at challenging times of life deeply needy, not only for social comfort but for the bonds which are forged in some challenging work or struggle. There is a distinction to be made: some who flower within fraternal action nonetheless have their own lights, talents, and direction to sustain them and to make them fertile in other realms when the great moments end, while others find nothing as profound as the movement. Passionate adherents to the cause or sect clearly fall along a spectrum on which only a close and cold-eyed observer could place them until the great events have passed.

I am not unusual, I think, in that when I survey the landscape of memory I find a disproportionate number of pictures of myself in groups: neighborhood gangs of kids, school and local clubs, athletic and other teams; later on, social movements and service committees, neighborhood get-togethers, and team projects in professional life. Because I have been a teacher at times, I have also had the pleasure of close and lively classes, where a sort of fraternity occurred among students and with me. Because I was an academic bureaucrat for years, I saw the currents of cooperation (or resistance) in committees and task forces. I worked with community arts groups: I saw the remarkable efficacy and occasional adjustments to peculiar temperaments with which they worked together. The painters and novelists were habitual workers-in-solitude but would define how they were willing to act as a community while music, theatre and film artists were expert at organizing, focusing a group on intense collaboration and even a shared passion, then dissolving the project to pass quickly to the next. The range was always surprising: on one hand a few anarchistic individuals or organizations—leaders spoke of their task as "herding cats"—but on the other hand many of the arts professionals whom I observed were among the best multi-tasking managers of simultaneous working groups, audiences, and community supporters that I ever saw.

Even in my remembered childhood groups—perhaps especially in them, now that I think of it —each member had a vivid and distinct identity in the gang's eyes, sometimes for qualities that would have seemed trivial to outsiders but were desperately important to us. Danny was famed for his bad temper, Billy for his fairness and athleticism, affable Butch for offering the back yard and multiple toys we wanted to use that year, and so on. Children change a great deal from year to year; even in the same coterie each successive stage recognizes and exaggerates the latest evolution of individuality ("Look at Brendan's muscles!" "Roger has a girlfriend!"). Where enough activities and groups are available young teens, especially the girls, buzz from group to group like bees among flowers. Because of this evolution of identity, new brother- and sisterhoods have great power for the young, and mass movements often have speed and energy because of their participation[4]. The pleasure and the sense of terrific revelation that marks adolescent fraternities arise from the fact that selves are both developed and recognized for the first time in a sort of public space. In our society, the in-school and out-of-school life of many adolescents is a rapidly stirred stew of small groups that form and shift and re-form, with individuals buzzing among and between the social pods, eager or frantic to enter and act. When the energy of adolescents and young adults is focused on a great Cause, the almost unbelievable physical vibrancy and wholeheartedness of youth itself flows into the movement.

In moments of adult fraternity, the realization of self through common action and the pleasure of recognition—of radically knowing others amidst their passions and of being known oneself in that realizing moment—remains central. We might assume that because the adult self is more fully established, tied to place and social status and responsibilities—in a word possesses a less inchoate identity—he or she is less needy, less susceptible to the fraternal appeal. In general, I believe that is true: investment in these stable bonds is a tempering, slowing factor. Just because of these external stabilities the adult self is hidden away from the leaping fire, finds it hard to communicate his or her specialness, is less intense in the instinctive desire for the constant fraternal stream. Medieval theologians had a theory that every single angel, having a slightly different mind from the next, was a distinct species; and Hannah Arendt has reflected that adults who are reflective become almost separate subspecies of humanity, each a little different from his or her neighbor, with whom really intimate communication is difficult. One of my poems says the same thing:

> Like angels, adult selves
> Emerge as separate species,
>
> Characteristic systems
> Of love, irreducible;
>
> Each one the intelligence
> Of the sphere it half-creates. [5]

However, when the adult does commit deeply to a group or cause, the result may be powerful and lasting because it is a selective commitment of a consistent identity vis-à-vis those others. In my experience, the more mature an adult is, the more important a tested set of friendships becomes, and the deeper the pleasure of communication about life with life-seasoned minds:

> When children dance in rings
>
> And old men lean to hear
> Each others' judgments, secure
>
> As household gods in their world,
> The no-longer young grow lonely
>
> For such a song as Dante
> Heard when the angels wheeled:
>
> The song of differences

Made perfect, in which we greet

What each of us became
Or never could quite reach....

Within the fraternity of a movement some participants, whether young or older, may discover the most profound of their friendships. As a result of these and other pressures from within the maturing self, some experiences of fraternity can engage mature adulthood as powerfully as the years of youth; that mature capacity tends to be less volatile than with youth, and patient.

2. Chains of Argument

To return to the second aspect of the *eros* that arises in groups that pursue a common goal, many associations of all sorts elaborate their doctrine, and hence their claim on allegiances, over time. Religious movements and long-lasting political reforms usually follow this path; revolutionary or reform movements spreading from nation to nation almost invariably do so; and sometimes a whole nation develops an ongoing national narrative. Key principles and documents, turning-point events, collective traumas, and national heroes crystalize the fraternal claims of the sect or nation. This process has clearly occurred in the long chain of movements, revolutions and ideologies that looked directly back to the French Revolution and its sequelae; it has occurred in American history, involving competing versions of what the nation "stands for." The American narrative at the nation's founding arguably centered at first on political liberty, a universal but imperfectly applied principle of equality, and widespread opportunity for modest prosperity. As we point out later, there was also an extremely cautious affirmation of national fraternity amidst great freedom to associate for various limited purposes. Of the elements of this narrative, the most dramatic came to involve the meaning and application of equality, not always conformable to ideas of liberty or property rights, but (as De Tocqueville saw) the great inescapable world ideal that Americans were trying out before other nations. The history of the equality ideal in the U.S. involved many currents, like a river fed by successive tributaries: in the first years the expansion of the franchise to non-property holding voters, then (triggering and following the Civil War) the freeing of negro slaves, then contentions related to immigration and the nature of the national heritage (including the questions of post-slavery status of blacks), then enfranchisement of women, then further struggles toward racial equality and lately legal equality for homosexuals. The mid-twentieth century saw expansion of some of the same principles that make up the American narrative through institutions for international order and commerce and in support of the western side of the Cold War. As we observed earlier, fraternity as the third great idea of the revolutionary period was ambiguous because equality remained in question in so many ways; the world idea of equality has advanced but imperfectly and extension of the "spirit of brotherhood"— realizations of active fraternity—are inextricably entangled with divisive battles against economic and social inequalities.

In action-oriented groups that endure, for example religious sects and self-reflective polities, it is often not the original key ideas that energize the group but the constant re-thinking of the guiding doctrine, which revitalizes the relation of members. In the modern era, as democratic values spread and democracies and republics have prevailed as political models, the internal and international dialogue has necessarily expanded to include, more or less, the whole public of each nation: *Who are we in this nation? What is the nature of our community vis-à-vis others?* Within some nations, and certainly in U.S. history from the first, there have been intense arguments about who the national *we* are (equal or not, white or mixed, European or "rainbow" in culture, global or self-isolating, and so on). In the American case the argument appeals to guiding principles, differently understood, and the quasi-sacred documents of our founding. In other nations, as described earlier, remote myths of founding, historical traumas, or revolutions more radical than the American may provide the key themes. From time to time American orators have announced that the vast westward expansion to a manifest destiny, the Civil War, the Civil Rights Movement, or the end of the Cold War are the heart of the narrative that should unite the citizenry, propositions accepted as grounds of discussion even as the meaning of that narrative was debated. Less successful keys have been the religious uniformity of the nation (non-denominational but Christian), northern European racial culture, and unfettered capitalism.

In such organizations as ideological political parties and reform movements, members continually affirm their guiding principles but also evolve their positions as issues evolve. The actors may be individually self-realized in their participation, and certainly know their comrades; they argue about new aspect of their philosophy and their movement has milestones to which they can return for guidance or encouragement. What I call below symposial moments of fraternity are those in which a revelation of identity or discovery of mutual bonds occurs at the same time that some truth or guiding mission is at the forefront, affirmed by group effort. The old-fashioned sense of the word "discovery" is the one I want here for both the brotherhood and the understanding evolved: "discovery" once meant simply that something was uncovered to view, and has come to mean that the hitherto unknown is pursued with some difficulty until unearthed. Both meanings apply.

This process of developing a narrative, usually to sustain unity but sometimes stumbling on issues that splinter the members, is common among both large organizations such as nations and the more passionate sort of small organizations. This makes examination of intense small orders useful even for understanding large-scale historic eruptions of fraternal emotion. It often appears that what happens is that the characteristic enthusiasm and swelling loyalties of an energized small group are suddenly cast onto a larger stage, engaging a wide public. One of the first questions that immediately rises for the society involved is whether this is positive or destructive to other loyalties; a second question is whether the public or some new or old institution will sustain the narrative taken over from the originating cell. Seeing such an elevation from small to large fraternities, Edmund Burke fumed at the French Revolution for abandoning settled social orders to follow the turbulent spirit of the Jacobin clubs, "adopt[ing] all the crude and desperate measures suggested by clubs composed of a monstrous medley of all conditions, tongues, and nations."[6] The twentieth and (so far) twenty-first centuries are too well acquainted with communist, Baathist, and other movements holding power in which the small party-cell's emphasis on unalloyed loyalty and atonement for incorrect thinking have been made tyrannous principles of government. One of Burke's concerns was breakdown of tradition, which sustains the roles of subordinate orders, which in turn are sources of balance in society; his comment prefigures the part of political theory well developed since, how "civic culture," sub-societies from kinship networks to churches and from social clubs to competing political parties assure participation in local government and train citizens in political action. This is a usual realm of practical fraternity as distinct from familial relations, which we explore in a later section on the "Third Sector," voluntary associations, in public life.

Supposing that intense but not uncommon small group experiences cast onto a larger stage explain much of what we experience in moments when fraternity is a dramatic public revelation, several literary symposia let us glimpse the leaping flame of shared participation in the unveiling of a truth or meaning greater than the selves that pursue it. Indeed, one of the symposia that we will consider below, John's Gospel account of the Last Supper, has been ritually repeated for two millennia in Communion ceremonies where brother- and sisterhood is part of a sacred *agape* or divine communion.

There is one great element of difference between the classical talking-parties and many other experiences of fraternity, including the great eruptive historical moments: symposia were designed for carrying on friendship and for sharing leisure, with the pleasures of music and food as well as wine; they were not set up for, nor were their passions triggered by, taking action. That is a tremendous difference, for the emergence of fraternity in purposeful organizations may arise from sharing of ideas but more often arises when there is shared effort and even an element of risk: risk as well as talk is how we open ourselves to brothers and sisters. The symposia that I will discuss are literary artifacts rather than records of historical action, but they contain action in the Aristotelian sense of a change or movement; they present a passionate, partly competitive intellectual pursuit and at several points intra-group competition for status or the love of the leader. As with organizations that engage in action that serves a meaning or principle, symposia must keep moving or lose participants' attention and loyalty to the task; in moving they unmistakably reveal and release personality. The model is useful because, as suggested earlier, sustained fraternal action in the world usually requires that the group develop some myth or story of its progress and the significance of the collective experience.

The second aspect of the difference between the literary symposia discussed below and action-based fraternities is that the great divisions in organizations, whether parties or sects or nations, are most often due to struggles for power. A symposial debate may involve competitive egos, but is play, sometimes turning into a serious lesson. In organizations with a longer term active purpose, differences about the ruling narrative are taken on passionately, for they help to anchor loyalty to this or that faction and this or that course of action even though the deepest motives for difference, such as competition for status, lie elsewhere. The great ideologies of churches and states have generally been transformed to defend those in power and to suppress rival arguments; apologetics is the function of most of the party or church intellectuals, who challenge (when they do so) only within safe limits and carefully adjust the official doctrine. The leadership in these mature power structures rarely cares much about the doctrine for its own sake, but a participant in the organization who wishes to identify himself with its deeper truth or vision finds that he can be admitted to higher levels, a coterie of more mature discussants whose status he puts on. Now and then, however, a member arises who objects stubbornly to inconsistencies from within the framework of the ideology or to corruption in the leaders—a Luther or Trotsky—and the power struggle among leaders is followed by a division over doctrine that legitimizes each side. Sunni against Shiite or Adams against Jefferson, the competitions have as much to do with power as with truths held, but allegiance is courted with the help of myth and argument. Obviously, not all organizations develop their myths very far: the local baseball team may have its memorable moments but no epic connections for casual fans; an army regiment may have a heritage and even great *esprit* but solders are not encouraged to imagine that it has an adjustable ideology.

In American political experience, the major political parties have almost always been broad alliances of interest groups and regions that announced principles as part of their courtship of partisan loyalties, but shifted positions from year to year and compromised when in power, so that it is easy to see them—even their turbulence—as the symposia of the season but not to see them as engaged in long or coherent dialogue. At election times, some of the most passionate adherents take up the party's philosophy of that moment and in that sense propose a narrative of national ideas, but the parties have never consistently embodied even their own narrative.

Great public eruptions of fraternal idealism seem, at the time and in memory, to have a profound, unfolding significance that sets them apart from humdrum daily history. Neither the ordinary flow of communal life nor ordinary politics have a single argumentative thread: a hundred agendas and side deals are being pursued at a time. But in the moments of crisis when we notice fraternity as a dramatic truth and discovery, an answer to some great questions seems to be at hand. When the historical development of that moment is retold by participants, with all of its competing appeals and pressures folded into the tale, the telling begins to resemble the unfolding dialectic of a symposium.

Symposia were rituals. In the eruptive fraternal moments of history and in uncountable teams and clubs, fraternity emerges as a value distinct from the subject addressed, and sustaining it becomes a goal in itself for many members. Rituals or ceremonial routines are soon adopted, although they may be as lightly official as the Friday night gathering of an office team for beer or comical celebrations recognizing leaders and outstanding followers when the year's sales results are announced. When a strongly fraternized group is disbanded, even when its cause has been successfully achieved many participants grieve both the lost comradeship and the lost sense of significance. When movements succeed in their goals, some members may even resent the success of their cause or deny that full success was achieved. Others will argue that the group should take advantage of its unified strength to set new goals. If these tactics do not suit, the veterans may schedule regular reunions to commemorate the cause, their heroes, and their own continued bond.

The issue of ritual repetition and revivals is too large and rich to detour for here, but it is worth noting that very often in politics, in plans for reforms or revolutions, and sometimes even in the inaugural stages of warfare, a repetition with mythic overtones pulls recruits to the new cause. Tocqueville, elected to the newly created French legislature in 1848,[7] was struck by the degree to which fledgling legislators around him were, in effect, play-acting roles from the first Revolution. Few had experience in any sort of legislature; such rituals as calling to order and magnificent speeches absorbed them. They had no notion that in established legislatures almost all the real work is done off the floor, in side conferences or coffee shops where deals are struck and difficulties worked out. According to Simon Shama, many of the original French revolutionaries of 1789 were equally self-dazzled, taking up poses they attributed to classical heroes, as if their speeches "were to be recorded by a new Tacitus."[8] In later revolutions, the revolutionaries' arguments about theory and strategy have often been colored by the desire to imitate: a theory of revolution is in effect the script for playing the revolutionary: successors of Marx, Lenin and Mao have sometimes argued theoretically correct strategies furiously.

To consider a very different venue that illustrates how and why rituals arise from symposial moments, schools and colleges are unusually rich in rituals. By their nature they deal with groups and make constant use of collective psychology to shape behavior. They make constant use of large events like graduations, but also practice innumerable smaller rituals of support for athletic teams, competitions for honors, appeals to class and house spirit, and so on. They use the natural sociability of youth as an instrument for shaping adult habits and, more simply, for getting everyone to work together. Over the course of a standard modern primary and secondary education, at least in the U.S., the different exposures to varied styles of community that occur are beyond counting. They range from simple extensions of maternal caring in early grades to parades, holiday pageants, orchestras, student governments, sports teams, and neophyte professional cadres. The levels graduate and build (often involving parents and/or a wider community) so that imagining a young adult in a new social circle involves a paradox: on one hand, youth's emotional and physical spark makes truly new things possible, painting their experience with fresh colors as if springtime had arrived. On the other hand, a modern youngster's models of interaction are never wholly new, but a flowering previously shared by many others, colored by family, friends and gangs of friends, the tribe or town, and in our example many classrooms.

What happens in the symposial moment? To start with, as in other fraternal moments there is an intensification of instincts for observing each other and enthusiasm for the topic or challenge at hand. When it occurs, the participants seem suddenly more gifted and the current of understanding and enthusiasm for what they understand together can be described as a leaping fire or as an electric current. Members may see themselves as continuing a larger myth or ideal community in a newly active way: the nation, the Body Of Christ, the Folk, The New Order, Manifest Destiny, Church Tradition, the Proletariat. If they do not feel that context at the time, they may impose it in memory. Thus, for many participants in the U.S. Civil Rights Movement, the solidarity among blacks and whites was not only completion of a deferred national destiny but an enactment of relations that would be imitated by the whole nation afterward. The larger myth turns the identity and story of the specific group into a chapter in a larger tale, raising the identities of the actors and their peers to roles in history.

The sense of being part of a Great Moment is sometimes more important to followers than to leaders, for the leaders often receive great satisfaction from leadership itself and may need to be reminded that the common purpose is larger than their role; they may also see that the great emotional moment that thrills participants is in a sense only a moment onstage, a useful public occasion but a temporary culmination. The pleasures of fraternity also differ for leaders and followers because the leaders are often parental and in any case monitors of the shared goal, sustaining group morale while possibly insisting on a strategy that costs members discomfort. They filter what they hear from the brethren and from the world outside the group, standing a little away from the group passion even as they feed it, more exhilarated by their control of the action and by members' admiration than by the joy of belonging that followers may have. As leaders, they already have acceptance and visibility and may fight furiously to sustain that status.

In some lasting movements, it might even be useful to speak of three levels of myth or history: 1) an overarching image (the Mystical body of Christ, the Triumph of the Proletariat, Equality); 2) a story or texts left by the Founders (the Acts of the Apostles, the Federalist Papers); and 3) the evolving current story of the group as it interprets itself to itself. Under the double roof of the mythic idea and the heroic forerunners' history the personalities and factions of the Founders become touchstones by which the current group describes and judges itself. If the group has an elaborate ideology, factions in the current group may praise or damn each other by identification with earlier factions, as Jeffersonian or Jacobin or Trotskyite.

In a mature brotherhood-in-action, as in a dialogue, ordinary members may share the sense of leadership responsibility and some of the leader's freedom of expression. As is true even in an adult family, brothers and sisters may expect to exercise responsibility and even leadership. In most of the fraternities that interest a reader of history there is continual tension, sometimes divisive but often creative, between each member's impulse to follow loyally and that of taking a larger role: there will be brothers or sisters who dissent from the leaders, claiming to do so on behalf of the cause, while others who insist on complete solidarity. Every society has formulae and processes for channeling these tensions, for a degree of leadership by followers and subordinates is crucial for success in most efforts. Choosing properly when to follow and how to lead in team roles is one of the skills—really a stance toward participation rather than a specific skill, but one that needs practice—that young people are taught and that different organizations try to modulate among members.

Within moments of symposial fraternity the flowering or revelation of identity may come from temporary abandonment of an unsatisfactory self or from what might be called self-creation through the action of that moment. Within the group there arises a comradely competition to serve notably well, perhaps exceeding one's expectations of oneself as well as that of the peers. Based in part on that dedication to appear well before the others and an assurance of acceptance for that effort, the bond that grows will feel like friendship, though diffused among many "friends." For those who are insecure it may be a relief that the bonds and mutual claims of the fraternity are both justified and tacitly limited by something external to their own worth, the worthy cause. For others, the benefits of belonging may far outweigh any intrinsic attraction to the cause. For both kinds of participants, intimacies become available that could not be found otherwise, and as a result they grieve for the lost comradeship when the group disbands.

Glenn Gray, writing about the almost ecstatic bravery that sometimes comes over soldiers in combat, suggests that the individual's fear of death recedes because the comradeship— the unit— is immortal[9]. This leads individuals to sacrifice themselves willingly for the others: the individual's death does not destroy the life of the platoon or unit in which he is most intensely himself. A martyr may feel the same, he suggests, but in a far lonelier context, for his comrades are not likely to be close behind him, needing to be saved by his risk.

Gray's inference about the effect of group immortality is worth pausing to consider further for a moment, for it suggests again the wide range of intense experiences that "fraternity" can cover. In combat units, there are often moments in which an individual risks himself with such unusual flair or lack of hesitation that he exemplifies, even more clearly than his comrades, Gray's surmise that the immortality of the group has lifted his fear of personal mortality. An example in recent wars might be the individual soldier who makes a lone charge against a machine gun nest that has been pinning down and killing his teammates. In older wars, the archetype would be the soldier who picks up the banner from a fallen flag-bearer to sustain a charge: flag-bearers were special targets, so that the gesture clearly embodied the *elan* of the whole unit at increased risk to oneself. Everyone else in the unit, all of them under fire, have sworn fealty to the nation and in the seasoned units that Gray describe are full of loyalty to each other, but that lone attacker or that volunteer flag-bearer is seen as filled with a moment of higher courage on the unit's behalf —"above and beyond the call of duty"—a wonder even to the comrades in the same battle. (Stephen Crane's hero in *The Red Badge of Courage* picks up the unit standard from a fallen comrade and charges with it in a fury of courage that he does not quite understand, but his comrades praise him and he is proud for having done it.) Behind the lines, thousands of soldiers have taken the same oaths and are part of a large military fraternity in service of that immortal thing the state, but their relation is far more abstract than this connection to the immediate comrades.

In Gray's memoir there is a glimpse of one of the other faces of fraternity. He was an intelligence officer during the

American invasion of Italy in World War II; while examining caves near a battlefield in search of deserters he came upon an aged hermit who was puzzled by the noise of combat. The old man did not know that there was a war going on. The two men, a philosopher by training and a hermit, had a conversation for a few hours about timeless issues, utterly freed for a moment from other constraints: *Who am I? What am I here for?* Hannah Arendt, introducing the paperback issue of *The Warriors*, comments, "This is fraternity." [10] Whether in such moments of colloquy between the two seekers after understanding, or in the furious comradeship of battle, the assertion and revelation of self to comrades, non-erotic and non-possessive, is central to what fraternity offers.

The same sort of assurance that one lives through the group that Gray posits may operate on a less dramatic level in many cultures where individualism seems to be of less moment than in the modern West and (to Western eyes) death seems to be treated as less momentous. Perhaps a customary expression of the same mechanism occurs in some of our common rituals of comfort in bereavement, or even resignation to aging: the comfort of fellowship, the sense that we undergo things together and indeed as part of natural order, comforts us rather than any new insight into the meaning of that order. One is reminded of Tolstoy, who began to feel the emptiness of philosophic explanations of life, joining the activities of his peasant tenants in order to share their simple acceptance of life. Tolstoy wished to join them in that peace, and seems to have succeeded in doing so, but did not share an exactly identical religious faith. It is the peace of fellowship rather than the specific faith or ideal that offers release from personal misery in such cases: the Truth or the Cause is only the sand particle around which the pearl of comfort forms.

Chapter 4. Two Ancient Models: Plato's *Symposium*, the Last Supper in John's *Gospel*

The greatest of the symposiums is Plato's. What I wish to pick out from it, at the cost of some repetition of material in the previous chapters, are moments that can serve as images of the processes of small-group fraternity. Plato's *Symposium* is a particularly interesting model because it displays what it dissects: eros, which is both desire and the fervor of relationship. The work stands as a useful model of the fact that continuous exploration of a fraternal group's mission and its mutual regulation by myth or theory can prolong fraternal feeling, sustain enthusiasm and create shared memories or even institutions. To treat a work of literature in this way is to propose that elements within the story can stand as a system for similar experiences outside it. In sketching Plato's dialogue, I am not so much interested in the content of the arguments as in the interactions within the small group, where the energy of brotherhood is both visible and part of the subject matter discussed.

Symposium's story is framed: it is a dialogue within a dialogue. It starts when the narrator, Aristodemos, is asked by a younger man, Glaucon, about the conversation at Agathon's drinking party, which he has heard about and assumes was a recent event. Aristodemos reconstructs the whole series of arguments, which occurred years before. The *Symposium's* arguments have already been winnowed to their memorable essence: the story has become its own myth, and Glaucon is about to enter its mystery. For my purpose, the frame offers a useful reminder that bright moments of fraternity take on a dramatic shape in the memory, and for some participants become touchstones by which friendship or significant action in society are henceforth measured. Because few details are sketched, minor details of dress or a slight gesture become portentous, as we will see later when Agathon changes his seat:

> Then Agathon said, "...I notice how [Alcibiades] reclined between me and you in order to keep us apart. Then he shall gain nothing by it, and I will come past you and recline there." [1]

In *Symposium*, the speakers are historic personages who are also in character as eloquent speakers, for they all represent intellectual disciplines: the healing arts of the physician, the argumentative skills of the professional rhetoric-teacher, and those of writers, philosophers, and politicians. Although the dialogue does not say so explicitly, it becomes clear that their specialties are disciplined expressions of eros, that desirous love which is also the topic of their dialogue.

A useful further aspect of the framing dialogue between Aristodemos and Glaucon is that the oral tradition of Agathon's banquet becomes an invitation to join the circle of disciples, those who love the activity of philosophy and therefore Socrates. Aristodemos laughs at himself, as Socrates often does, but then recruits Glaucon:

> I used to run all over the place...but I was more miserable than anyone–just as you are now, when you think you would rather do anything than be a philosopher.[2]

The importance of witnesses, the power of the retold story, and above all the instinct that brings a likely recruit are significant here just as they are in the stories of Jesus' recruitment of several disciples in the Gospels. Key figures arrive to the feast as if brought by some fate or because the leader sees their special capacity. Many epic stories dedicate long narratives to the gathering of the heroes, whether to sail the Argo, besiege Troy, man the Pequod's whaleboats, defeat the Lord of the Rings, or join the Seven Samurai. Some tales involve a search for the exactly necessary person for the team, without whom nothing will succeed: thus, Nestor uses a trick to force the unwilling Odysseus to enlist for the Trojan War, who in turn uses a trick to find Achilles in *his* hiding place. But in many cases of eventually fateful enlistment there is no explanation but coincidence that in retrospect seems fateful.

There is both recruitment and coincidence in *Symposium*: Aristodemos says he fell in with Socrates and invited him to Agathon's feast, but when they arrive Agathon assures him that he had tried to find him to invite him. Aside from the courtesy, the sense of an almost fated coming-together is intensified. After a ritual invocation to the gods, the participants agree explicitly on the topic: Eryximachos, taking a suggestion from Phaidon, proposes that the topic be praise of love, and Socrates, their intellectual leader, seconds the suggestion, assuring that it is the one thing he knows about!

Even before the friends confirm their topic, they have defined their rules for working together. In many fraternal efforts, as in most organizational action, an agreed-on process and goal are a routine and welcome channeling, like the rules of an athletic contest. Most of the symposium's participants had drunk hard the previous night so that tonight they agree to be temperate, pleasing their minds while resting their queasy stomachs. To focus on talk they send away their flute-player. In what follows the participants cooperate but display competitive gifts. Competitor/collaborators, they are also artists: each differs from previous speakers by using his unique art while complementing truths that the predecessor spoke. This dialectic, which Plato manages as no one else ever has, as a social process resembles the mutual exhortation and channeled competition that mark good teams in sport or great jazz combos, each stimulating the other to play so well that they expand the bounds of their skill. When this occurs, the experience is not of strain but of rising exhilaration. The individual actors outdo themselves, taking energy from each to each, as if—as Plato says elsewhere—a leaping flame passed among them.

Because there will be competition there is a bit of verbal jousting among the most talented players at the outset: Agathon responds to Socrates' complaint that he cannot compete against the poet's verbal talent by challenging Socrates' false modesty:

> "You are a scoffer, Socrates!" said Agathon. "Well, we will come into court before long about this, you and I, on our claim for wisdom, and the judge shall be Dionysus."[3]

Although we may not associate playfulness with some of the great mass movements and revolts of history, there has usually been a considerable measure of playfulness and fantasy in the early stages, whether the crowning of a pretty street girl as Goddess of Liberty in the Paris of the 1789, or the natural-seeming linkage of "hippy" dropout culture with the anti-war movements in the United States in the 1960's. Even crowd violence often has its element of play, whether giddiness at the animal power of so many bodies and throats combined, or the playing out of cruel fantasies as effigies are burned, buildings vandalized, or individuals tortured amidst laughter. In American tradition, the Indian disguises of the Boston Tea Party were fantasy with a message; in later years, the mobs that poured tar and feathers over enemies represented the cruel turn of play. In his history of the French Revolution, Simon Shama dispels the notion that the Revolution had innocent and murderous stages in turn, demonstrating that it was often murderous from the first[4]. At the revolutionary moment, though, and in memory, even the cruelty seemed festive: two sides of the same coin, a currency too easily exchanged.

When there is no friendly competition to serve the common goal, fraternity is experienced less intensely. On the other hand, when the competition ceases to be bound by tacit or explicit rules, or where victory over the others is a ruthless goal, the result is paralysis of the group. Even in friendly competition, the disinhibition of the festive setting or the fury of the game always threatens to unbolt the gates. Much of the pleasure of the game is precisely in the channeling of the energy unleashed; children are often taught competitive games as means to understanding control of temper, rules, penalties, and tolerance of defeat, while occasions when an adult in a friendly game loses his temper or cheats are preludes to his losing friends. At a feast of arguments like *Symposium*, in parallel with physically difficult games, there is a double struggle against the intellectual opponent and against the difficulty of the subject at hand. At the same time—and this is hard to put into more precise words—the brother- or sisterhood that emerges is felt to assure the authenticity of the truths uncovered. The participants see the object of their attention together and through each other's eyes. As they interpret their vision to each other they are also more visible to the others as persons: this is a great strength that comes of self-challenging work together. On the other hand, sects or parties dedicated to some change or revolution are often so profoundly inward-looking, constantly re-examining and monitoring adherence to their ideology, that they can be paralyzed by disputes over the correct doctrine.

The play of competing forms of expertise is *The Symposium's* way of representing the visibility of each to each that occurs in deep experiences of fraternity, the revelation of secret selves, emotions, passions, and gifts in a way that meets the occasion yet is deeply personal. As I indicated earlier, one reason why youths seem to run quickly and naturally through a myriad of small fraternities is, in part, that identity is forming in so many different ways that the need to reveal one's newest self and to be accepted is relentless. Recognition, the chance to be truly known—even for one's hidden dreams and forbidden angers to be known—is one of the gifts that fraternity offers. A youth who does not find that fraternity among adolescent friends because of isolated location, race, sexual preference, or special talents or handicaps sometimes develops a deeper understanding of his own inner life and is often deeply selective and deeply appreciative of communities and friendships in later life. Referring back for a moment to our discussion of individuals in fraternal outbreaks, the "organizational junkies" or "true believers" are on the other extreme of the spectrum, having no worthy selves in their own eyes without the cause and the group identity. Many truly creative souls, who may have great strength of identity, and many youths who are starting to listen intensely to their own souls, oscillate between self-discovery in isolation (perhaps in art or scientific studies) with intense sociability. They seek out like-minded people and their get-togethers have the sparkle of relief, of letting go after strain. Many artists alternate periods of solitary work with exuberant socializing, which may have also been true of some of Plato's discussants. Occasionally, artistic temperaments— not always the greatest talents, but with the artist's ability to turn full energy to the moment—mark the fiery leaders of movements, for they, like actors entering the stage, can commit themselves wholly, enacting the charisma that ignites a group.

To return to *Symposium*, the opening speaker, Phaidon, offers a lovely encomium of love–his version is homosexual– as the power that raises individual souls above their natural level to achieve generosity, loyalty, nobility of soul. For our use of the dialogue as a model, it is a reminder that all forms of love have, or claim to have, the ability to raise the individual above the level of usual talents. Moreover, "being in love," like conversion to great causes, puts one under an umbrella of expectations that in this case are described as entirely praiseworthy. Next the sophist Pausanias, like professors of later eras, divides the topic: *eros* offers several observable types and the elevating passion is not the one usually observed. He suggests therefore that there are two loves, a higher kind that Phaidon described and common sexual passions that evince no such nobility.

The next speaker should be Aristophanes but he has the hiccups from overindulgence. Eryximachos, a physician, has also been acting as the symposiast or overseer of discussion, whose job is to keep the arguments on track and the friends in harmony. He advises Aristophanes to try to sneeze as a cure, while agreeing to speak in his turn. In Eryximachos' discourse eros is the principle of harmony and balance, a source of healing, in effect the symposiast of life itself.

After a fit of sneezing, Aristophanes is ready to speak, He makes a joke that could undercut the whole preceding discourse of love as an elevating passion and principle of harmony: he suggests that curing a hiccup or scratching where it tickles–i.e., meeting bodily urges that are uncontrollable and even ridiculous--may have more to do with a satisfying life than any nobler impulse! Eryximachos rebukes him, for like the team prankster or class clown, Aristophanes' wit threatens to derail the group from its purpose. Yet Aristophanes is not the least valued nor least perceptive speaker: he keeps the physical and impulsive behavior that eros causes in the foreground. Admonished to be serious, he proceeds with a hilarious alternative myth: eros is an expression of pure emptiness, a divine punishment. Humans were once made like large spheres, with two sexual organs apiece. Some of the spheres were all-male, some all-female, and some mixed. But humanity offended the gods, who split us in half. Since then, eros is merely each divided sphere's longing for its other half.

Moreover, mankind has not reformed, so that unless we behave better we may be split again with the result that we will look like reliefs carved on a wall! This tale is one of divine action, but far from the tacit self-congratulations of Phaidon it reflects the awkward or seamy behavior of actual lovers while picturing the depth of their need as the work of divinities. Aristophanes joins Phaidon's praise of homosexual love, claiming that the boys who are best suited for it are descended from male/male spheres; in doing so, he introduces the issue of *political* eros by suggesting that those same boys are the ones most likely to become leaders in manhood.

Taking Aristophanes' speech as a guide to additional fraternal themes, three lessons are easily drawn. The first, which may seem to contradict much of what was said above, is the lightness with which the fraternal affiliations may begin. Many an organization swells its membership simply because it offers a place to go to and people to be with, and many a revolt swells because it entertains the restless and momentarily rootless. Reasons for belonging may be as unconsidered as scratching an itch at first, no matter how grandiose the slogans or manifestoes of the organization, nor how deep the angers that finally break out. On the other hand, the great themes of would-be leaders may be diverted to light satisfactions, the circuses that appease the mob.

The second lesson is about humor. It is generally forbidden to loyal members of the group to notice awkward or self-serving behaviors of devotees except as that noticing furthers the members' allegiance to the cause. There can be great laughter and affectionate teasing in many groups, and indeed that intimacy is one of the fraternal pleasures, but the group has tacit rules about when and where the members can laugh at each other. Above all, the purpose for which the group exists is not to be ridiculed. Ridicule of the leaders may be allowed but usually as a privilege of the most supportive colleagues, perhaps reserved for ceremonial moments like the comic "roasts" of our days or the Dionysian festivals of the Greeks.

The final lesson I would draw from Aristophanes, the lesson that Socrates draws, is that great and mean passions do not signal two different kinds of love at work as the speakers before Aristophanes argued, but response to the same emptiness. In a practical community context, we may speak of good and bad fraternity as one group or party is constructive and the other not, but which is which is often debatable, and the motives of members might be more similar than we like to think.

Humorous arguments generally cannot be answered, but only transcended. The next speaker, Agathon, does not try to deal directly with the threat of Aristophanes' vision. Rather, he rises to the tragic poet's height, praising Love "as it is in itself," not as it effects humankind. For him, as for Lucretius writing about Venus centuries later, eros is the creative force within all order. Subsuming the idealistic descriptions of love in previous speeches, Agathon describes Love as source of meaning, harmony, fruitfulness, beauty. It has the four great virtues: temperance, justice, wisdom, and courage. His sublime view should have disheartened the following speaker as a competitor, for the eloquence of his vision seems unopposable: Surely, if there is any profound truth about Love, it must be this!

Socrates knows that the tragic poet has ignored the comic poet's truth. He resolves the competing visions, but first reinterprets the group's task, or rather redefines it to suit his own approach:

> I was a fool when I told you I would take my turn in singing the favours of Love...I did not know how an encomium was made, and it was without this knowledge that I agreed to take my part in praising...I take it back now; I make no eulogy in this

> fashion....However, the truth, if you like: I have no objection to telling the truth, in my own fashion....[5]

Rather than speaking on his own authority, Socrates, although in effect the leader of this company, interrogates Agathon to make him identify contradictions inherent in his views, and then reports the theory of Love he obtained in a dialogue years before with the priestess Diotima. Socrates' answer thus possesses an authority beyond his own although she teaches him through dialogue, his own art. Given that his view of eros is that it is a seeking after truth/beauty, and that he has announced at the outset of the dialogue that it is the only thing he really claims to know about, it is fitting that he portrays himself as a seeker who found instruction. It also notifies us, however, if we were not fully aware from the discourses of Phaidon and Agathon, that to *explain* love (or even love's power over humans) is to explain a divinity, which is beyond our power. Diotima meets the challenge of the opposite views of love, i.e. that it expresses noble desire for beauty or the commonest sort of emptiness, by explaining that eros is a demigod, an intermediate power between the earthly and the heavenly, seeking the beautiful in ascending levels but never reaching it. This explanation sustains the idealism with which Phaidon fathered the chain of argument yet acknowledges that eros is driven by incompleteness.

Among the many sorts of love that might be described as work of a demigod, a power that yearns, the brotherhood of a group committed to action is one: the unfilled common purposes creates the eros of the group even when from moment to moment there is also enjoyment of friendship. The notion of a demigod has a particularly close fit with group enthusiasms. Writing centuries later, Plutarch considered the story that a voice was heard from the sky announcing the death of the god Pan. His explanation was that many local gods and heroes whose cults had arisen and faded were not expressions of that timeless divinity which wears the names of high gods such as Zeus and Aphrodite for its different aspects in our lives, but demigods: intermediate spirits who exist for a few generations and fade away. While they thrive, they fill cults and movements with their energy; but they eventually pass away or desert their devotees. It is a demigod, a fiery but time-bound divinity, whom we see in the fraternal outbursts that mark history for a generation or perhaps for a century.

The intellectual poem of the *Symposium* is complete at this point; yet there is a final act to the drama that is of great interest for our use of the dialogue as a model. There is a commotion and Alcibiades enters: a handsome politician and brilliant student of Socrates later accused of vandalizing gods' statues and still later exiled after leading a disastrous expedition to Sicily. He would end as a traitor in service to the Spartans. When the politician enters several things change. First, the focus is back to sexual love, in this case Alcibiades' affectionately rueful praise of Socrates' refusal to be seduced by him. His praise is combined with an astute recognition that the Silenus-faced Socrates is in fact a sensual man under reason's power rather than indifferent to desire. There is also a literal rearrangement of positions: Agathon, the speaker of greatest persuasive power and noblest vision, moves to the other side of Socrates as if to counterbalance Alcibiades: philosophy sits between poetry and politics.

Alcibiades praises not love but Socrates. Alcibiades' politic art is to know others' characters including the weaknesses that will serve his ends, which are self-serving. (The poet Donald Justice has remarked somewhere that Alcibiades should be a figure of terror to educators, for despite brilliant gifts and the tutelage of the greatest moral educator ever, he turned evil.) Alcibiades' praise of Socrates is relevant to the earlier speeches of *Symposium* in that it is about seduction. Personal virtue such as Socrates possesses is needed to approach the higher loves: Alcibiades' interest on the other hand is in domination and he makes his personality shine. He brings us back from abstractions to personal desire, and to the bonds created by personal charisma. Soon after he finishes talking, a group of revelers breaks in, and the scene of dialogue becomes a drunken party. A feast of reason turned orgiastic is the way that some would describe the course of the French Revolution from high-minded declarations of the Rights of Man to the Reign of Terror. As the party ends, Socrates is awake and sober and is trying to explain to the two poets that comedy and tragedy are essentially the same, an argument appropriate to Dionysus' presence. Aristophanes, having drunk deeply, expresses the great artist's ultimate indifference to critical theory by falling asleep.

Endings are important in symposia. If they do not end in disorder, they end in some sort of dismissal to the world of action. Socrates' other great pupil, Xenophon, also wrote a *Symposium*, where Socrates holds forth on education for a father who wants practical advice. Xenophon's the final scene is one where the host brings in a pair of dancers to enact Dionysus' courtship of Ariadne. The erotic scene, prelude to the enduring and faithful marriage of the god with a mortal heroine, stirs the younger men, who decide it is time to go home to their wives. Socrates walks home talking calmly with an old friend: the symposial moment is ended but two forms of permanent relation are resumed.

John's account of the Last Supper

The story of the Last Supper as told by John is that of a seder rather than a drinking-bout, and the form is that of a master instructing disciples rather than unfolding argument, but it is in the broad tradition of symposia and dialogues, which the ancients including other scriptural writers used in a variety of forms. Jesus discourses as he sits or lies on a banquet couch next to his favorite, John. His address, complex and beautiful, is about the unity of the disciples in the face of the world's adversity, a discourse prompted at key turns by Peter's requests for clarification. Like Plato's *Symposium*, the discourse heightens the same unity that it analyzes but the great difference is that it is about how the community will remain connected as it acts in the world. The shared pursuit of an idea in a philosophical symposium, wonderful as it is, does not raise the issues of courage, effectiveness, or sustaining unity against pressure that action demands. Beyond this great difference the similarities to Plato's *Symposium* are numerous: a teacher of great virtue divinely instructed on the topic, a traitor on hand, and (as told in Luke's Gospel) a mob scene follows in Gesthemane, where Jesus goes to pray and the Apostles fall asleep full of wine until a crowd arrives to arrest Jesus and a brawl occurs in which Peter cuts off an opponent's ear.

Among the elements in John's account most relevant to our theme is, first, the command to "love one another." It is given within the context of the group's bond with the leader and its mission but is not conditioned on particular roles that individuals may play, nor on their future interpretations of the group' ideology. In the history of Christianity's founding, this state of unity became difficult as soon as the disciples went forth to proselytize, as the story of future apostle Paul's desire to enroll Gentiles over Peter's opposition was to demonstrate. But dogma, in the ordinary sense at least, is not central to the unity that Jesus describes: rather, mutual love is the antidote to divisions over dogma and strategy. In arming the apostles for their mission, Jesus sets up a complex set of relations that must guide them: with him, with the Father who has given him authority, with each other, and with the world, which will recognize their distinctive unity and hate them–a hatred which in its way is welcome, for indifference is much more destructive to serious causes than is active hostility.

Jesus at this moment is what Plutarch would have called the Apostle's demigod, the hero whose immediate charisma is to be replaced by an inspiriting power which he promises will come, that of the Paraclete or "Advocate," here no further defined. An important feature of their enduring strength together is what is now called, perhaps bloodlessly, servant leadership: a large literature among Christian organizations (and beyond, including some current writings on non-profit leadership) exists on leading to serve others in an exemplary humility of style that underlines the primacy of serving over personal status. Jesus is not only *close* to the least member of their company but identifies himself as lowest in whatever hierarchies they imagine. He dramatizes the mutual humility of their order by washing the feet of the group disciples over Peter's objection.

This model of leadership is powerful by assuring the leader's full identification with the least significant member of the group. Peter is the foil who constantly defines the wrong ideas of leadership: the future leader of the sect has the instinctive partisanship, the practical energy and the taste for command that make him an inevitable leader, but he is filled with conventional notions about hierarchy, loyalty, and the perquisites of leadership. As the narrative makes clear a bit later, Peter is jealous of John (one cannot help thinking that John, or writers in his tradition, took special aim at institutional thinkers in writing this narrative). When Peter objects to Jesus' washing of the disciples' feet, unable to accept the action as the lesson it is, Jesus tells him, "Unless I wash you, you have no share with me."[6] His response is that of the loyalist who follows before he understands: "Lord, not my feet only, but also my hands and my head." Jesus tempers this true-believer's instinct for the external: "He who has washed his feet is clean all over."

Peter's compulsion to be in the forefront is not a bad trait in a disciple or leader, in fact is inevitably found in most leaders, but Jesus subjects it to two disciplines: a desire to serve the cause more than one's own status, and what we would call a democratic conviction rooted in the Jewish Covenant: all believers are equal, and the leader must humble himself because God finds every soul worthy. The Peter of John's Last Supper is devoid of his leader's vision even though his loyalty is boisterous; he is humbled by rebuke, but his sincere love for Jesus will force him to serve as commanded.

Peter's humbling is part and parcel of John's teaching. Like the future Church, Peter is repeatedly tempted by, and must be weaned away from, styles of leadership that contravene the spiritual purpose for which leadership is given. As the *Acts of the Apostles* shows, his first instinct after the Resurrection was to consolidate successes and maintain walls of exclusion for his band rather than allow Gentile converts to ignore traditional Jewish rituals. These are the instincts of a leader who understands the natural dynamics of doctrine and ritual to unify an organization; Paul would soon make doctrine a source of wider affiliation in an unexpected way.

In early church history, if one imagines John's gospel and *Acts* as a single story, Peter is not displaced from authority but given instruction. He is not a subtle learner and in John's narrative grows strident under the pressure of his confusion and rebuke. As for Jesus himself as teacher/leader, throughout the Last Supper narrative Jesus subordinates both group satisfaction and his own ego, in the narrow sense at least, to the necessities of his mission and the slightly complex guidance he offers. I say "narrow sense" because he feels exhilaration at the final act's inexorable dawning, the working-out of his Father's will. "When [Judas] had gone out, Jesus said, 'Now the Son of Man has been glorified....'" [7]He has no illusions about the weaknesses of his brethren, predicting that the loyalist Peter would deny him, but that does not undermine his profession of love nor his repeated command to the disciples to imitate his mutual love: "I give you a new commandment. As I have loved you, so you should love one another."[8]

Jesus' leading is that of one delegated, perhaps like an elder brother charged with his father's authority. He prays to the Father,

> While I was with them, I protected them...guarded them....I am not asking you to take them out of the world, but I ask you to protect them from the evil one....[9]

Members in any group may take courage from their common mission and from their leaders that they feel they would not have in their own right. It often happens that the sheer energy and power of the conviction that they carry into the world makes them persuasive. In revolutionary times, they discover that the world is full of people who have awaited just such a message as they bring. Jesus promises this courage and this secret effectiveness, without mitigating the unpopularity and difficulty of the mission, by assuring that the Advocate will come. The disciples may not have worldly force but will be marked by a connection to human depths and powers beyond their own gifts: "....When the spirit of truth comes, he will not speak on his own, but he will speak whatever he hears...."[10]

None of this is legalistic, despite the extraordinarily delicate balancing of the relations that Jesus offers: for, in the end, truth will judge the world: "I come not to judge the world....on the last day the word that I have spoken will serve as judge." That sense that the truth is present but not yet wakened in many hearts, and that spiritual connections are an invisible medium in which souls move to each other, sustains the believer on his or her mission. (To describe the sense of an invisible social medium of powerful currents, some eighteenth and nineteenth century thinkers used imagery of magnetic currents as described by mesmerism to describe a common spirit flowing among those who felt its power.)

There are two other moments in John's narrative when Peter, the loyal but unwise disciple who would (and will) lead, is in the forefront. One occurs when Jesus explicitly confronts Peter with his implicit claim to love him more than the other disciples do: "Simon Peter, do you love me more than these?" (13/21)[11] It is notable that Jesus does not say in turn that he loves Peter any more or less than the others. Rather, he turns Peter's ferocity into a command that responds to Peter's nature: "feed my sheep...Follow me!" This is the lesson that Jesus taught by symbolic action in the washing of feet, but now Jesus makes it an explicit command, which is the sort of direction that makes sense to Peter. It explicitly transforms love of one leader, Jesus, to responsibility for the group.

And there is the final note, about John himself. When Jesus, resurrected, reappears and commands Peter to follow him, John also follows. Peter instantly asks, "What of him?" Peter can't, even now, let go of hierarchical issues nor his instinctive jealousy of John, whose place in Jesus' eyes seems to have no relation to professions of loyalty or to the services he can do. Jesus answers, "If it is my will that he remain until I come, what is that to you? Follow me!"[12] (21/22) The repetition humbles by its plainness and also by its opaqueness. The hardest thing, sometimes, in any organization of people with powerful feelings about each other, whether among saints or families or jealous schoolchildren, is simply to accept that one's place in the movement and in the father's or mother's or leader's eyes is not entirely in one's power. One's place in the organization, one's virtue or usefulness or even complete authority, never fully controls the bonds that hold the members together. As in any group there are loves among group members, and sometimes currents of respect or popularity, that transcend the group loyalties in unseen ways. Sometimes these affections become sources of bitter division because one would-be friend or lover is jealous, or a leader is jealous of another's popularity. In royal courts in previous eras, where the ruler's friendship meant power, differences in affection from peers or leaders could have savage results. In this dialogue there are mysteries of affection, but it is not for the group or any jealous member to envy or to judge.

The two dialogues we have just outlined illustrate patterns of interaction within purposeful small groups that are universal, but in these cases the leaders and the willing participants combine to discipline the group process, subjecting it to the pursuit of truth about a great ideal in one case, to revelation in the second case. They remind us of the universal fact that keeping purposeful organizations on track is a challenge both for leaders and followers. Even aside from the internal competitions, contradictory agendas arise as individuals and communities mediate among other claims on their loyalty: family, clubs, friends, lovers, other causes, the nation, greed, or other gods. Fraternities that have been gathered for a complex or difficult purpose therefore often evolve methods and teachings on to how to balance other claims. Inherent in the group dynamic is competition for status and for authority, for personal rivalries may break even highly idealistic organizations, but in successful cases that competitive dynamic and some balance of other claims are channeled as members challenge each other to perform well.

Chapter 5. The Crowd and the Vigil

The famous historic eruptions of communal passion in revolutions, crusades, and riots are special cases of crowd emotion: mutually exciting, often memorable, sometimes enthralling and occasionally terrifying. Often these moments allow an assemblage of the like-minded to celebrate brotherhood and enmity to opponents in the same fiery breath. This alternation or double-sidedness is true whether one sees the eruptions in historical accounts or close: the French Revolution, with its idealisms, its great declarations, its pageantry, its mobs -and its mob-supported Terrors, is the paradigmatic historical image of crowds changing history. Its positive images of revolutionary brotherhood have echoed seductively in revolutionary idealism for over two centuries, often sentimentalized in literature or films about the generous natural bonds among the workers, the peasants, or the People's Army. The French Revolution's violence and the wars that followed spawned the first wave of a usually reactionary literature on mass hysteria, mobs, and political extremism. On all sides, writers have wrestled with volatile public emotion as a key to modern politics: not merely as a momentary chaos of local mob powers, as with classical instances, but as a key to how (and whether) enlarged populations with an expectation of sharing authority continuously could support a stable polity.

The energy released in crowds is exhilarating and terrifying. For many participants, and sometimes for popular memory, the moments are uniquely bright or searing. They may be revelations of how we—the *we* of the charismatic moment— are one social body, a beautiful or tragic but very powerful One. The eruptive moment may seem a revelation of ignored truths about human nature, either its nobility or its savagery:

the best of times and the worst of times, with a meaning to be debated for generations to come. As indicated earlier, it is often a time when youth sets the tone, whether in hope or anger or both: as Wordsworth recalled of the French Revolution,

> Bliss was it in that dawn to be alive,
> But to be young was very heaven![1]

The sense of revelations and the note of youth are linked: the eruptive moment of fraternity may astonish everyone, but the sense of something utterly new revealing itself is likely to be most felt, and most welcomed, by the young. Still, it takes an old or very cynical mind set to be wholly immune to the fraternal blossoming.

Fraternal emotions obviously come in a wide range of kinds and intensities, some of which we have discussed above; they also arise in small or large groups or assemblies that we describe as crowds because they do not have an apparent internal structure nor long endurance. That makes them seem different in kind, whether an easy congregation of neighbors to a community picnic, the animal explosion of a revolutionary mob, the terror and exhilaration of the cavalry galloping to a charge, or the highs and lows of rabid fans at a fierce sports competition. When denizens of a city or nation are deeply stirred by an outbreak of fraternal emotion they assemble spontaneously and they find or invent symbols to imagine their cause together, structuring what they already feel is a shared story, prolonging and justifying their passion. In this vein, revolutions and revolts and sometimes the beginnings of wars often involve an exuberant outbreak of artistic and celebratory fantasy, with songs, pictures or pageants invented to express the feeling of liberation born when so many hearts join in the same emotion. These displays are usually evanescent, but when we find a truly thoughtful exception to the inarticulateness that is inherent in a great crowd's gathering the event is that much more memorable, a culmination as much as a new beginning: it takes on a long life in memory, giving birth to anniversaries or even to lasting institutions. A brilliant example is Dr.King's March on Washington, where leaders and followers had been highly articulate for many years beforehand about their mutual bonds, their common purpose, their large religious and democratic vision. There are many moments in religious ritual, feast days with elaborate costumes and ceremonies, which aim for a sense of culmination and renewal of fervor at the same time. They standardize and re-manufacture the quest for story and imagery that marks the crowd's exuberant fraternal moment. Culmination and renewal combined, marrying climax and future, is an essential function of such repetitions, rekindling communal passion to sustained devotion.

The outbreaks that make us look at fraternity as an eruptive factor in history involve tribal migrations, mass pilgrimages, violent mobs, and mass demonstrations. In almost every explosive instance, either manufactured for our excitement (as at a sports event or play) or in politics and war (where collective exuberance or ferocity is also manufactured but heightened by the fact that risks and costs may be serious), the crowd's moment is dramatic: the multitude feels its power, and the energy of the human pack in pursuit enhances the sense of individual strength. The personal enhancement that arises, which may include release from inhibitions to ecstatic joy or violence, is not entirely different from the effect that we see in well-coordinated groups whose members unite their efforts for a deliberate end, but that purposeful fraternity persists over longer time periods and may use moments of excitement as a tool, not as its emotional center. The "crowd," on the other hand, is short lived and largely without internal structure though it may have aims to accomplish for the period of its existence. Individuals in the crowd look to their fellows initially and crucially for confirmation that they are all *together*, for what follows is a sense of power. The exploding crowd which so fascinates us in history is not "efficient" except at celebrating or at tearing things down: it is like the wolf pack, not in its hours of shrewd selection and pursuit of a vulnerable caribou, but as it rushes in for the kill. We find a managed and artificial version of the crowd's power to rage, sorrow, hope or wonder in football stadiums and political rallies: the audience joins the team on the field empathetically as audiences at a dramas do but with simpler emotions, for the player on the field or the stage actor is concentrating on skills and timing and calculated bursts of intensity while the crowd's emotionality is usually that of freed emotions without preparation for systematic action. Along with "brotherhood" and "fraternity," then, *crowd* is the third term for fraternal emotion that must be considered because it applies in the most dramatic moments.

One of the most impressive, but eccentric, broad-scale works on crowds is Canetti's *Crowds and Power* (German publication 1960). Underlying his work is a deep awareness of the way in which crowds have been manipulated in modern politics, especially in some of the great fascist and communist movements. (A contemporary writer would add virtual manipulation of mass audiences by media even as the subjects of manipulation sit at home as a great and growing part of the subject.) The power of the physical crowds organized by movements like those of Mussolini and Hitler was twofold: they were means of directly threatening their society (and sometimes of destroying enemies physically) but at the same time underwrote a claim to represent the mass of the population, embodying in their marches or roars the aroused national spirit. The intention of crowd organizers was to demonstrate, by fearsome and exultant *fraternite*, that their party held the reins of the masses. It was undoubtedly helpful to them that even some of their enemies imagined modern mass societies as crowds in every respect but physical assemblage: anonymous and undirected. Facelessness is a characteristic that many thinkers fearfully or scornfully have attributed to modern mass man; facelessness is the characteristic of a crowd that implies freedom to act destructively without penalty. Enlisting the psychology of the mob as well as the threat of actual mobs seemed a uniquely fitting strategy for manipulation of a mass society. No doubt seasoned political and military leader have always been aware of crowd psychology in their cities or armies, but the era of revolutions and the ever-increasing sense of the masses as a sleeping crowd have made manipulation of the masses by crowd psychology a defining factor in modern history. Canetti makes this underlying terror of the masses as an ungathered crowd explicit: he sees all modern democratic and pseudo-democratic movements, along with mass armies, as the spirit of the crowd breaking through previous bounds of class and culture:

> Since the French revolution these eruptions have taken on a form which we feel to be modern....The history of the last 150 years has culminated in a spate of such eruptions; they have engulfed even wars, for all wars are now mass wars. The crowd....wants to experience for itself...its own animal force and passion and...will use whatever social pretexts and demands offer themselves.[2]

Yeats, looking mainly at the Irish political situation in 1920, expressed the fear that temperate citizens were paralyzed by uncertainty while fanatical spirits—the revolutionaries he viewed as full of intemperate crowd passions—were poised to act with disastrous effect: "The best lack all conviction; the worst/Are full of passionate intensity." [3]Yeats's take on his own nation's turmoil was quickly read as an expression of the world's political malaise.

Crowd emotions are mysterious because they are instinctive and like other instincts are not immediately clear to individuals who are swept by them. They involve animal surges, making members capable of frenzied energy; they awaken the animals nearby and like other instincts firing they overcome inhibitions. Animal metaphors for crowd emotions have abounded from early times, as have images of madness, drunkenness and sexual frenzy (stories of the bacchae combine all three). Conservative analysts of the French Revolution like DeMaistre used language suggesting that crowds become female (i.e. subject to hysteria) while the late nineteenth century theorist Gustave LeBon (*The Crowd: A Study of the Popular Mind*, 1896) proposed that the crowd becomes a collective beast. Although it is hard to define what a collective animal would be, there are some insects for which the description of a whole hive or nest as one animal elucidates their behavior; we might imagine many crowds as swarms, in a process that like the swarming of bees may have a useful purpose or may simply be a furious chaotic response to disturbance of the hive. The reactionary critic imagined a sullen collective beast whose instinct was to destroy, usually dormant but too easily awakened and manipulated.

The instinctive ability to collect in voice and action that we see in crowds, the quick swelling of emotion, and the exuberant physicality of that awakening, make it undeniable that animal energies and volatile social instincts are awakened in crowds all at once, but it is easy to add gothic or romantic overtones to the fact. Although we often use animal imagery for moments of frenzy, mammalian "crowds"—the wolf-pack is the instance just mentioned—often show skillful cooperation and judgment. The pack that cuts out a sickly caribou from its herd does so patiently and by strategy, dashing as a mob only for the kill, when furious suddenness

115

overwhelms the victim's resistance with the fewest possible injuries to the attackers. Packs devolve into frenzy at such moments and there can be no doubt that energetic action in a human mob involves our most feral selves, but whether panic or intelligent strategies steer the ferocity is not predetermined: close explanation of riots and revolutionary upheavals usually shows that some leaders and agitators have had clear intentions whether to reform, overthrow, revenge or pillage for profit.

Crowds and Power roots the sweeping energy in the sense of body, although in a peculiar way. Canetti identifies fear of physical closeness to others as a source: the crowd both enlists and overcomes that fear for a moment, creating a powerful release. I suspect that only a European of bourgeois background would identify that source, for the sense of desired physical distance varies by culture and by age of participants, but it is clearly true that the mob's physical intimacy generates power, exhilarating or terrifying. Rooting some of the crowd's power in mutual physicality is clearly correct, for even groups dancing together demonstrate that proximity and some repeated theme or motion create currents through a club, cult or village. Presumably, Canetti is also right in suggesting that crowd fervor can build on bonds or separation anxieties from childhood, and that (in freudian terms) the id, the unconscious "animal" self, is often close to the surface in a turbulent crowd. Destructiveness and cruelty like that of animals in a rage are easily unleashed in crowds, although one reason is that the least temperate individuals, with a grudge or a wish to vandalize, take the lead because they are safe in crowd anonymity.

Parallels for human crowd behavior have been sought in chimpanzees, baboons, and bonabos, the closest ape relatives of humans, which can exhibit both social generosity and collective savagery. Because it is instinctive, a human crowd may be ecstatic or violent by quick turns; but, being human, it also can exhibit laughter, wonder, sorrow, pity, adoration—the whole human range, in swiftly spread contagions of laughter or weeping at a theatre, a game, or a funeral. Canetti, like most other writers on crowds, is of course most attentive to the violent potential, and pays special attention to the sense of power that a crowd may have along with what he sees as an inherent desire to enlist more and more members. This causes him to recognize but virtually discount crowds that unite for fervent but controlled purposes like performing a symphony or attending a memorial ceremony after tragic disasters. In his sense they are hardly crowds at all.

Canetti describes a pure case of the crowd (an "open crowd") which always seeks to enlarge itself and where many members are attracted and exhilarated by achieving equality with the others, where before they were inferior or powerless. He then describes a variety of structured or "closed" crowds: in his elegant system, any social grouping is a crowd of sorts. This analysis tends to make fraternities based on agreements to work toward a goal seem attenuated but is valuable in emphasizing that a reservoir of "crowd" power is always more or less present in almost any social setting, any shared work. Even in dry bureaucratic workplaces or on a quiet night at the local tavern the flow of fraternal and animal spirits is present and may be awakened to a more intense level. We speak colloquially of the "crowd" for groups of youthful friends and for the local tavern's regulars because these are loosely structured and have no defined purpose but come together repeatedly and do have their own chemistry. Even when a group is highly structured and hierarchically controlled, as in a large office or factory, less formal crowd-currents flow. They take root in informal and accidental matters: courtesy or lack of it, easy or grudging cooperation, acceptable dress, and so on. At certain moments "the crowd" will enforce a fashion or penalize a behavior. Treating all types of social organization as "crowds" points up a crucial theme, that a large part of our ritual life and of our educational efforts, even of our play, is devoted to eliciting and channeling crowd emotions, internalizing passions that we learn in groups so that each individual pursues collective goals with or without the presence of others. In this vein, school classrooms, sports teams, scout packs, and religious rituals induce the young— but not only the young—to conform with approved groups, internalize their purposes and rules, yet learn to resist contagions of group emotion as need requires.

> The human pack, when it is wise, pits
> long sight against the moment's cry,
> holds to purpose beyond the blood-surge,
> that soaring climax of the hunt.

Sometimes, we know, the heroic individual is one who by talents or suffering, perhaps persecution, has learned to see things differently from the majority around him. How to create a balance of brave loyalty in unison with teammates and brave independence from them when they fail to pursue the proper course is the perennial issue for training leaders and soldiers. It seeks a combination of temperance and focused fury, a combination that involves training in strenuous action but also indoctrination in controlling ideals:

> Whether obedient boy scouts
> or thoughtful misfits (with their long
> hatred of bullies) are likelier
> to reach this militant temperance
> is not the question: we can't raise
> outsiders. Hence the sacred pause,
> the lone vigil before knighthood.[4]

In the soldier moving into battle, the football player awaiting the snap, the actor entering a climactic stage scene, we want the crowd's intensity with tempered control: the channeled passion, not panic or loss of skills. We want leaders and followers who commit full energy, perhaps their lives, to the necessary pursuit as the moment requires, but do not do violence to the common purpose. One of the common themes of popular drama is the lawman or reformer who must stand against his own "crowd" (as Gary Cooper's heroic sheriff does in *High Noon*) because he is loyal to the very values that the crowd has claimed to revere. As I said earlier, wolves know how to protect each other and find the weak caribou; humans admire the individual who absorbs the best of his crowd's desires and makes them a controlled strength.

It is not only crowd vs. individual, of course, that interests us. It is the juxtaposition of this or that small crowd to the largest crowd, the majority, that makes the fraternity of specialized groups dramatic and sometimes impressive. Many important political and social reforms involve small, dedicated associations that decide to move their society in a direction that it has not wished to consider. Civil rights, gay rights, environmental action—the list of causes pushed by small fraternities against the preferences of the majority crowd over the last century alone is long, and the pattern in fact is standard for social change in democracies. The small group members, more informed on their issue than the public, support each other until some disaster or a widely recognized injustice causes the wider public to accept that their issue must be addressed. Long-time workers in the vineyard of their cause, they are ready with facts, figures, materials, positions, and leadership for their suddenly swelling numbers[5]. If the tight little faction achieves wide support the lonely pioneers who were once "extremists" are a band of prophets. Until then the fraternity of the small group defends them against the less focused crowd, the majority.

In the mid-1950's, a widely popular treatments of American culture was David Riesman's *The Lonely Crowd* (1950) a title that caught the perceived homogeneity of Americans and a great contradiction, that a nation celebrating individualism was in fact conformist, fad-ridden and filled with directionless individuals. This conformism did not deepen bonds with fellows but reflected an inward emptiness, so that the crowd was faceless as crowds are, and not a true community: the members were from the "lonely." American life was conventional and its members lacking "inner-direction," afraid of deviation from the crowd. Consumerism and media were accused of supplying periodic doses of collective excitement that sustained the conformity, holding the crowd together with transient materialistic passions.

I write this at a point in history where social media are so intensely used that they arguably overmatch the impacts of older mass media, the movies and radio/TV. For several generations starting in the 1950's, many critics bewailed the easily audiences whose suppressed frustration with life and ineffectuality were satirized in movies like Payevsky's *Network* (1976), in which a crazed network anchor encourages millions of people to shout from their windows "I'm mad as hell and I won't take it anymore!" without changing anything. That old film seemed profound at the time as a reflection of popular alienation in a world of mass manipulation through TV, but today I take it as also a drama of resentments and frustration that can be awakened in any population, even individualistic and originally optimistic Americans, facing whatever promise life did not deliver on.

More to our point, digital social networks are now pervasive, redeveloping and adding to their number constantly, so that virtual crowds gather for an unimaginable variety of purposes: play, romance, education, or agitation for some cause. The variety of virtual crowds suggests that the passivity of the mass media audiences criticized since the 50's was partly an artifact of the non-interactive nature of the media involved; it also highlights the fact that there have always been virtual as well as physical crowds whom we call the various "publics," i.e. those who "consume" rather passively but follow the news of politics or fashion or the arts in detail. This notion of "publics" within the general public is one that I return to later; here I would simply point out that digital crowds must join the list of types of crowd (to use Canetti's language), and that they encourage individualized inputs and responses as the stereotyped enlistment of mass audiences does not. In revolutions and uprisings of the last decade, the cell phone alone has changed the speed of events by wildfire spreading of news that in an older era might have been suppressed by authorities. The potential is such that authoritarian nations including China impose heavy censorship of the internet. Whether this much more interactive connection makes the "crowd" in the U. S. (or elsewhere) less "lonely" and more inner-directed or simply more varied in its consumerism is an issue that as far as I know is still to be determined.

Injecting the rise of social media into the conversation does not diminish the wonder or alarm we might feel when an energetic crowd organizes, whether in person or virtually. The virtual crowd and the brother- or sisterhood felt within it are so easy to establish, at least where the internet is unrestricted, so free of social risk, that the connections must be somewhat evanescent, perhaps illusory: but on the other hand, we have numerous anecdotal examples and some conspiracies and lone terrorists who have followed obsessions on the internet with little other human contact. When I have consulted college students about this, they report that their cell phones, internet capacities, Facebook and Twitter keep them connected with family and friends in different locales, and that organizing a game or party is made vastly easier, as is keeping up with news (for those who care to do that). In all these respects, the social capital created is clearly positive and in fact unprecedented in its breadth if not in its depth. At the same time, however, they all have tales of friends who use media rather than face-to-face connection out of fear of direct contact. Some develop digital personas quite different from their actual identities, released to fantasy selves as some are in physical crowds. When and how these powerful engines for connection, conversation and collaboration affect our notions of bonds within groups and among nations is an evolving question, in which virtual crowds, swiftly communicating "publics" on some issues and themes, become more important.

In the virtual realm as in physical realms, small as well as large crowds may gather; the ready availability and intimacy of social media mean that any number of people can weigh into discussion of an ongoing event. They blog, they comment, they "like," they tweet, they may form a public opinion almost instantly. In political campaigns and celebrity talent contests, the mass of responses can be tallied, the consensus reported and reacted to in hours. A crowd of sorts, a momentary plebiscite on who sings or argues best, for example, is reported. At the same time, however, recent cases of "lone wolf" or small group terrorism demonstrate that an individual or a few friends working their electronics at distance can pursue their curiosity and be converted, enlisted, indoctrinated, and advised in tactics for an attack. They can experience conversions that previously required person-to-person interaction. I suggested above that it is not unusual—quite the opposite, part of what we educate our children for—to create situations in which an individual embodies the passion of the officially sanctioned and approved crowd that is not present. The same process must apply to one who has the internal command necessary to resist the crowd that is present around him but is intent on action against it in obedience to an opposing ideology. In other instances, as far as can be figured in cases of individual terrorist attacks, e.g. bitter young men attacking their schools, the violent actor may (or may not!) claim some ideological allegiance as fashionable for such acts, or may google and emulate previous killers: personal rage and emulation of other killers seem to have been essential, but it feels like crowd madness as well as personal madness when we inspect it.

What is new about social media connections as crowd activity is that the connections are swift and intimate, so that plots, seductions, bullying, propaganda and sinister enlistments can begin in secret, while the political promise (or threat) lies in the same speed and fluidity, and the same privacy of contacts, even if, as we have learned, service providers and skilled hackers can find out a great deal when they choose a target.

The political and social gift is that innumerable human connections and shared interests thrive in the same virtual space. In the cases that worry us most, a translation occurs from audience member of a web site to fantasy affiliate of a secret society, moving the acolyte to act in the real world. In the new universe of so many media, distinctions between information sources, audiences, passionate participants, and individual enlistee begin to blur: they become a crowd of uncertain extent.

We must add that although translations from audience membership to deeper allegiances are a dramatic aspect of the rise of social media, they are arguably an enlargement of a process that has occurred from time to time with audiences of literature, music, and some broad shifts in political opinions. Recipients took the message to heart, felt their affiliation in spirit with other readers or listeners, and in sentiment joined a public in which physical crowds, if any arise, are a late manifestation of how many hearts and minds have been touched.

Social media "crowds," as they seem to be developing in their endless variations, undermine the notion that crowd mentality is essentially derived from physical energies, even though mammalian fury or hilarity obviously roars through some physical gatherings. The physical commitment, plus instinctive delight in the power of the mass, can energize or terrorize, especially if the crowd is new or strange. In such matters as political participation, committing oneself by attending an emergency meeting or marching in a demonstration strengthens the commitment of the acolyte members of the party or movement, and of course those joiners are not frightened as bystanders might be. The crowd emotions of an enduring movement may change over time, for physical participation in meetings and demonstrations are planned and the participants develop a calm habit of planning and undertaking them. It is often the case that social media expressions, including "tweets," Facebook postings and blogs among the passionately committed are *less* measured than face-to-face collaboration or even a grand crowd's demonstration would be. The audience of human sheep who are said to be hypnotized by mass media and consumerism obviously exists and may well be a "lonely crowd"; yet in the face of the buzz of social media it appears that the uniformity and passivity of the mass media audience was assumed too easily because the media themselves did not admit interaction. Most of what is visible on social media is banal and fugitive, neighborly self-reporting and passing opinions, but while hardly profound in most cases it offers the same casual life sharing and conversation about the day's news that marks every marketplace or chatty city corner in the world. That is why its support of, or substitution for, ordinary civic interaction is a matter of powerful importance, and why the nature of digital crowds is potentially important for fraternity. In the virtual crowds of social media, as in physical crowds, instinct is clearly not triggered only by rage, fear, or proximity of other bodies—though all these occur—it is aroused and becomes infective by power of imagination.

To pursue the social media question just a bit further: there are always crowds within crowds, small crowds within larger, that have a life and conventions of their own. One of the remarkable and surprising facets of social media is that in theory almost anyone can join any online crowd or group; another is that ideas and attitudes that were largely invisible or conventionally censored by government or by the majority of a society become mainstage themes, open to general view. This extraordinary potential for openness and speed of connection can be put to good or bad use.

One example of the latter, much in the news as this is written and with many aspects unresolved, occurred during the 2016 American Presidential election, when Russian hackers and intelligence agents attempted to influence the election, first to undermine likely winner Mrs. Clinton (a longtime critic of the Putin) and eventually in favor of Mr. Trump. Throughout history, competing empires have understood that they could weaken their rivals by stirring distrust or discontent among potentially disaffected classes or ethnic minorities in the opponent's territory; stirring that trouble is a longstanding role of intelligence operatives as well as of propagandists. In the 2016 election, the Russian interference sought out social factions and fringe political movements that had been relatively invisible to mainstream media and much of American of society, and further were conventionally disapproved of, such as white supremacists and American Nazis. The Russians and willing Americans also highlighted (and sometimes invented) confrontive messages promoting such movements as Black Lives Matter that would be particularly offensive to clients of Facebook who had been targeted as likely to be offended. Hostilities and paranoias that had been in the shadows appeared on the mainstage, taking over much of the narrative and the electoral debate, clamoring in angry rallies but laying claim to much wider support by manipulation of "likes" and intemperate tweets.

In the long-ago era when "social media" meant landline telephones and local talk radio, there existed, as will always be the case, innumerable corners of social interaction in which half-truths and forbidden jokes and trade in topics "improper to discuss in public" thrived. In the whites-only country club it might be racial jokes, in the lady's bridge group it might be a ladies-only discussion of choice undergarments but spiced with the latest marital scandal. In the men's locker room it would be an off-color joke or rough mockery of the latest antics of a local leader. Urban myths and nasty rumors were always part of the current and still are ("Obama is a Muslim" may live forever in the backwaters of the white Deep South!). Sometimes real issues or real confusions amplify the sullen, timeless conviction that all politicians are crooks, that foreigners or big business greed ruins jobs, or that pushy feminists are destroying the family. In general crowds, like the societies they draw from, obey a number of instinctive conventions about what is permissible at the moment and proper to place in front of the majority, but social media "crowds" operate both amidst and out of sight of the conventions. Most societies, whether clubs or nations, are defined by assumed common values, common purposes and boundaries, but social media make societies porous in these respects. As a result, sustained friendships, easy organization, and communication in emergencies are made easy, but the channels open to paranoid convictions, furies or rumors that fringe groups or political manipulators sponsor. The general society becomes more like a randomly collected crowd, unsure of its conventions and its membership. It suddenly understands—society does, which always assumes a fictional consensus about most issues and about culture—that it is riven by divisions and hostilities. As a result, it cannot move to deliberation or coherent action. It is distracted, less able to act civically and democratically, which is what the hostile intelligence operation and the would-be autocrat both aim to achieve.

Crowds can be manipulated partly because they are curious and urgent to know how to act. Even in turbulent physical crowds there is almost always an immediate struggle to find out what is happening, or supposed to happen, what story to imagine: "What's going on? They say the prisons were thrown open...They say there is firing in the central square...." This used to be physical sharing of rumor, now it flashes on cell phones. Crowd emotions, momentary intensifications of connection, are moved by news, spectacles, circuses, funerals, dramas, or even a touching photograph. It is what one would expect of deep instinct in a species marked by imagination and sociability combined. For this reason, a crowd like its individual members can run through a whole range of human emotions from violent to compassionate, from sad to silly, in a short space of time. The crowd is surprising in the speed of its imagination: we might expect susceptibility to impulse in the assembled members to spread gradually, but the crowd tends to see at once, the mass picking its cue from the quickest. Because of this speed and cueing, the crowd can turn angry or panicked, horrified or brave in minutes as it becomes imaginatively caught up in the drama of its own moment. The one human trait missing, despite the quickness of apprehension involved, is reflection. A crowd may certainly know things collectively: later in this book I'll discuss the philosopher Shaftesbury, who posited that society has a *sensus communis*, a common judgment, of many matters. However, the crowd is often taken by surprise, caught by its own passions, because collective thinking is vastly slower and more difficult than collective feeling.[6]

Section II: The Poetry and Paradoxes of a Flowering Ideal

…the Poet binds together by passion and knowledge the vast empire of human society, as it is spread over the whole earth, and over all time.

Wordsworth

Chapter 6: The Mutual Dynamic of Rights and Fraternity

One could reasonably ask whether a topic as varied and universal as I have taken "brotherhood" to be could have a history at all. If it is true that everyone has experienced fraternities, and that the fraternity motif can be found across the vast range of human sociability, and if it is also true that such varied experiences supply muscle and blood to the metaphor, fraternity as a range of experience cannot have a history. But principles and theories of brotherhood do have histories, both in the world of intellect and the world of institutions, and there is a modern political history of great importance whose signal event was the French declaration of *fraternite* as at once a national and a universal rallying cry. As the chapters immediately following attempt to show, experiences of fraternity were illuminated by the democratic political ideal in new ways. The ideal of political fraternity itself took on, in turn, new and expanding implications.

The first chapter of this section offer a sketch of the ideas that over several preceding centuries fed the revolutionary impulse. The succeeding chapters examine a few English and American writers, mostly poets, who wrestled with fraternity as a newly politicized theme. These chapters are intended as suggestive case histories. The usefulness of literature in pursuit of our topic arises from the nature of fraternity itself: Fraternity as a theme of democratic politics may be a principle that individuals or a society hold and express through habitual cooperation, but it includes a potentially fierce commitment tested in crises or in the face of great injustices. In these moments, pursuit of fraternity may lead to dramatic questioning of the very meaning of human connection.

To follow that claim a little further, fraternity as a democratic political ideal has involved paradoxes beyond the political realm, touching ideas of self, of cultural values, of daily behavior. In the cases we follow here, the sentimentalist philosopher Shaftesbury strives to unite immersion in civic life and a new respect for the rationality of the common judgment with neoclassical ideals of self-cultivation and virtue. The great English poet Wordsworth and some of his peers represent the Romantic discovery that identification with *miserables*, their most oppressed and degraded fellow citizens, might shake their confidence in themselves and in what it means to be human. A group of nineteenth century American poets, the "Fireside Poets," are described as trying to shape an American sense of bonds that is universal rather than tribal in its democratic principles; and then Walt Whitman is described as a preacher of universal love struggling with issues that such preachers always face. Finally, a chapter points out a twentieth century tension between the artist's independence of audience or societal values and his or her defenses of freedoms of thought when this is under assault.

New Implications of Democratic Fraternity

Fraternity takes on new implications in the context of both democratic political ideals and pragmatic experiences of democratic rule. The fraternity motif colors perceptions of human nature as well as ideas for the ordering of nations. Taken as a political ideal, fraternity raises more deeply the question of how the individuals connect their personal development to the value placed on human beings in general, a remarkable historical development. We have long understood that the themes of liberty and equality penetrate societies in ways that early proponents may not have expected. Those two ideals, acted upon as political principles, began to color perception and action on matters of race, gender, migration, property, empire, manners—in the end, a wide range of substantive social issues. Liberties that might collide are mediated by law in societies that aim for justice and order, but at the individual and community level the conviction of liberty, especially after oppression, penetrates the soul: the romantics felt this and insisted on its deep importance. Those who achieve a new liberation acquire intrinsic power and a new expressiveness; an example is the courage and desire for self-reliance that newly freed American slave communities exhibited from the moment of emancipation. By the same token, the ideal that gives a people equality under the law, crucial as that legal principle is, soon requires that social and economic inequalities be addressed because legal equality is so easily compromised in practice. Equality becomes an active conviction with implications that reach into the home and marketplace as well as the law court. A parallel dynamism is implicit in fraternity, which becomes a source of high vision and personal unease that the poets might measure better than the political philosophers can.

Fraternity, to be less romantic about it, leads to new orientations of collective as well as individual values. Individuals and even societies wrestle with what the range of their human sympathies and loyalties *mean*. One of the issues is how deep personal emotions relate to collective life: sorrow for private losses or sublime wonder at a natural scene color the understanding of human experience generally, but the fraternity motif recognizes sympathies across distances and in effect finds what is communal in both private and public moments, saying: *this is what our brothers and sisters also undergo.*

Again, a basic issue for any ideal, and certainly for fraternity, is how to strike a balance: how do I balance the multitude of loyalties that I may be asked to follow? Ultimately, if the "spirit of brotherhood" guides decisions, it will involve awareness of ethical obligation, generosity in understanding others' situations, and realism about the costs or feasibility of mutual action. One part of this question of balance is intrinsic to political fraternity and was especially important for the American poets discussed below: how to formulate community and national loyalties in a way that is also an affirmation of universal equality of rights, for there are necessarily tensions between the service I would give my home community and the needs of my neighbor's community.

If one defines fraternity broadly, as that which movements and nations claim is their conviction of brotherhood—an inconveniently broad definition but the one that fits the history—the political theme of fraternity arises in the eighteenth century as a universal but also fashionable ideal drawing from Renaissance humanism, the Reformation's emphases on individual conscience, and Enlightenment fashions of rationalism and sentimentalism. As an ideal and appeal, it rippled through audiences of readers and political idealists who shared liberating ideas and imitated each other in action from nation to nation and continent to continent. Over two-plus centuries from the first great revolutions, fraternity under various names has usually been a concomitant appeal to the irresistibly spreading democratic theme of equality. Sometimes it has supported the drive for economic justice, as in international socialism; sometimes its passion supported ethnic or national independence, e.g. liberty from colonial control. Commonly, these themes have been mixed. And, while brotherly passions have united each party in revolts, wars, pirate raids and so on from the beginning of history, the great spasms of fraternal emotion in the modern political contexts, supporting the people and their rights, have almost always attempted to appeal to audiences beyond the nation or class that is in revolt.

One can imagine modern history as a landscape swept by waves of fraternal enthusiasm, often different in purpose but similar in the passions evoked, flaring in revolutions and warfare but also expressed in reform movements, in the arts, and in creation of pragmatic mechanisms for cooperation or neighborly help. The history is less often a story of majorities against self-serving individuals (kings or tyrants, though there have been many of these) than a history of competing brotherhoods, involving ethnicities or regions against their nation, peoples against empires that ruled them, sects against sects, class against class, or slaves against masters. Even some of the movements that have refused notions of universal rights have shown the perceived need to advance arguments for a historicist right, a collective destiny for the nation or race that overrides the rights of lesser brothers, so that the Reich can advance over its enemies, the dictatorship of the proletariat can erase resistant classes, or Manifest Destiny can excuse North American genocide. Apocalyptic religious kingdoms like ISIS follow a comparable pattern, cementing a brotherhood according to rules revered by many while erasing opposition or tepidity ruthlessly. On the other hand, part of the "spirit of brotherhood" story across the centuries had been the generous support of liberation efforts by outsiders on grounds of principle, empathy, or faith in progress. This was a powerful aspect of the excitement that the American and French Revolutions created: enlistment of volunteers as well as sympathetic writing and theorizing have been typical expressions of support for those who are struggling to rise.

The interconnection between rights and fraternity developed over several centuries as one aspect of great intellectual and political changes. To begin with, while the exact relation of the principles can be debated, democratic ideas of equality came to involve appeals for brotherhood as those claims unfolded amid controversy. In the mind of a religious or philosophical thinker, brotherhood might be the founding principle and equality of rights would follow from it, but in actual political situations the practical exercise of rights, persuasion of assemblies, leadership roles, and distribution of benefits are continually negotiated. In that context, brotherhood is the reminder of connection that one side or the other in a contest will offer to obtain more general sympathy for its cause. When division is especially bitter, a shared understanding of the necessary of unity in the society and of common values within the whole society may temper the extremism of the parties on each side. The "spirit of brotherhood" in these cases is not an enthusiasm but a source of long views and temperance, where absolute suppression of one side would end the prospect of restored peace and neighborliness. Unfortunately, history offers numerous examples of societies where one side in a controversy marks its victory by eradication of the opponents. The crucial difference is that the revolution which understands rights and even humanity to belong to all sides—a principle of fraternity—is less likely to seek to wipe its foes from the earth and more likely to achieve peace for both sides.

To say that brotherhood correlates with equality of rights because at least one side appeals to that motif amidst controversy is admittedly a simplistic starting point, but it alerts us to the fact that fraternity, if basically established in a community, can operate even when it is not understood in the same way by all participants. Settling a contest under the aegis of fraternity becomes part of that community's history and of its ongoing interpretation of itself.

That fact, that fraternity is often a tempering principle is important because the ideal has flowered and grown more complex over time, involving rights that can be in conflict and claims that are historically new to many societies. These might include the rights of women, unprecedented sexual or religious freedoms, or tribal rights of cultural preservation within non-tribal nations. Fraternities of various sorts exist across dividing lines even in rigidly class-organized hierarchical societies, while few egalitarian societies are wholly so, so that a habitual conviction of underlying brother/sisterhood can temper conflict even where there are different views of rights. However, equality is the reigning theoretical idea in most modern democracies, so that brotherhood themes are unavoidably intertwined and their expansion to defense of new rights or as a tempering influence in new controversies is inevitable.

To take the connection of fraternity with human rights a step further: an earlier chapter noted a movement among Italian and Latin American scholars who are investigating fraternity as a combined practical and intellectual project. They argue that equality and liberty, the other principles of the famous French triad, cannot be well understood without taking fraternity into account. This is obviously true as a practical matter, for (as a simple example) a society that privileges liberty to accumulate wealth without concern for community—a common error in American history— eventually must make choices: either to reinforce class and economic disparities at the cost of strife and aggravated inequality, or find measures of redistribution for mutual welfare. When the latter choices are made, recognizing mutual economic or other obligations, fraternal arguments make the compromises involved more stable even if they were initially forced by one side. In a longer and more fundamental view, neither liberty nor equality can be understood without consideration of the community in which rights are exercised and the imagined social orders that defend each kind of rights. An egalitarian society, perhaps more than any other model, must be marked by generosity and mutual concern if it is to preserve basic rights.

Another preliminary observation is that the modern history of the fraternity motif is inherently entwined with the question of how average person can participate in his/her community's self-governance. Again, the theme of equality implies that all must be enabled in law, but fraternity is often the motif under which individuals acquire both skills and opportunities to act with others. Fraternity become the principle, although it takes on many names, within which the citizens differ peacefully over issues and serve their community. We return to this below, examining how Shaftsbury sought to combine classical tradition with democratic communal wisdom; we will later take note of Tocqueville's wonder at how American commoners "associated" for projects that elites would lead in other nations. The whole tendency of the imaginative side of modern democracy is to demonstrate that the lives and communal interactions of ordinary people have an intrinsic depth and importance, like the actions of the kings and heroes of old.

A third observation—really an assumption—is that as nations grow more complex in their relations, expressions of "the spirit of brotherhood" will be embodied in specific systems of cooperation within and between communities and nations. Many of these systems and institutions will implement technical arrangements like climate monitoring, development loan banks, or anti-dumping regulations for sales of international products, but many will be regularized mechanisms for mutual help, e.g. to meet epidemics or natural disasters. The first great examples arose in the eighteenth and nineteenth centuries, e.g. the International Red Cross; by the mid-twentieth century and up to the present, the growth of international NGOs and IGOs has represented pragmatic extensions of fraternity even admitting that major power strategic competition during and after the Cold War and rich nations' desire for economic expansion were preeminent motives. Like philanthropic activity generally, these institutional arrangements sometimes supported unequal economic or political power by easing symptoms of injustice but not the underlying ills, but many of the systems have provided local investment support, health services, and agricultural improvement for many beneficiaries. There are times of war or political retrogression when such networks seem only a cobweb, easily broken when the nation-states resist them. But like spider-webs they tend to be spun where opportunity allows, and many are not nearly as frail as my metaphor suggests.

As part of this long process of creating mechanisms, ever since the Enlightenment many specialized publics interested in specific world causes and philanthropies have grown up, supporting specific expressions of the "spirit of brotherhood" in various nations and internationally. There also developed, especially in the twentieth century, a much wider public whose world contacts derive from travel, entertainment, arts and news media. This wider public contains many segments in realms from environmental activism to soccer that can serve as reservoirs of support for specific causes. Enabled but not determined by law, the international networks resemble and overlap with the official sectors that mark advanced democracies. As random as this web of institutions and audiences may seem, it is notable how suspicious of it—the organizations, the accessible media, and even the potentially satiric arts that flow—are the world's most repressive regimes.

Intellectual backgrounds of "fraternite!"

The unmistakable moment when fraternity in a democratic political rather than theological sense erupts into history is the French Revolution. The ideal, or rather the great slogan, was not followed up by much discussion and theoretical definition, which is why recent scholars call it the "ignored" principle. To those who announced it, the slogan was an invitation to join their vision, and optimistic thinkers and actors flared with answering enthusiasm across the world. The French revolution triggered a quarter century of warfare marked by the rise of Napoleon and the final victory of the reactionary powers, yet its spirit and themes were continually reechoed in Europe and the Americas and have continued across the globe to the present, providing rationales for revolt and creation of constitutional orders among the colonized and tyrannized.

That eruptive French slogan reflected several previous centuries of transformation in how humanity—sometimes only European humanity, and the individual more than the collective—was imagined. To summarize simply what the Renaissance, the Reformation, and the Enlightenment contributed to the fraternity motif, we might picture a rather sleepy late medieval kingdom in Europe around the early 1400's. In this kingdom many individuals had rights, but these were almost wholly defined by rigid class privileges and by traditions, which created the immediate fraternities that most people belonged to. The nobility had extensive rights to rule and to ownership of almost all land that was not the Church's; they understood their class status, knew what was due them, and fought to retain their class rights vis-à-vis the kings, the Church, and when necessary the commons. Their brothers were not fellow inhabitants of their region but lords of comparable level elsewhere. Burghers in the cities, too, were a commercial class protected in local roles and traditional occupations organized into guilds and ward organizations. In some places, rural yeomen or small landholders were sturdy classes who held rights to common land or to parts of the harvest they gathered, as defined by tradition. At the same time, while ranks and traditional roles defined the fraternities of what we would call secular society, the Church included all souls in the heavenly democracy of the saved, for which the lower classes must wait in docile humility. The secular and religious orders of society were theoretically inextricable, the power of the prince twinned with that of the Church. The social hierarchies of earth mirrored the hierarchies of the created universe, The Great Chain of Being, so that they altogether radiated a certain fitness among the parts and the whole. The spirit of future nationalism was at best nascent;

identification with a clan, a common dialect, a city, or the region more often powerful.

Nostalgia for aspects of this all-encompassing ideal of order, a grand and pervasive imaginative framework for all of life with assurance of happy complementarity among classes, would underlie conservative responses to reform and revolution for centuries after it fell apart. The old medieval order contained many of the connections that political fraternity grows from: neighborhood and regional stability, routines of work together, kinship networks, preparations for local defense, longstanding religious observances, and so on. These were separately viable in many places for centuries to come but ceased to be parts of one system.

This old order was always in considerable measure a grand unifying fiction. The rulers were a volatile warrior class that settled dynastic issues and border claims by force, while high religious offices in the deeply hierarchical church were often awarded politically. Europe was roiled by crusades and campaigns against Muslim powers, by famines, by regional heresies, and by devastating plagues that displaced populations and decimated institutions of mutual help like hospitals. If we examine the art of the period, most of it is religious and was funded by the rich to celebrate themselves: the groups we see on church or palace walls are favorite saints and attendant angels joined by the patrons who funded the artwork, praying at a saint's deathbed or below the Cross. Other common images are processions, images of clearly classified social order whether of pilgrims (as in Chaucer) or *en route* to the grave where Death, the ultimate democrat, praises the humble peasant but mocks the proud lady. If we turn to literature, much is satire against the princes or churchmen who fail the demands of their status. The life of the cities and highways, on the other hand, as seen in Villon and Rabelais, is comic turmoil, for the roads and the cities were full of people who had broken away at least temporarily from traditional roles and locales.

If we scroll forward two centuries, the old image of what society should be like has not changed entirely, for social imagination is nostalgic and many provinces and country towns had changed little in day to day life; yet in fact the old order had shattered. What the Renaissance brought was the elevation of man, especially the individual, as a figure of dignity in himself—"what a piece of work is man!" as Hamlet says, in a speech that echoes Montaigne. For our purpose, it is important that although the image of human nature was secularized in the sense of being separated from a status of salvation, the human was not desacralized. To be human was not less valued, at least in theory, but to be semi-divine, due to the human power of reason and the record of magnificent accomplishments.

In this transformation, admiration and indeed worship of the ancient classics played a tremendous part, for the world of the classics as understood in the Renaissance was a world of heroic actors and thinkers. The realistic lives of contemporary nations, their borders shifting and nobles quarreling, were rarely in the forefront of European imagination in literature or art compared with models drawn from the classical world to apply to their own, for the classics offered a common treasury of themes and shared intellectual points of reference.

As with the elevation of innate human dignity that marked the Renaissance, it is easy to summarize several aspects of the Reformation that prepared for the modern political fraternity motif. The emphasis on individual faith in Lutheranism, and then on personal conviction of salvation in Calvinism, represented in effect a claim for individual rights of conscience. For, if God commands that men and women should come to belief or strengthen their faith by reading scripture and finding inward assurances, they must have an inherent right to do these things. The argument of rights of conscience was implicit even if the instinct of many reformers and their converted princes was to impose the true doctrine harshly, just as Catholic princes defended their orthodoxy by use of the Inquisition. Across the spectrum of Protestantism that developed, only a few small sects argued for innate rights of conscience—an anarchic principle! but all claimed that they acted as God commanded. However, the principle of free conscience was implicit even if freedom to discuss or write might not be tolerated; and the various new churches were so stubborn that especially in Protestant nations a tacit tolerance crept in where theory called for suppression. (The Roman Church did not recognize that "error has rights" in matters of conscience until the 1960's.)

After the first half century of religiously motivated warfare, the Peace of Augsburg (1555) set down the principle of *cujus regio, ejus religio*—whoever was ruler of a nation could choose its religion. *Cujus regio* was obviously not a religious principle but a formula for peace among neighboring nations. It assured the unity of state and church assumed to be necessary for order within each kingdom, but as dynastic successions changed and borders of empire varied across Europe, a tacit acceptance of differing creeds arose in some nations, with rising cynicism about the clerical establishments. (The most famous useful conversion was that of Henry IV, the protestant winner in France's civil war who agreed to official Catholic hegemony because "Paris is worth a mass.")

A second aspect of the Reformation relevant to both the experience of fraternity and its power under democratic conditions was the new importance of the local congregation, led to a significant degree by lay persons and less closely directed (if at all) by an episcopacy. In Lutheran and Calvinist communities, and then in many smaller denominations such as Quakers and Anabaptists, the congregation was central, expanding leadership ability across class lines and expanding the authority of the middle classes over their societies. These versions of Protestantism involved their members actively in expressing their personal spiritual state before others' eyes, an element of mutual revelation that as noted earlier is often important in fraternities. In some cases, membership was selective, following upon interview and observation of the candidate by peers in the congregation. An emphasis on preaching over ritual in some sects combined with the greater literacy needed to read the Bible arguably strengthened unity until, as sometimes occurred, independent reading and thinking led congregations to divide.

Protestant congregations often fostered strong notions of individual and collective responsibilities to the larger community expressed by civic leadership. We will note below that sentimentalism, popular in the eighteenth century, encouraged benevolence based on optimism about human nature. The sterner protestant creeds did not share that optimism but had long promulgated civic virtues and active charity, especially for those who achieved worldly success. (Among Calvinists, a believer's prosperity and his community leadership were both signs of probable salvation.) Thus, the "protestant ethic" offered models of philanthropy and exemplary citizenship that jibed extremely well with social values and civic behavior that were to be encouraged by the Enlightenment's more secular rationalism and sentimentalism.

The next great periodization that we use to summarize wide intellectual trends is the Enlightenment. The emphasis on science, reason, and natural law ethics that prevailed among the philosophes (along with anti-clericalism) supported the notion that humans are equal in nature, no matter how their cultures might warp that nature. The growth of the known world and its many peoples had had an effect, for "mankind" was the worldwide species, truly visible for the first time. Universal, too, and multi-cultural in their way, were the moral judgments that the great writers made: Voltaire's Candide visits Brazil, where Jesuits were guiding Indian revolts against their colonial masters; Samuel Johnson begins "The Vanity of Human Wishes," a poem on the inevitability of disappointment, by surveying mankind "from China to Peru," for all peoples learn the same sad lesson. Across Europe and amid the elites of the colonies an international readership with democratic tendencies had arisen, made up of great numbers of middle and sometimes lower-class persons—literacy the only required card for participation. The audience included intellectual leaders but also many people of ordinary station, increasingly including literate women, who appreciated both the idealism and the satire in the stories they read and took an interest in debates about politics and the world's news. Part of worldwide "mankind," this audience sometimes reached a consensus on political and philosophic issues, and when it did so it had informal power: its enthusiasm and laughter were feared by those in high places.

An especially important element of the Enlightenment for our topic is sentimentalism, which I try to appreciate in a chapter below on Shaftesbury. Sentimental philosophers emphasized the innate similarity of human instincts, not only of reason but feelings and sympathies. Their views coincided with a new interest in childhood, and how education and experience (including exposure to benevolent Nature) shaped social and moral instincts. Obviously, a philosophy that sees human compassion, love of the beautiful, and disgust at evil as universal instincts sets the stage for an enriched imagination of brotherhood. For the sentimentalist empathy, even across social and cultural lines, is a natural and instinctive use of imagination, so that empathetic identification becomes central to fraternity in the Enlightenment and Romantic eras. The issue was not merely philosophic: sentimentalism affected manners, aesthetic judgment, and popular arts, and was reflected in a new elevation of Benevolence to a mark of high character, a source of the ideal citizen's happiness as well as that of society.

One further aspect of the great transformation that occurred in the later Renaissance and the Enlightenment needs to be mentioned, a concept that carried on powerfully in nineteenth and twentieth century thought and up to the present: that is the idea that shared *culture* is the base of social solidarity and the richest expressions of community. Experts differ on how to define "culture'; it has a variety of meanings, and the term is sometime used for ideals of national character or typical character of a tribe or long-established regional society. The set of relations that we call a culture are a natural base for explaining experiences of brotherhood: to share culture often means easy attainment of intimacy with fellows from the same setting while difficulty in working with persons of an alien community may be explained as due to differing cultures.

It was only during the Enlightenment that the various complexities of culture as a context for all aspects of daily life and thought began to become a pervasive interest, with the concept becoming even more important in the nineteenth century and remaining so today. Whether in ancient eras as summarized by scholars, or in what were once called "primitive" societies studied by anthropologists, cultures are imagined as organic in that great social elements reflect each other and lend coherence to the whole. If the great values are not in harmony, they are called the characteristic tensions or polarities of that society. In a shared culture, the contexts of daily life are largely familiar, and their stability is emotionally and practically valuable. "Culture" taken broadly can include the manners that make citizens feel mutually respected, the familiarity of folkways, styles of family management, typical humor, and customs of governance: together they create a presumption of belonging and mutual loyalties.

Starting with the consolidation of nations in the late Renaissance, philosophers, artists, and some political leaders expanded ideas of ethnic or national culture to the realms of aspiration. They aimed to picture but also to enhance what German or French, British or Italian culture could stand for, often a national essence superior to rival cultures. Ancient customs, old victories, heroic myths and founding heroes stood for the essential strength of the Folk, now become a modern people but with the old steel in its character; the greatest poets of the language, especially the makers of epics when they existed, voiced the enduring spirit and intrinsic grandeur of the civilization. In many instances, that cultural spirit could be explored as a spur to unification, as with early nineteenth century Germany and Italy. In eighteenth century Great Britain, notions of culture supported the imperial balancing act that restrained the restless Celtic regions at home and yet could guide the governance of a far-flung empire. (As the American colonies demonstrated, their conviction that its citizens should have "the rights of Englishmen" caused political disruption, but most of the culture persisted in English ways.) In many colonial territories, the ruling elites who oversaw enslaved or oppressed classes of different races saw themselves as counterparts of the elites in the European homeland, linked by old family ties, racial purity, and an imitative colonial high culture.

Part of the historic argument about the competitive destiny of nations as well as about their core values came to involve ideas of culture: the appeal to national culture highlighted aspirations based on what had been in place for a long time or needed restoration, in either case focusing struggles over what parts of cultural heritage were most crucial: common language, a religious, the King, the Constitution, traditional classes, the unchanging peasantry, and so on. In this context, perhaps especially in empires, the high culture of music, literature and architecture might be especially celebrated, although some living artists would be suspect if they were dismissive of the official culture. In the American setting, high culture discussions after the revolutionary period increasingly evinced a desire to express a distinct American cultural identity, assumed to be an expression of triumphant nationhood.

Powerful and invigorating as this process of claiming and expanding cultural heritages was, it had a dark aspect as it emphasized differences and aimed at superiority. The ancients had often believed in cyclical history (nations rise and fall as if by fate) and in national characteristics shaped by geographical conditions or climate. By the nineteenth century, and well before Darwinism gave the idea a pseudo-scientific impulse, the underlying assumption of celebrants of national culture was evolutionary in that the accomplishments of various peoples were taken as evidence of innate character or capacity. Race classifications were increasingly assumed to underlie the national traits made visible in cultures. As a result, even thinkers who might admit "all men are created equal" as to theoretic rights would affirm, on the testimony of science and history, that the more civilized (European) nations deserved empire and that the Negro or the Indian could not properly join the club. In the late nineteenth century and in early decades of the twentieth century, it was not uncommon to see in textbooks and similar displays a procession of human evolution in which one end shows an ape that learned to walk on two legs, then a Hottentot, then other negroes, and up the line past American Indians to brown and yellow Asians and a blondish northern European at their head. Except for the ape, the line was a ranking of cultures based on perceived primitivism and placed the brown and yellow lower than Europeans because they had been conquered by Europeans, a proof of evolutionary superiority. Many thinkers ranked rival cultures among the European peoples as well, with the implication that some part of the difference of Irish, Italians, Serbs, Spaniards or Jews was "in the blood," lessening whatever fraternity claims were in the air by strengthening ethnic claims and discounting the claims of "mankind."

Despite misuse, and regardless of whether "culture" is seen as organic or something looser, the deep webs of interconnection that the concept covers are obviously of immense value. They are valuable to long term members of the culture and a challenge to those who encounter them as strangers, whether as travelers or as native infants. Appreciation of or even defense of different cultures, and facility at interacting with them, must obviously be entailed in worldwide defenses of rights and in extensions of the spirit of brotherhood. Among western peoples in the nineteenth century, to generalize about a complicated story, ideas of culture were likely to be debated in the context of nationalism and sometimes of empire. In the later twentieth century and up to the present, expanding notions of human rights have come to include the right of original peoples, marginalized minorities, and ethnic communities within larger nations to maintain a distinctive culture as an intrinsically valuable heritage of their community. If a people loses its coherence as a distinctive culture, that is seen as a loss to human culture as a whole as well as to that people. Within a nation, recognition or celebration of a minority's cultural heritage is often an expression of equality and respect. This is what is intended in the U.S. when Black History Month or Hispanic or Chinese cultural festivals are supported. The shift to preservation of heritages is a widening of the vision of rights to include sustaining specific cultural communities as contributing to human heritage in general.

Utopianism

If the pre-revolutionary eras described (and oversimplified) set an implicit context for the meaning of *"fraternite"'* another relevant trend, rooted in the Enlightenment but very much a feature of the post-revolutionary eras, is utopianism. New and optimistic theories of society, sometimes followed by actual experiments in small communities, promised that reformed principles of social relations could improve the lot of mankind. Utopian visions, especially in religion, were not new, but utopias on "scientific" or philosophical propositions about social order—theories such as limiting or punishing crime differently—were new on the scene. Interest in them was a sign of the invisible brother- and sisterhood of optimism: it also reflected a new conviction that human nature and possible social orders were more plastic than tradition or old doctrines suggested.

It is tempting to dismiss the utopian spirit, for those who became disappointed with results and those who had always distrusted it were alike dismissive. But a utopian willingness to invest in new social structures has been recurrently powerful, essentially representing waves of hope among those who were not part of the current game of power in their societies. It is also an evidence of how truly, in the first years after the French Revolution, fraternal arguments became contagious, for the essence of utopianism is a re-arrangement of social bonds guided by a new theory. On several occasions but especially after wars, including eventually the two World Wars, dismay at the human and economic costs of war has led to wide enthusiasm for institutions that reflected goals of brotherhood and above all peace, which—because so many failed—seem utopian in retrospect. In the nineteenth century Europe, which featured so many repressive regimes, failed revolutions, weak reforms, arm races, and continued colonial expansion, the examples of practical or utopian counter-efforts now seem pitifully weak: the start of international aid organizations, socialist world congresses to address economic injustice, disarmament conferences, anti-colonial conferences, and so on. Yet some of these offered models for the political future and/or created continuing nongovernmental organizations. In light of the failures it is easy to dismiss the number of prominent movements and individuals who tried to lay the basis for unprecedented peace and drew upon the plethora of theories and conferences. Exemplars of the nineteenth century dreams who had twentieth century impact included Nobel, Carnegie, Wilson, and Ghandi.

In 1880, Friedrich Engels wrote a short history of socialism and communism in his century. *Socialism: Utopian and Scientific* traced the energy as well as some ideas of socialist movements from early utopian thinkers to the "three great Utopians,"[1] Saint-Simon, Fourier, and Owens—figures whose disciples rode the wave of enthusiasm that the French revolution engendered. Following these, Engels traces the development of his and Marx's "scientific" socialism, centered on the rise and bonding of the proletariat. Engels' history is helpful here because he values the waves of hope and imaginative vision on which his utopians rode. Later critics including later socialists might see these early visons as "insane," but

> For ourselves, we delight in the stupendously grand thoughts and germs of thought that everywhere break through their phantastic covering, and to which these Philistines are blind." [2]

The point we take here is that the utopian strain carried through the decades, echoing the exuberant conviction that new and liberated communities lay just over the horizon. It would be hard to imagine a modern revolution or great social movement that has not had at least a utopian overtone, an imagination of better communal lives to be achieved a new

149

rationality, productive of deeper social friendships across the board, is introduced.

Returning to the early post-revolutionary era, even the Americans, whose theories balanced mutual competition and distrust of the citizenry with the need for collaboration, were increasingly unified over much of the nineteenth century by rhetorical assurances that their national vision would be the model for the world. Their expansion westward became a project that patriotic enthusiasts cast in an ideal light, as Whitman was to cast American personality itself as holding utopian promise for humanity.

Counter-narratives and Contrary Versions

After the initial revolutionary period, a thorough history of the fraternity motif would trace, alongside repeated revolutions, and amidst remarkable international campaigns like those against slavery, widespread elaboration of group identities along national, ethnic, and racial lines. Alongside the contagious fraternal impulses against oppression, racist and nationalistic versions arose that offered defenses of slavery or imperialism. Rising nationalist ambitions elaborated Nordic or Anglo-Saxon superiority, the Slavic soul, Japanese racial essence, and so on. Many of the theories, as indicated above, were dressed in Darwinian pseudo-science, but that science cut both ways: a conviction of inevitable progress that had arisen in the Enlightenment was strengthened by evolutionary theories, giving some reformers confidence that they were marching in an irresistible cadre with other visionaries. As the American poet James Russell Lowell put it in an 1845 poem against slavery, enlisting the spirit of the age, "the energy sublime/ Of a century bursts full blossomed." [3]

During most of the first century of revolutions, and sometimes up to the present, the struggles for human rights and for independence of subjugated nations were combined. European revolutionaries in 1789 and 1848, and many other national revolutionaries up to the present time, proclaimed basic rights due all humans for nations hitherto oppressed by kings or imperial power. These were liberal in the nineteenth century sense: although some of the nineteenth century revolutions addressed the misery of peasants, slaves or ethnic minorities to a degree, liberal leaders tended to trust that limiting the king or nobility, installing republican institutions, or extending the franchise more widely where representative institutions already existed would accomplish what the revolution could not do immediately. Nineteenth century liberals tended to favor assimilation rather than distinct political status for ethnic minorities or immigrants, and free trade with loose reins on capitalism. Old class distinctions based on inherited status and new elites created by new wealth were tolerated if the welfare of the general populace could be improved. The notion of international brotherhood and innate rights was a usual and often eloquent conviction, but empires were not abandoned. By the end of the nineteenth century, however, competing fraternities were eroding both liberal convictions and the power of liberal leaders in the politics of many nations. John Lukacs' *Budapest 1900* outlines some of the counterforces at work in the admittedly complex example of Hungary, secondary center of the Austro-Hungarian Empire at the century's turn. Lukacs argues that Hungary and Budapest exemplify crosscurrents that were affecting much of Europe. The revolution for Hungarian independence led by Kossuth in 1848 had failed but gradually resulted in near-equivalent status with Austria in domination of an ethnically complex empire. Liberal ideals had won partial reforms that dampened their revolutionary energy. In Hungary, the liberals had welcomed assimilation of minorities into Hungarian culture ("magyarization"): Jews, Austrians, Germans, Czechs, Serbs, and Ruthenians joined the social mainstream, especially in Budapest. However, the Jews (who thrived in the commercial realm that the Hungarian gentry had traditionally scorned) were resented and the other groups began to press for national rights, not assimilation. Native Hungarians increasingly emphasized their national differences with Austria despite their raised status, and labor unions, though internationalist in their socialism, argued against free trade in order to protect their workers from foreign competition. Neither the upper and middle classes nor the workers were in sympathy with the peasants, who were deeply conservative in social views and religion. Splintered nationalisms and class/cultural loyalties, particularist values, had begun to undermine the ideology that proclaimed universal rights and imperial fraternity. Lukacs argues that similar crosscurrents were at work in Britain's relation with Ireland and among numerous other countries. Micheline Ischay, whose *The History of Human Rights* I have relied on heavily as background of this chapter, argues that by 1918 two ideals embodied and celebrated in Wilson's Fourteen Points, national self-determination combined with individual rights, in practice were often mutually contradictory:

> By founding the principle of self-determination primarily on ethnic and cultural—rather than democratic—rights within given borders, Wilson inadvertently offered equal moral weight to irreconcilable conceptions of national autonomy. [4]

Even as we recognize the accuracy of Ishay's observation, we must repeat that in real communities and states, as in individual lives, there is always a process of mediation among values and loyalties. The mediations and casuistry that seek a balance are often made difficult by competing vision of fraternity. Tribal rights, ethnic loyalties, an external threat and sometimes other traditions can seem to be absolute values at moments of controversy, sweeping off concern for minority or individual rights. Moderation in pursuing the claims of one's own faction—which some will take as betrayal of the brotherhood! —is the sign of great security on the part of a leader and of his/her society.

To consider Ischay's example of Wilson at the end of World War I for a moment further, the years immediately after fighting ended displayed remarkable outbreaks of optimism accompanied or succeeded by revolutions and civil wars. Giddy exuberance at a war's end is usual for victors, of course, but Wilson's arrival in Europe with the Fourteen Points in hand was indeed a moment of almost messianic enthusiasm for the structure of peace he offered, one of the historic "outbursts" we have found so striking. Wilson felt, probably correctly at that moment, that the great majority of ordinary people in Europe and the U.S. were in favor of his "peace without victors" On occasion, he urged squabbling delegations at Versailles to respond to what he saw as a world outcry and historic opportunity. Not everyone, certainly not his fellow heads of state nor his political enemies at home, shared the vision, mocking his self-righteousness, but for a historic moment the optimism he represented was widely, even giddily, shared. By the end of the Versailles negotiations, a peace with punitive reparations had been signed, a peace that observers like the economist Keynes damned as sure to lead to future wars, while political enemies in the U.S. laid plans to prevent American acceptance of the League of Nations. At the same time, ill-fated socialist revolutions were occurring in several European states where the old regimes had lost credibility, civil war was raging in Russia and would soon break out in Ireland, and anticolonial agitation was rising in India—a full range of eruptions involving different notions of social justice or national identity amidst ebbing dreams of universal peace.

If the great model of the early nineteenth century and some later revolutions had been essentially republican, focusing on basic individual political rights, the rising fraternities of the late nineteenth century increasingly involved competing nationalisms, ethnic splintering, and oppressed classes in revolt against foreign and local elites: often industrial workers in the nineteenth century, more often peasants in twentieth century Latin America and Asia. They would rise in opposition to capitalist elites in the advanced nations and against dominant landowners in nations that had been or still were colonized. The massive literature produced by socialists, anarchists, and other reformers represented ideals of brotherhood among the lowest social levels and, usually, a classless future, a utopia tailored to the people.

Over the nineteenth and into the twentieth century, socialists and labor advocates undoubtedly bore the main responsibility for expansion of human rights ideals and equitable social policies in the "advanced" democracies, including improved economic and living conditions of workers and protection of women and children. In European countries and in the U.S., pressure from socialists helped to lead to adoption of reform agendas (e.g. by the Progressive Movement in the U.S.). In the U.S. this occurred without much wider adoption of the underlying economic and social ideas. Many of the great revolutions of the twentieth century, including Lenin's takeover of a liberal revolution in Russia and a spate of failed revolutions after World War I, were self-proclaimed uprisings in favor of oppressed lower classes: some gave priority to redressing old oppression and redistributing wealth over defense of universal or personal rights. Later in the twentieth century, especially as the great empires broke up, the four themes of ethnic independence within nations, nationalism, personal rights, and redress for previous oppression were often in tension. In the dramatic example of India, the agitation led by Ghandi aimed at national liberation from

British rule, but the newly independent nation fractured instantly on Hindu/Muslim lines while Ghandi's own profound concern to raise the Untouchables and other bottom castes made only modest headway and their status remains a major challenge. Currently, the Near East is in turmoil as increasing numbers of religious and ethnic communities claim independence and sometimes superiority vis-à-vis each other; the extreme movements are hostile on sectarian grounds to individual rights that the West has considered central, including freedom of religious choice and the rights of women.

McWilliams' study of American fraternity ideas documents with American examples the almost universal discourse among reflective statesmen, intellectuals and artists that marked the later nineteenth century concerning what ideals of justice and solidarity would make modern societies workable, undoing the worst evils of capitalism and the miseries of urban and rural poor. Pragmatic international efforts were especially prominent following wars, which temporarily exhausted the animosities of opponents and made the costs of conflict visible. The modern pattern of organizing to serve the wounded in wartime and to respond to international "humanitarian" crises began to emerge in the nineteenth century with the International Red Cross and treaties such as the Geneva Convention (1864) on treatment of prisoners of war. International reform organizations devoted to specific rights violations in areas such as the Congo[5] slowly proliferated in what we now call the Third Sector. The rise of international intergovernmental organizations (IGO's) can be traced to trade and maritime agreements of the later nineteenth century, to relief efforts during and after World War I that depended on volunteers but necessarily worked with governments, and to agencies created before and after the First World War, including the World Court, the International Labor Organization, and the failed League of Nations. After

World War Two, the founding of the United Nations and economic agencies such as the World Bank along with trade and currency pacts addressed the apparent lessons of the League of Nations' political failure and also those of the worldwide Depression of the 1930's, which was understood as a failure of the world financial system that required systematic safeguards for the future. The great experiment along the same line that marked the later part of the last century has been the European Union, which imposes regulations for human rights and against political corruption alongside the economic structure.

As the institutional systems just mentioned were being implemented in the mid-twentieth century, decolonization was underway in the old European colonial possessions. The liberation movements involved usually declared universal principles of human rights (a standard facet of constitutions) and expressed fraternal enthusiasm for their new nation, but often in fact were conglomerations of ethnic groups or tribes that had to struggle for unity and often fractured. Simultaneously, the Cold War emerged as a state of mutual threat encompassing almost all "advanced" nations; the ideological arguments (which must be distinguished from the facts on either side) involved opposed models of fraternity and opposing accusations of violation of rights. In practice, Cold War alignments and commercial globalization meant that the industrialized northern hemisphere nations continued to intrude both their economic prowess and political influence into the so-called Third World, mostly nations of the southern hemisphere. Frequently, as Ishay notes, Cold War alignment outweighed professed concern for rights of any sort: both the democracies and the communist bloc supported dictatorships that ignored their professed values. However, even though many of these interactions were driven by military strategy and/or an essentially imperialist desire to control resources, they often included support for economic development and initiatives in health and education that often have continued to the present and represent pragmatic extensions of the "spirit of brotherhood."

Add to these massive changes in the world system the incalculable effects of the rise of communications media and transportation, making alien places and foreign cultures more recognizable to each other: these are important if mutual human recognition is in some sense a bed rock of fraternal behavior. Mutual recognizability clearly has not prevented wars and oppression, yet surely a partial restraint against these is the weight of collective perception, enabled by the worldwide flow of imagery and messages. From World Cup football to the Olympics, from international scouting to Rotary chapters, from images of Hiroshima to those of the Twin Towers falling, the "other" has become potentially present to eyes and ears as never before. Although there have been exceptions including dramatic recent terrorist acts (which *aim* to be widely seen in order to dramatize the attackers' unbreakable will) most of the great governmental crimes against humanity of the last century and to the present in "advanced" states have had to be thrust out of sight by the perpetrators and denied in tightly controlled media.

We can sum up this thumbnail sketch of ideas concerning fraternity by saying again that it runs in ever closer parallel with the political history of human rights but includes elements of mutual understanding and expressions of charity that legalistic formulations can only suggest. In the more advanced nations, considerations of equity and broadly shared necessity have resulted in rights to social benefits including basic education, health insurance, and retirement systems, while protocols among the nations have defined rights of refugees. As the questions of minority and cultural rights have emerged, including increased concerns for women and children, for more advanced education and for preserving heritages, the picture of rights becomes more fully humanistic.

Here are sections of the 1989 *UN Declaration of the Rights of the Child*:

Principle 2—The child...shall be given opportunities and facilities...to develop mentally, physically morally, spiritually and socially in a healthy and normal manner and in conditions of freedom and dignity....

> Principle 10—The child shall be protected from practices which may foster racial, religious, and any other form of discrimination. He shall be brought up in a spirit of understanding, tolerance, friendship among peoples, peace and universal brotherhood, and in full consciousness that his energy and talents should be devoted to the service of his fellow men.[6]

There are very few nations where this picture fits the prospects for all children and history offers little assurance that progress in this direction is inevitable. Yet this statement is remarkable in that it argues an enlargement of the imagination of rights and of the emergent human who is assured them: an enlargement that will be defended not only by contests in courts but by charity, wisdom and cultural respect. Further, the mark of healthy adulthood is taken to be willingness and ability to serve fellow men.

Constant negotiation or mediation must occur to sustain political fraternity when the rights of individuals, the cultural rights of ethnicities and/or original peoples, and rights of self-determination among peoples and aspiring nations lay claims to be recognized. At the great moments of fraternal enthusiasm, for instance when a new nation emerges from colonialism or a suppressed people or tribe finds it voice for recognition of its distinct heritage, the exultation of moment obscures any sense that some principles and some loyalties will be in in conflict. As Ishay's comment cited earlier reminds us, many exuberant historic moments offer examples of combined principles that soon collided with each other. Each of the values mentioned has been celebrated as an irresistible principle firing the energies of brotherhood so that temperance in pursuit of them is a difficult challenge. The enlarged, humanistic idea of "mankind" that we described earlier becomes crucial, for it implies willingness to combine empathy, principles, and compromise within the diversity that every modern nation unavoidably confronts.

Chapter 7. Sentimental Tactics: Shaftesbury's Chapter Headings

The waking share a world in common.
Heracleitus

Although a profound vision of human brotherhood is present in many religions, including the three Mosaic religions, and upright judges and kings are always commended, the great creeds have rarely admired the horse-trading and worldly dialogue that makes a civil society work. Those daily, often near-trivial (but in the mass crucial) interactions entail one end of the spectrum of fraternity, while doctrines of universal brotherhood represent the more sublime end. If one looks to literature or philosophy for images of relatively secular civil interaction combined with humanistic idealism, the first great figures after the classical era arise in the later Renaissance, especially Montaigne, the great exemplar of tolerant interest in all things human. We find a much wider field of writers and thinkers of that sort in the Enlightenment, when both wit and philosophical analysis looked to the real workings and daily manners of classes, cities, courts and empires. One of the most interesting and influential thinkers in this vein was Anthony Cooper, the Third Earl of Shaftesbury (1671-1713), whose philosophy applies to a spectrum of social experience, from private arguments about religion and politics to matters of artistic taste to finding inspiration for benevolence in Nature. Although followers systematized his philosophical positions, the synthesis visible in his works that I explore in the next pages is less that of theoretical principles than of personal strategies of argument for improvement of self and society. One can read the sequence of arguments that he offered as a manual of tactics for individuals who wish to benefit their fellows. The strategies are coherent from one level of discourse to another, implicitly linking the public person, the writer, the philosopher, and the visionary idealist as aspects of one politically responsible actor. As the ideal user of the implied tactics, we might steal a phrase from the poet Shelley: to be a "poet-legislator," whose imagination, passion, and skill in social interaction combine to enhance civility and justice in his society.

Shaftesbury's principal work, *Characteristics of Men, Manners and Opinions* (1711), now forgotten except by specialists, was a major source of the sentimental philosophies of his century and of Romantic idealism in the era to follow. Shaftesbury had both served in Parliament and frequented the clubs and drawing rooms of early eighteenth-century England: he is the first modern writer to grasp the importance of what he calls the "freedom of the club," the back-and-forth of political argument and even ridicule that characterizes the civic realm. That ongoing mixture of dialogue and debate mixed with gossip, talk of fashion and insiders' satiric laughter surely has always occurred in all human societies, but it becomes a centrally important activity of the whole polity, an expression both of community and of freedom, for Shaftesbury.

As Shaftesbury lays out his philosophic positions in *Characteristics*, they imply a series of strategies for debate and even reform of a society marked by powerful religious institutions but where politics has become essentially secular. This was the case in England in the early 1700's. Claiming to arise directly out of natural and innate feelings, sentimentalism could transcend too-narrow rationalism by recognizing universal feelings and instincts; it could override religious factionalism by affirming "natural religion," e.g. drawing from innate moral sense and from the inspiration of nature; and it could stand against oppression on grounds of universal humanity. Through these strategies, sentimentalism offered a wealth of social and political tactics in support of civil and (as we would say) open societies. Shaftesbury's era was sharply aware that theories of politics and theories of human nature go hand in hand: a thinker convinced that men would naturally act as wolves to other men (Hobbes' position) would support absolutist control, while thinkers in Calvin's line, convinced that free will is an illusion, would support a theocratic order. On the other hand, sentimentalist thinkers posited free will, the essential goodness of human nature, the centrality of empathy in ethics, and education of feelings. Sentimentalism often emphasized the emotional and moral growth of children, for if human nature is essentially social and marked by an instinct for morality and beauty, the emotional formation of youth becomes a vastly important topic.

With its emphasis on moral instincts, sentimentalism was the counterpart and complement to more legalistic reasoning about human rights that marked the period. For sentimentalist thinkers, the rights with which the Creator had endowed humans are understood and acted on due to imaginative empathy, so that imagination of humanity, including self-imagination, becomes a highlighted characteristic of the ethical person.

Characteristics was regarded by contemporaries like Leibnitz and Montesquieu as a profound and even poetical work of philosophy, yet less than a century later Wordsworth called it "unjustly neglected"[1] in his revised *Preface to The Lyrical Ballads* (1816). One reason for the neglect may be that both Shaftesbury's ideas and his implied strategies of persuasion became so commonplace as to seem unremarkable.

Another possible reason is that comparable ideas were more powerfully modeled in the works of Rousseau and later writers, with vivid characters to display them, albeit without the sense of interaction in "public space" that we find in Shaftesbury.

Shaftesbury was the grandson of a politically powerful nobleman, the first Earl of Shaftesbury, who had supported the rights of Parliament against Charles the First and then against Cromwell and became an important minister for Charles the Second. He was a patron of the great libertarian philosopher John Locke, who became the third Earl's tutor. The First Earl's opponents had been royal authoritarians around the first Charles and then Calvinist authoritarians around Cromwell. His grandson the philosopher had these opponents in mind as he made his arguments for free exchange of opinions. Shaftesbury the philosopher was an insider with access to free political dialogue as it occurred within Parliament and within the salons and clubs of his class, as well as within London generally. His intellectual sources include neo-platonists of the previous generations as well as Locke, but as one steeped in the classics his understanding of the "freedom of the club" as well as his ideal of moral self-improvement owes much to Athens.

In order to read *Characteristics* as a "manual of tactics" it is necessary to examine the progression of styles as well as topics in the sections of *Characteristics*, and further to assume that as in classical rhetoric different genres of writing imply different levels of truth, with impassioned poetic expression being the most elevated and powerful. The titles of the first five treatises (slightly shortened) are:

-A Letter Concerning Enthusiasm
-*Sensus Communis:* An Essay on the Freedom of Wit and Humour
-Soliloquy, or Advice to an Author

-An Inquiry Concerning Virtue or Merit
-The Moralists, a Philosophical Rhapsody

Traditionally, letters and essays are "low" style, familiar and matter-of-fact literary forms. These are the forms adopted in the first two pieces listed, in which fanaticism (wrongheaded "enthusiasm") is dissected and the free play of "wit and humour" defended. Then, as if the treatises which make up *Characteristics* were Platonic dialectic rising to more elevated levels, the "Soliloquy, or Advice to an Author," is essentially an exhortation to attempt self-knowledge with many reflections on taste and on literary models: taste here is an instrument, as well as a result, of self-formation. The oddness of the title–soliloquies are usually dramatic performances, not mediums for advice–alerts us that genres are being manipulated: the reader is being urged to participate in society in a way that involves dramatic imagination and self-knowledge. I should note, by the way, that the actual prose style of the first four treatises does not vary much, and the "soliloquy" is not in dramatic form, so that the notice about genre contained in the title takes on added importance.

The "Soliloquy"–in which, in effect, the would-be author is told how to advise himself–is followed by the more abstract and academic "An Inquiry Concerning Virtue or Merit." The "Inquiry" was the first treatise published but finds its logical place in the middle of the hierarchy of styles. By virtue of its theoretic ambition this treatise claims a rhetorical status above that of the "Soliloquy." By virtue of the familiarity of its intentions and method it tends to be quoted by philosophical writers as Shaftesbury's definitive statement of his system and was the expression of his system that followers like Francis Hutcheson codified. But in fact, the theoretical formulation is not the most powerful expression of Shaftesbury's position. That comes in "The Moralists, a Philosophical Rhapsody," a dialogue between two philosophic friends who have met in a mountain setting. The implication of the subtitle, as well as the speakers' appeals to the sublimity of the scenery around them (forerunner of a myriad of Romantic works) is that this is moral argument at a high level embodying the most admirable aspirations. It is philosophic argument that aims to motivate as well as to demonstrate, and its rhapsodic tone means to incorporate the idealism shared by the friends as inseparable from their theories.

Following "The Moralists," three essays, "Miscellaneous Reflections on the Preceding Treatises, etc." are supposed to be "modern"—i.e. confused and disordered, returning to the mixed level of satire and contemporary polemics. In fact, they offer an extended commentary on the ways in which arguments offered in earlier sections apply to political and religious controversies, and they answer possible objections. If the preceding treatises represent a dialectical rise to rhetorical heights, the placement of these pieces corresponds to the chaotic and comic aftermaths of the symposia we described earlier in this book. It may be worth recalling, as the deeply classical author may have, that the linguistic root of "satire" is *satura*, a mixed grill or hash[2].

To view this dialogic structure as a handbook for poets in society, one must consider what advice an eloquent citizen with a passion for virtue (a noble "enthusiasm") would take from each of its sections. The rising levels of style from the "Letter" to the "Rhapsody" offer a portrait of moral enthusiasm and rhetorical cleverness on the part of the philosophic good citizen: each level works because of the deeper enthusiasms and idealistic vision expounded at a higher level. Thus, the "Letter" identifies enthusiasm as a universal aspect of human character, including that of poets and religious figures who were not fanatics. Passion for a cause or great truth is crucial for society but must be understood and tempered, which requires self-knowledge of oneself as an enthusiast, the topic of the "Soliloquy" to follow later. The enthusiasm of the rational and virtuous citizen, sometimes expressed in satire or sharp dissection of other's ideas in free exchange, must outweigh the enthusiasm of the fanatic.

The argument in the "Letter" leads, in "*Sensus Communis*: An Essay on the Freedom of Wit and Humour" to a highly original vision of how the free interplay and conflict of opinions make society healthier. The free play of wit and humour includes, but is much larger than, carrying on arguments in good humor, though the latter is relevant because the reasonable enthusiast will use both reason (often satiric) and a balanced emotional temper against the fanatic. (Later eighteenth-century writers celebrated the "man of good humour" as a benevolent and sociable type.) The virtuous citizen who uses and encourages free interchange enlists the tacit approval, the basic rationality, and sometimes the laughter of the audience to support his side of a public argument. The key terms here, "wit" and "humour" have changed in nuance since Shaftesbury wrote: "Wit" included analytic skill, especially in verbal argument, as well as satiric thrusts, while "humour" carried the overtones of the old physiology of humours, bodily fluids and organs that created human moods and personalities: splenetic, cordial or bilious characters were dominated by the spleen, the heart, or the liver. Our different humours make our behaviors amusing to others (the source of our current usage of the word); they also generate different perspectives. The marketplace of free talk and testing of ideas that Shaftesbury imagines is one in which temperaments as well as arguments are important for the counterbalance they create, for both in politics (where we judge leaders as being to our taste) and in religion (where we have different inspirations) the sheer interplay of human types becomes a tempering factor.

Shaftesbury's argument for the freedom of wit and humour has long been recognized as a brilliant early defense of freedom of speech, rooting the defense less in rights of the individual than in social benefit, assuring that the result will not be anarchy (the great fear of authoritarians) but greater collective rationality. Shaftesbury's sources for this argument include English machiavellian republican thinkers like Sidney and Harrington and his own tutor Locke. Machiavellian republican theorists expected and tried to systematize a balance of interests or factions within the state: thus, Harrington formalized three competing classes of Englishmen in his utopia *Oceania*. What is original in Shaftesbury is his focus on the *process* of free dialogue at the communal and small group level, leading to an enlarged notion of what it must imply for the formation of citizens and for a newly significant factor, an ongoing and responsive public opinion.

In order to explain how free play of wit and humour improves the state over a long term, Shaftesbury argues that when these freedoms are allowed, a shared public judgment emerges--a common sense of the truth concerning whatever matters are open to public comment. This idea is of course powerful in several ways: it implicitly highlights the value of the judgments of the average practical citizen, and thus is democratic; it implies that inter-subjective judgment is dependable, and thus is friendly to empiricism and the rational spirit of the era; and it rejects the special knowledge claims of the religious visionaries, and thus is secular with respect to politics. Under the right conditions, with participation in dialogue by temperately enthusiastic and philosophic wits, the mechanism of free expression is self-regulating, a feedback mechanism for social sanity. Shaftesbury explicitly compares the exchange of opinions with trade; his vision of the mechanism correcting itself is surely one source of Adam Smith's later description of an "invisible hand" adjusting the economic marketplace[3]. The play of wit and humour tempers social excesses when the freedom to exercise it is present in a free market of discourse and debate, but obviously will be most effective when some citizens have the wit, the refined self-knowledge, and the idealism that shapes the conflict of ideas into a deeper shared wisdom. What is more, the *sensus communis* operates and persists dynamically over time: a new and expansive notion of communal memory is implicit in the idea.

Part of Shaftesbury's originality is seeing that these mechanisms of adjustment and judgment operate along a continuum that we might call the public, the private or informal, and the personal. The most public sphere, for example arguments in Parliament, ultimately derives energy or tempering from the informal world of "the club," whether in actual clubs, party caucuses, market squares, or friendships. The themes of the public sphere and the self-adjusting wisdoms of the private sphere, that of the *sensus communis*, are raised to deeper and comprehensive level in the poet/legislator, who engages in dialogue with himself in the most personal sphere. He aspires to taste, the goal of the "Soliloquy," and to high virtue, the vision of "The Moralists."

The "Soliloquy: or, Advice to an Author" takes up the question of how and why an idealistic citizen is to understand his own enthusiasms, imagine his own role, and improve himself as a moral person. These are all aspects of the pursuit of virtue, which is never purely personal but always that of an actor in society. Where Socrates had recommended mirrors as an emblem of self-knowing, Shaftesbury looks to classic dialogues as dramas that model internal as well as external discourse. The "Soliloquy" addresses the progress of taste along with recommending a few models, for Shaftesbury, though imbued in the classics, is convinced that the progress of the arts in England has improved taste and purged literary vices from the Restoration to his own day[4], with positive implications for public morality. A successor volume to *Characteristics* entitled *Second Characters* is one of the first modern philosophical efforts at aesthetic theory, interpreting and measuring the value of literary and plastic works of art as conveyors of moral lessons; here, too, the underlying conviction is that taste, understood as discrimination and self-formation rather than mere fashion, is crucial for the health of the public realm.

All these advices and theories place trust in human nature, trust that the interplay of personalities and argument can temper excess and that self-awareness will lead both to self- and social improvement. Neither a Calvinist nor a Hobbesian would agree to this dependence on human nature without the iron guidance of scripture or the State. The "Inquiry Concerning Virtue or Merit" argues that a benevolent social instinct is inherent in humankind, and further, that it overlaps with an instinct for beauty and order, so that pleasure and mutual need alike are naturally supportive of morality. Shaftesbury's argument is especially directed against Hobbes, pointing out that man is not necessarily a wolf to man, that both men and wolves are in fact sociable to their own kind or group, however savage to enemies or to sheep: indeed, war itself is in many respects an intensely social activity, involving great generosity among members of the same side.

Sentimental argument is always partly *ad hominem*. A sentimental philosopher certainly does ask, "Does this argument make sense?" but also and always, "What kind of person are you, who argue this position?" Shaftesbury points out that Hobbes in personal life contradicts his principles, acting with reputed good character and writing his book to educate fellow men, which would not make sense by his theory. If he were consistent, he should have tried to flatter mankind to make himself rich or powerful.

It is true that the sentimentalist's desire to appeal to the best aspect of human nature easily turns into a blindness toward the worst side, and sometimes engenders a rote gentility of expression that suffocates the unsavory side of truth. As an early example, the chief codifier of Shaftesbury's philosophy,

Hutcheson, read Hume's early *Essay on Human Nature,* and wrote the author to complain that the style of writing suggested too little admiration for virtue. Hume fired back a letter eloquently defending the philosopher's right to describe things exactly as they are. However, Hume did in fact adjust his style in later writings[5]. The correspondence suggests that from the first the manipulative aspect of sentimentalism was in play, appealing to the best in human nature but understanding that the appeal is at least partly a tactic, coaxing virtuous action from egoistic and conformist motives. Shaftsbury himself was clearly not a euphemist who evaded harsh judgments and satiric thrusts, but delighted in the chaffing, teasing, and critique of the "club," subjecting even religious ideas to the test of ridicule. However, as we not below, the fact that sentimentalism engendered appeals to self-image and social acceptability meant that it held its own temptations

Shaftesbury does not literally dramatize the day-to-day interplay that he praises, yet "The Moralists" and his following chapters called "Miscellanies" bring us close to it. The one part of *Characteristics* that is in actual dialogue is highfaluting, "The Moralists, A Philosophic Rhapsody," the subtitle of which alerts us that we have entered the realm of idealistic poetry. The dialogue repeats tenets of the "Inquiry"; it displays a degree of dramatic tension when two friends, the enthusiast Theocles and the more skeptical Philocles, debate a Calvinist whose politics are authoritarian. The philosophic friends wrestle with the problem of human evil amid a sublime natural setting where it is easy to believe that Nature is good. Their dialogue is recorded for the sake of a third friend, Palemon, who is disappointed with the lack of virtue he sees in society. This literary framework thus implies the transfer of enthusiasm from the natural setting (and "natural religion") to politics and mores. The differences among the friends are more of temperament than of theory, one having a deeper innate optimism, another more skepticism, the third a stoic's distaste for human moral frailty.

"The Moralists" introduces themes and stereotypes that would be sustained and sharpened endlessly in later Romantic works, in which relation to humanity is mediated through relationship with natural settings. The dialogists agree, as to a truism, that love of mankind and love of nature are two paths to the same state of virtue. Almost a century later, it ought to surprise the reader but apparently never does when Wordsworth stands above the rugged natural setting of ruined Tintern Abbey, joined by his best friend (his sister), feeling a divine spirit "interfused" throughout the universe, and hearing the "still, sad music of humanity." The natural and social aesthetic have been so habitually intermingled over the previous century that the instant progression from Nature to Humanity is felt as inevitable, not as an interpolation. In "The Moralists" as in many later literary pictures, the sublime supplies a moral inspiration that the observers will carry into public spheres, re-awakened to their own natural benevolence and to personal aspirations for virtue.

Although our sense of styles and genres has changed, and although the issue of how to relate public freedoms to religious beliefs is no longer the key issue in Western civil societies (though it is yet a great world issue), Shaftesbury's vision of how the linguistic tactics and guiding moral vision of the philosophic citizen can work in society remains unusually rich with implications. The outcome of his teaching, the ultimate purpose of *Characteristics* seen as a handbook, is a society in dialogue, in which both freedom and connection are nurtured. The mechanism of *sensus communis* is self-feeding and self-correcting, but most dependably so when actors of deeply considered enthusiasm are part of the machine, practicing its freedoms.

Political philosophers, including several who have explicated Hannah Arendt's notion of the "public space," have long regarded Shaftesbury as perhaps the first great expositor of the nature of public dialogue. Thus, Michael Denneny, citing Gracian's earlier identification of taste "as a faculty that perceives realities that were neither subjective nor objective," argues that the theme was "most fruitfully developed by Shaftesbury, whose thought has startling and profound affinities with that of Arendt."[6]

Wordsworth speaks (in *The Prelude*) of how the landscape is "half-created, half-perceived" by the poet's eye, which of course stands for the awakened capacity of all humans. The landscape is real and solid, but as a *scape*, having form and organization and perhaps beauty or symbolism, it is created, i.e. awarded its qualities, by the imagination. The process is akin to what occurs when an individual learns to perceive as an expert in fields such as medicine and art criticism: the physician literally sees more than the layman when he notes a patient's skin or gait, intuiting perhaps a fever or an old injury. In the case of a landscape, which is endlessly detailed and runs on out of sight, the perceiver creates its appearance in the degree to which it is a whole with aesthetic characteristics and integrity that do not exist until seen in that way. The same phrase (half-created, half-perceived) applies even more dynamically to social interactions. As they are perceived by participants but especially when they are expressed in speech or symbols, the shared perceptions and connections among the participants expand, growing more complex and richer with implication.

This is a common and usually banal aspect of what occurs when we meet a casual acquaintance on the sidewalk. Between two humans who happen to meet on the street, not to mention those who act within a group, there is a nimbus of taken-for-granted, presumed, half-perceived, and potential relations beyond what participants might describe if interviewed. The contents of your nimbus and mine—tacit assumptions, inchoate relations with each other, and half-sensed possibilities—contain a great deal of information in common, because we share the world in common and (in our example) a community in common. This realm of unexpressed common acquaintance with life is of course important to literature: the poet works within that nimbus of the half-recognized but intimately known aspects of life, awakening recognition of something important to all of us:

What oft was thought but ne'er so well expressed.
Pope

Sometimes what the poet offers is simply a sharper awareness of the weight of joy or sorrow that we can only point to, confessing the inadequacy of words:

But Oh, the difference to me!
Wordsworth

Shaftesbury's version of sentimentalism implies a resilient and inherently powerful social theory, if by that term we mean a theory on how to make society work for mutual benefit and that works better and better if everyone understands it. It works better the more consciously it is shared among as many citizens as possible. Its particular gift is that it extends to the halo of half-formed communication and tacit agreements, touching my desire for approbation and your enthusiasm to persuade me. It is ready to allow for another's wry temperament, matters of taste, and so on. Recognizing that society is pushed and pulled by "enthusiasms," it posits that onlookers form and have always formed judgments measured against the tacit knowledge of life that they can bring to the controversies of the moment.

The individual citizen's depth of instinct for the social, the good, and the beautiful, even if only half-aware, combined with the same reservoir in many others, can be elicited as a tempering influence, a deep reservoir of rationality—often "common sense" in the contemporary sense of that term, although Shaftesbury's term implies an ongoing dynamic process of judging men and issues. The Shaftesburyan never entirely disengages from humanity but shapes his own taste and that of his society, sure that human nature is inherently social with a moral sense and an aesthetic sense that can be appealed to. His idealism is potentially powerful over time because wide vision and enthusiasm are contagious. At every stage, the system is both inward and social, a template for the romantic hero and/or reformer, whose challenge is to sustain his patience with human nature as he encounters it.

A glance at works designed to guide young men in courtly society, like those of the 17th century Spanish Jesuit Gracian, shows that they recognized the importance of reputation and men's opinions but did not offer the same sense of public wisdom that *Characteristics* offers. Advice offered for success in a society in which power is concentrated in courts will be about cultivating exquisitely appropriate manners, seeking prudent alliances, and seeking hidden mainsprings of others' actions, behaviors that serve in a sphere where a few confer power and favorites shift. Shaftesbury's arguments reflect a societal process involving far more voices and minds. The dynamic of free exchange that he has observed was created by growth of commercial life, by experience of parliamentary government, by increased religious toleration, and by increasingly egalitarian social values. In a rigid class structure, superiors need not be courteous to inferiors nor praise their innate goodness, although when they do show those courtesies they are praised for it. But in a more democratic society, where commerce, elections, and a potentially noisy press exist, persuasive individuals must act as if fellow citizens deserve to be listened to and even complimented on the virtues they will show as he persuades them.

It is hard for moderns to grasp the novelty of Shaftesbury's appeal to *sensus communis*: it is not only popular opinion, which in many political systems of his era would have been scorned and in other cases distrusted as a problem for rulers: it is a collective rationality that has authority beyond the fashions and fads of the day. What is more, as will be mentioned below, the idea flowers in several directions: it provides a basis for democratic political theory but also suggests that cultures are in a constant process of dialogue and potentially full of wisdom. A couple of generations earlier, it would have seemed absurd to most European writers and thinkers to credit heavily the opinions of the commons; exceptions are writers familiar with republics like Machiavelli, whose Prince, a "new man" in supreme power, must attend to the perceptions of the populace to build consensual legitimacy. We need look no further than Shakespeare's *MacBeth* to find a dismissal of the commons' judgment in eras preceding Shaftesbury. In his most famous speech, MacBeth laments the emptiness of his life, saying that life is a grind of meaningless days,

> …a tale told by an idiot, full
> of sound and fury, signifying nothing.

The *Oxford English Dictionary* says that this is the first time that the word "idiot" is used in its modern sense of one born without full potential for reason, but in fact an older meaning clings to the word. An "idiot" was a person, usually illiterate, who could speak only his native language. (The Roman church had long included "idiot priests" who could say Mass by memorizing the Latin but could not read it.) What kind of story would a late-medieval Scots "idiot" tell? A tale of murderous heroes and warring clans, with witches, omens, and the loud fury of historically meaningless conquests—a tale like MacBeth's. "Told by an idiot" dismisses folk understanding, whereas Shaftesbury's century saw widening respect for the mythic depth of folk tales and ballads, while daring robbers from the folk traditions began to appear in literature as proto-democratic heroes[7].

Shaftesbury's intellectual descendants are found in two grand streams that are relevant to the theme of fraternity. One line of intellectual descent runs to Schiller, who explored the profound shared knowledge of life that is the wisdom of the folk as a touchstone for both art and political ideals. Beyond him the idea flowers as part of German idealism, for the deep old convictions of the people began to be seen embodying a national spirit evolving through history. One implication, especially as the nineteenth century produced its great movements and revolutions, was that history would validate the brotherhood of those who are swept into the movements that build on this sprit, whether for democracy or imperial destiny.

A second line of descent led to the Common Sense School of philosophers, dominant in England and American academies in the late eighteenth century. Shaftesbury's system was codified by Frances Hutcheson, a clergyman who posited that human nature is naturally good (he was also, fittingly, apparently the first philosopher to attempt to explain humor). Hutcheson's best-known successor was Adam Smith, whose ethical system was built on the natural operation of imagination on innate affections, or empathy: we understand what an injury to my fellow man is (and why morally wrong) by sensing how we would feel in the same situation. Smith is more famous, as noted, for an economic theory in which the self-adjusting principle that Shaftesbury imagined for free speech becomes a market control. Smith's most notable academic successors were Scottish philosophers, Stewart and Reid, who combined a Lockean emphasis on sense impressions with Hutcheson's assumption of innate moral and aesthetic instincts. Arguably, the grandest and most original embodiment of the Common Sense school's approach was Wordsworth's *The Prelude*, which narrates the growth of the human mind in stages ("spots of time") when intense sense impressions trigger and intermix with innate moral or aesthetic impulses in a long process of maturation to adulthood: it is poetry's greatest contribution to the long debate over nature vs. nurture in human formation.

The Degradations of Sentimentalism

It is necessary to say a few more words about the degradations of sentimentalism, for they illustrate the social dynamics involved, which easily lead to phony appeals to fellow-feeling. The major ideas have become ingrained in western thought in many transformations, and a few should be mentioned as having special reference to the U.S., where optimism is a national characteristic. At the most innocent level a conventional sentimental expression, say a Mother's Day card, recognizes through a conventional gesture an emotion most people cannot express fully. As noted earlier, often even the great artists don't explicitly express the deepest shared emotions: rather, the poet's metaphor or the great composer's music awakens recognition in the audience. "Sentimental" in little ceremonies refers to a conventional symbol or gesture that giver and recipient agree to take as intended. The gesture touches what I called the nimbus of unexpressed interactions: my flowers and my card for mother point to a large realm of feeling.

A sentimental gesture may be perfunctory, or it may be of great sweetness to those involved. In an artwork, on the other hand, when a piece is "sentimental" it relies too heavily on a standard image and its conventional emotional claims. Thus, the picture of a rural Thanksgiving table is sentimental in which the turkey is perfect, the kids are all clean-faced and eager, grandpa and grandma are smiling and there is no Aunt

Alice scowling at the gravy dish nor a lean-to collapsing outside the farmhouse window. Many Romantic poets recognized the combination of sincere emotional burden with inarticulateness that we find it in ordinary characters: Burns's country swain has no urbane language for the vividness of his love, who is like "a red, *red* rose/That blooms in summer." The repetition tells the intensity of his love: he can *see* that brilliantly red redness, like her beautiful, beautiful splendor. Japanese haiku and related forms often recognize this sort of deep inarticulate emotion by a sudden juxtaposition of images that bring back a heartache or open a sense of eternity. Whether this sentimentality is authentic or banal in literary works depends greatly on the verbal handling and the *personae* involved. In the Romantic writers, sentimental simplicity often implied a new level of respect for humble lives.

There are scales of appropriateness even in conventional sentimentality, depending on the persons involved and the deeper issues. We sympathize with a child who has lost a pet gerbil and praise the rodent's virtues as a dear companion because the child's sense of loss is so sincere, while a grownup with the same effusions would be comic. A movie criminal who will steal or murder but is rhapsodic over an aquarium fish (as in the movie *A Fish Called Wanda*) is comic; the James Bond villain who strokes his heavy-furred cat while torturing the hero is sinister because he takes pleasure in the opposites, beauty and cruelty, together.

We also set aside, as perennial and conventional, the declarations of mutual esteem and faith in others' character that are an ancient tactic in negotiations, sales, and electoral campaigns. A declaration of admiration and liking for the other is a common prelude to deal-making, as it is to seduction. In politics and many other settings, it is a rare orator who does not compliment his audience; what sentimentalism as popularized from the eighteenth century to the present added to the timeless ploys of negotiation was a lexicon and an easily oversimplified theory about everyone's basic goodness. Several centuries of fashionable sentimentalism, promoted as self-ennobling idealism by philosophers, religious figures, and other popularizers, encouraged—at least in the U.S.—a rote positiveness more recently buttressed with echoes of Buddhism and pop Freudianism. The extremely long list of those responsible includes R.W. Emerson, Dale Carnegie, and endless media gurus counseling avoidance of "negativism" and boosting our self-approval.

In political speech, admiration of the good character of the nation (excepting the opponent and his supporters, an inexplicable exception) is a commonplace, often apparently sincere. Thus, when former President Gerald Ford explained that he would not cease public appearances after several assassination attempts because "Americans are good people" it was hardly relevant, since eccentrics like Squeaky Fromm (one of his would-be assassins) were not representative of the people or any movement. On the other hand, when George W. Bush was required to express official regret for the torture at Abu Ghraib prison during the Second Iraq War (without admitting that his administration encouraged torture) he said "Americans are good people"—camouflaging the issue for his American audience, for the phrase or something like it has become a comforting political mantra.

The most common degradation of sentimentalism has been that practiced by the censors of propriety. The sentimental philosopher's *ad hominem* question—What kind of person are you, that you make this argument? turns into a convention that one's character is defined by what one allows oneself to see, never mind the speaking what one knows. It follows that one's morals or manners are defective if one admits even to understanding violent or brutal or explicitly sexual emotions (again, never mind feeling them!) and one must not describe these in public argument or popular art. The timeless human disinclination to face unpleasant truths encourages the argument that the depiction of ugly facts is a sign of low character: thus, a social critic becomes, in the words of Theodore Roosevelt, a "muckraker." At worst, the standard for acceptable speech becomes Thumper the Rabbit's rule: "If ya can't say suthin' good, don't say nuthin' at all." Idealism degrades to self-congratulation, while pursuit of taste in the arts and decency of expression become conventionality, enforced by official or social censorship. In corners and behind hands, of course, the nastiest of rumors, jokes and judgments are still exchanged. Rejecting these hypocrisies, by the mid-nineteenth century Whitman would declare, "I am no sentimentalist, no stander above men and women" in that he speaks frankly and does not put on the air of moral superiority.

Chapter 8. Poetic Nightmares and the Paradoxes of Fraternity[1]

> It was the best of times, it was the worst of times.
>
> Dickens

The English Romantic poets responded to their era's bright ideal of fraternity—the emergent brotherhood of nations and of liberated peoples within the nations—with powerful enthusiasm, which the wars and reversals of the era tempered but did not destroy. The erupting conviction of brotherhood was especially attractive to poets and other artists because art seemed a way to shape the forms and sentiments by which humankind could achieve a deeper brotherhood. However, they rediscovered a perennial truth with shocking force: that the bright ideal of realized individuals finding brotherhood in liberty opens to view a darker communion with guilt, despair and need. This discovery, the public fact that so many of their brothers' lives were desperate and the private fact that they must share and mirror the others' despair—i.e., face what blighted bodies and souls might tell about their ideals and the meaning of human existence—is expressed in some extraordinary passages describing lost souls or maimed bodies. These are often nightmarish dreams or moments of disassociation, in which the narrator is dizzied or floats in a sea of faces and bodies. Dreams and madness were of course ancient conventions, and "gothic" and grotesque imagery was familiar, but after the Revolution the misery and the disintegration of identity involved in these dreams infect both the poet and ideals of society. Even when the dreams and visions are offered as personal experiences, they are infused with implications for universal human connection. They suggest that an important dimension of the power of art would lie in translation of these visions of shameful and horrific life into a deeper affirmation of common humanity. That translation could not be based on pity from a distance but on a taking inward, an empathy with hopelessness that for the m0ment could shake the poet's sense of his identity. Both the poet's story of his own despairs and the pitiable characters whom he meets amid city or country degradation must be so honestly handled as to produce, in Wordsworth's phrase, "relationship and love."

The paradox of fraternity emerged as an unavoidable fact in Romantic poetry as *fraternite'* emerged as a central political problem in history. The ecstasy of fellow-feeling sparked by the early stages of revolution admitted how deeply men had been and normally are divided. That man's need for fellowship and shared visions create "enthusiasm" was an eighteenth-century commonplace, but the revolutionary spectacle exposed both violence and depths of need, rooted in human nature, too profound for sentimental optimism to discount. Brotherly feeling comes to include identification with the poor and victimized along with hope and pity for them, which sometimes stand at a distance. The extremes of idealism and degradation, polar revelations of universal human experience, became central to poetry. Exploring the darker side of brotherhood, sharing miseries that had blighted souls as well as bodies and admitting the threat to the poet's sense of his own life's meaning emerged as a challenge as powerful as advocacy of liberty in the state.

What had occurred was the emergence of those whom Hugo was to call *les miserables* as an unavoidably combined moral and political problem, touching the vocations of the poet as well as that of the would-be reformer. As Blake and Wordsworth saw them in London, the city's poorest were even worse off than the rural poor, for their existences seemed more shameful than the meager but traditional lives close to Nature that rural villages showed. When the *miserables* surfaced into the political daylight, writers demanded in their name not only legal justice but that personal dignity which each human owes to his fellows. For the first time in history, as Hannah Arendt has written[2], pity became a public, political virtue rather than a private moral sentiment. Robespierre demonstrated early that purgation of hypocrisy could itself be a hypocritical act, but in a sense the persistent autobiographic moralizing of the early Romantics is a Terror turned inward to expose and purge the poets' selves as a prelude to brotherhood.

Confidence in the ability to imagine humankind itself had been shaken, and this was particularly true in encounters with city life. Wordsworth describes his first entrance into London as entrance to a cave, which is seen by the entrant first a chaos of gothic shades, then as sterile stone, and only finally inhabited by less frightening imagined shapes. The "curious traveler" entering the cave first sees "a canopy... Of shapes and forms... That shift and vanish... Like spectres (*The Prelude*,VIII . ll.569-572)".[3] As the eye adjusts, the scene stands "in perfect view/...lifeless as a written book." But a "new quickening" occurs that "Busies the eye with images and forms,"

> A variegated landscape,—there the shape
> Of some gigantic warrior clad in mail,
> The ghostly semblance of a hooded monk,
> Veiled nun, or pilgrim resting on his staff:
> Strange congregation! Yet not slow to meet
> Eyes that perceive through minds that can inspire.
>
> (ll. 581-89)

The very existence of this complicated figure tells a good deal about the combined vibrancy and threat that the city offered. The cave in the extended simile eventually fills with medieval images, knight and giant, monk and nun: a Chaucerian humanity that tells us that the city is full of exotic human types and tales once the poet learns that the city is neither haunted nor sterile. At the same time, the city repeatedly offers the poet moral shocks that literally daze him. Thus, a young prostitute blaspheming undoes his sense of human connection:

> I shuddered, for a barrier seemed at once
> Thrown in, that from humanity divorced
> Humanity, splitting the race of man
> In twain, yet leaving the same outward form.
> (The Prelude VII, ll. 385-88)

Later, when the young poet had come to understand the life such girls led, he feels not division splitting humanity but "sadness."

Wordsworth's shock is not simply that of a conventionally moral young man encountering the worst degradations of the city: it is a momentary fracture in the poet's sense of what a human being is. He has grown in both aesthetic and moral dimensions as natural impulses and healthy social contacts formed his humanity, and in that sentimental era he expects to connect with others by empathy with their similar nature. For the moment he can't imagine himself and the cursing whore as having the same humanity. His later sympathy and "sadness" require reflection to achieve, with understanding of her likely background. His "sadness" does not entirely close the distance, for it is an expression of pity and an acceptance of tragedy. Pity, though a great virtue, is often ambiguous in that it often allows the pitier to keep his social or economic distance from the sufferer and sometimes to deny equality of humanity. This is not Wordsworth's case, for he wants to affirm human unity, but is one of many examples of an issue that sentimentalism and the Enlightenment's new emphasis on the growth of human character introduced: what happens when innocence, such as that of the beloved and sheltered child, encounters death or evil? How shall elders introduce these harsh facts of life and how manage the shock, despair, or trauma involved? This became a recurrent question in literature as well as in theories of child-rearing. The same interest in the collision of innocence with life's evils sometimes extended as well to adult characters embittered by a lost romance or disillusioned by a failed political dream. Wordsworth's word "sadness" has its current meaning of sorrowful mood but carries, as well, an old implication of somberness, accepting the universality of loss and the need for optimism to be balanced by realism.

In much of the emerging political theory of the era, and in the literary celebrations of country life, democratic values were pictured in such customary fraternities as neighborly cooperation among farmers, conversation among travelers, and free intercourse of opinion in a local tavern. But the new sense of pity and terror at lives emptied of meaning creates an opposite community that we might call the City of Night, which is frightening and sometimes invades the City of Day, as in the passage just cited on the young prostitute. The poet, matured, must engage both cities, communing with the despair of his fellows while bearing a political vision of confidence and shared dignity. Each vision raises the question of how it can be reconciled with the other. In the actual flow of city life, as opposed to country settings, the chaotic stream of passersby and the obvious misery of some inhabitants are such that celebration of communion with all humans often occurs in moments of solitude, not amidst the crowds. Thus, in "Tintern Abbey" it is an isolated landscape of mountains and ruins that causes Wordsworth to hear the "still, sad music of humanity." In London itself, an ecstatic embrace of humanity occurs while the sun is rising but the city has not awakened in "Composed upon Westminster Bridge":

Dear God! The very houses seem asleep,
And all that mighty heart is beating still![4]

If we keep in mind the problem of reconcilement, of return from night visions to the daytime city and its less threatening but still complex positive fraternities, we can better appreciate the importance of the literary use of dream conventions. These assure the reader that the vision holds deep but only partial truth. Descriptions of trances, dizziness, near-madness and nightmares signify that the visions arise from intense moral sympathy, an imaginative sensitivity intrinsic to the poetic gift. The poet is morally and psychically at risk, troubled by more than the terror of the moment, because he must integrate his connection with naked misery, futility, or death-in-life into his larger, waking imagination of mankind. An image of this integration into the City of Day though narration occurs in *The Rime of the Ancient Mariner*, in a passage that Wordsworth had suggested to Coleridge. The Mariner stands as a living soul among ghosts who work the ship as he sails home. He has been saved by his love of beautiful water-snakes, but he will continue to live among terrifying, silent wraiths until, brought ashore, he begins testifying to his surprising salvation by love of the beautiful even amidst his own misery. As with the Mariner, so with the visions of lost souls, whether in the real city or dreams: the fraternity of lost and living is sewn in the testimony. The visionary conventions of the nightmare or disassociation promise the poet's return from the risk of identification with blighted souls to the daylight sphere of relationship and dialogue.

The City of Night is a sphere of risk to sanity and moral coherence because it resonates with the poet's own fears and weaknesses, and the worst of these is that his life is as meaninglessness as those he pities. The distortions of humanity seen in dreams and among the *miserables* undermine the poet's ability to imagine an ideal of human nature. In the philosophic tradition of sentimentalism, in which ethical impulses are based on empathy with others, seeing extreme horrors does not only excite sympathy: it threatens to pollute the imagination. Thus, Shelley's Prometheus:

> I behold such execrable shapes,
> Methinks I grow like what I contemplate,
> And laugh and stare in loathsome sympathy.[5]

It is the Romantic poet's fate to enter such worlds and his gift to unite the pitiable scenes with his wider and nobler vision of human community. The Romantic visions undoubtedly draw on deep, perhaps primordial, experiences of fear or alarm in unfamiliar cities, dark places, or meeting stranger faces. For the romantics, the implications of these fears are almost always loss of coherent identity as well as loss of ideals. Ghosts imply the threat of death but also unassuageable nostalgias for lost loves or lost chances; the maimed stand for the inherent incompleteness of human hopes, the distorted faces or bodies for what passions have done to each life. The threatening implications for an ideal of humanity and for communion among men is almost always at least tacitly present, and for these poets it is an issue to be resolved by some return to wholeness, whereas earlier and later writers using the same conventions might not share that post-revolutionary anxiety to resolve the paradox. For Wordsworth, as indicated, the anxiety to integrate the oppositions is explicit, a philosophical challenge addressed in the Christian apologetics of *The Excursion* (1915) regarded as his major long poem in his lifetime. In autobiographical *The Prelude* (drafted in 1805 but not published until 1850, in the author's old age), the encounter is more nearly raw: an encounter with a blind beggar on a London street who carries a sign explaining his story, is terrifying: "an apt type/ his label seemed of the utmost we can know..." The poet's mind "turned round/ As with the might of waters," and he gazes "As if admonished from another world." For Blake on the other hand, the extremes are truths of Innocence and Experience, to be understood in their constant opposition. He walks nighttime London

> Where the chartered Thames does flow
> And mark on every face I meet
> Marks of weakness, marks of woe. [6]

In Blake's city, as Experience understands it, hypocrisy infiltrates everything, though Innocence does not understand. The official expressions of benevolence are cloyed with pride; the soot-blackened cathedrals, are "dark, satanic mills"; and as for pity,

> Pity would be no more
> If we did not make somebody poor....[7]

Many romantic visions of luminous or horrid faces occur at moments when the protagonist has been examining his life intently and has discerned something alien in his own being. The strangeness of others' faces reflects something frightening in the discovered self. The visions may have the effect of breaking down the strangeness that divides men, and may heal divisions within the self. This sort of healing self-projection occurs in Whitman's "the Sleepers," when the poet gazes on his city's sufferers while they sleep and soothes them with caressing gestures. Another, less restorative self-projection occurs in the series of nightmares that DeQuincy experienced as he approached middle age. In the first nightmares, human figures were dwarfed within the sublimely threatening architecture of Piranesi's *Antiquities of Rome*: human aspirations dwarfed by time itself. In the second series of nightmares, memories of the young DeQuincy's futile search through London streets for a prostitute who had befriended him transform into a phantasmagoria:

> Perhaps some part of my London life [searching for Ann among fluctuating crowds] might be answerable.... upon the rocking waters of the ocean the human face began to reveal itself; the sea appeared paved with innumerable faces... imploring, wrathful, despairing... my mind tossed, as it seemed, upon the billowy ocean....[8]

The third series of dreams showed cruel Asiatic civilizations, in which individuals counted for nothing, and the dreamer is finally "kissed with cancerous kisses by crocodiles." Each of these dreams offers a version of the terrifying submersion of the individual, first by time and then in the flow of souls and finally in the jaws of those alliterative reptiles. The latter two dreams have an erotic overtone that DeQuincy emphasizes by tying them to Ann: individual souls are dissolved except for faces in the ocean, they are kissed and infected and no doubt will be devoured. As it relates to a fraternity ideal, which values and preserves individuality within its community, the nightmare (like the city in which Ann was lost) absorbs and cancels the individual. And yet, of course, both fear of absorption and the fact of death must be common to humanity and therefore a piece of the fraternal vision whether of the day or night cities of the poetic vision.

A remarkable passage of counterpoint to the horrors of DeQuincey's dreams occurs in an essay by Charles Lamb, "Witches, and Other Night Fears." Lamb had real madness in his family and worked at a profession that was almost a literary byword for anonymous dreary city life, that of a clerk in a mercantile house. Yet he parodies the dreams of Coleridge (which DeQuincey was imitating) to express his own healthy self-acceptance. The ability to enter into brotherhood of an enduring sort depends on self-acceptance, just as enduring friendship does; and that self-acceptance must reflect accurate awareness, and some taming or reconcilement, of whatever grandeur or pitiableness our lives really show. Lamb could measure his own life, which held family tragedies and urbane delight in friends and the theatre; he knew better than to measure the city by its extremes. Recording his childhood fears, Lamb mentions recurrent dreams of horrid faces. He drops a shrewd hint that the intensity of his nightmares had to do with the isolation of children in the nursery at night. However, he reports that the dreams lost their terror when he understood that they would not harm him and that having nightmares was not unusual. At the time of his writing, he says, he dreamt mostly of architecture. As in DeQuincey, this may indicate a sense of the individual's smallness on the stage of history, or it may suggest Lamb's constant identification with London, whose permanence he would find more comfort than nightmare. Admitting his admiration of Coleridge, he offers his own dream of the ocean. He is not a lost soul in the swirl nor are there ghastly faces in the waves: he is a god surrounded by Nereids. They bear him up the Thames, their numbers diminishing as they do so until they deposit him onto the dock at Lambeth as plain Charles Lamb. The dream suggests confidence in his identity and acceptance of it, with small regret at the loss of his divinity and his Nereids. He steps ashore a little humiliated, but he cannot support that self-image of his divinity in the city. Shedding the glorious trappings is in effect a comment on the self-advertisement of Coleridge's and DeQuincey's reported dreams. He admits his lightness compared with Coleridge yet his journey is profoundly as well as superficially comic: his dreams have led him, modest and laughing, into the human city, a return to the city of Day that no other romantic colleague accomplished so directly. For Lamb, as Coleridge described him, "No sound is dissonant which tells of life."[9]

Dream sequences and myths of descent into underworlds are ancient literary devices; what the English romantics mentioned here give the reader when they adopt these conventions is distinctive because the implications for human brotherhood and human liberation, the revolutionary themes and the ideals of their era, are immediately present. In one sense or another they tend to point the way to a reconciliation of the opposite visions in a deeper sympathy for humanity. A couple of modern versions of similar moments demonstrate the difference in nuance: once these descents are familiar, the poets feel no compunction to wrestle with the reconciliation, repair the vision of what man is. One of the most famous modern passages occurs in Eliot's *The Wasteland*. His narrator observes the stream of commuters entering the commercial district of London:

> A crowd flows over London Bridge, so many,
> I had not thought death had undone so many.[10]

The bankers and clerks are the living dead in a city and era of pure spiritual exhaustion, meaningless by loss of myth, religious faith, even natural vitality. *The Wasteland* does not repair its bleakness, nor is the narrator spun round and dizzied by the death in life that he sees. The second line is a quotation from Dante's *Inferno*, from the moment when Dante first walks among the dead including the millions who are like particles in a sandstorm because they have made no decisions in life that would lead them either to Hell or Heaven. The quotation is exactly apt, but the meaning of that vision of ghostly London—exhaustion, loss of self, meaninglessness— is one that the Romantics established.

As a final example, a brief poem by Ezra Pound surprises us by following the pattern of Wordsworth's "Westminster

Bridge." Pound's haiku-like *In the Metro* describes the crowd surfacing into daylight from the Parisian underground, presumably at morning. In the tradition, and especially for Pound, we might expect the pale faces to wear traces of the darkness they bear. And indeed they do not "appear" but are an "apparition," the word we use for ghosts. But what the poet suddenly sees is ecstatic, a vision of blossoms: the beauty of humans in sudden connection.

> The apparition of these faces in the crowd;
> Petals on a wet, black bough.[11]

Chapter 9. The Light of American Firesides

Washington's "Peaceable Spirit"

The term "fraternity" with its overtone in English of unions created for limited purposes is especially useful in examining the American version of the theme because fraternity has been largely absent in American political discourse. Alongside conventional appeals to patriotism and celebrations of the nation as a great family (more common in later twentieth century rhetoric of racial harmony than earlier) we find constant reminders of the contractual and purposive context of the nation's origins. The ambivalence is especially obvious in the first decades of the republic's existence, when different implicit and explicit models of national community were in competition. After the Civil War, with prospects of geographical division ruled out, the question increasingly arose as a matter of shared cultural values and/or ethnicity: what bonds will sustain this violently confirmed Union? The correlative question, reflected in Jim Crow laws, anti-Asian laws, and anti-immigrant movements was: who is to be excluded? Although there is no doubt that Americans even in the colonial era began to see themselves as having a distinctly independent character compared with their English contemporaries, the colonists whose descendants created a nation were steeped in differing regional and sometimes religious loyalties. Egalitarianism erased old class distinctions, while regions changed character with citizens' mobility. The nineteenth century began to see numerous efforts in the arts and in political rhetoric to establish a traditional sense of nationhood as an inheritance, arising from possession of the land and common domestic values. In this chapter we look mainly at few poets who stand for a great many voices exploring this national project. We should begin by recognizing that the dialogue about inheritance and explicit affirmation of bonds is still ongoing, is arguably in itself an American cultural characteristic. For this reason, the early American political philosophy of limitation on society's claims is important not only for political thought but because the same cast of thought has often been extended to social imagination generally: notions of limited government and of strong individualism have been in centuries-long tension with fraternity.

In the French Revolution the ideal of equality ignited a vision of fraternity among members of unequal classes, but in the American tradition equality did not carry that message as clearly. Class divisions were less rigid from the first, except for that of slaves. English concepts of individual liberty and eager defense of property rights, combined with the dissemination of settlers across wide territories, encouraged sentiments of independence and affirmed that citizens (white males) might well see themselves unsubordinated to others' privileges. Whether they could be asked to support other regions or even their neighbors (having cast off English rule) was open to question.

Before exploring the early American hesitance concerning fraternity it is worth emphasizing that the discomfort has not disappeared. In their classic study *Habits of the Heart: Individualism and Commitment in American Life* (1985)[1], Robert Bellah and colleagues described Americans who lent time or money generously to good causes but resisted generalizing from their own motives to obligations that society should accept. There was no commonly agreed on theory of mutual obligation nor of social benefits that the whole society rather than charitable institutions should provide. One of Bellah's concerns following the study was that the unexamined individualism even of generous

Americans undermines society's capacity to act collectively for meeting basic needs. The individualism of Bellah's respondents reflected a mindset typical of mainstream American thought from the founding of the nation: individualism limits the abstract claims of brotherhood even when it may fulfill the impulse of brotherhood in volunteered concrete action.

In the early decades of the American republic caution about fraternal appeals in the political sphere reflected regional suspicions, resistance to anything smacking of taxation, and the elephantine presence of slavery. Moreover, at the theoretical level, the founders' ideas of government reflected the heritage of seventeenth century English machiavellian republican thinkers like Sidney and Harrington, carried on by Locke among others. These writers envisioned political communities in balanced tension, designing rules and branches that could resolve conflict without destroying the structure. Competitive branches provided means to resolve the fully expected competition of classes and regions well as checking excessive power in any branch. The founders' theories arguably tended to legitimize the social contests that they moderated: the American founders, fulminated against parties and factions not for expressing different interests but for their inherent tendency to go too far, undercutting balances that government was structured to achieve.

An example from the Washington's career serves to illustrate the uneasiness of fraternal themes and the care with which they had to be addressed. Following his surrender of military command, Washington issued a circular letter, "Advice to the United States"[2] in 1783. He stated that he intended to address "four things...essential to the well being...of the United States as an independent power." The fourth is what we would call a fraternal spirit:

Fourthly. The prevalence of that pacific and friendly disposition, among the people of the United States, which will induce them to forget their local prejudices and policies to make those mutual concessions which are requisite to the general prosperity, and, in some instances, to sacrifice their individual advantages to the interest of the community....

One expects a peroration about the new national spirit to elaborate this item of "Advice," but he cuts the topic off: "On the three first Articles I will make a few observations, leaving the last to the good sense and serious consideration of those immediately concerned."

Washington's resignation of the topic to "those immediately concerned" is startlingly instructive of the care with which such appeals were to be handled. Washington did not truly abandon the fraternal subject in the pages that followed this passage: the most fervent part of his appeal for justice, one of his four "Articles," is an argument for keeping faith with the soldiers who had served him and the fledgling nation's army. Elsewhere in the "Advice" he warns against the danger to all if any state should fail to obey the new national authority as it exercises its given powers. Thus, the emotional debt to the soldiers and the relations of mutual interest that support fraternity are espoused, but national sentiment beyond those considerations is left to others to manage tactfully.

There was surely a deep shrewdness in Washington's relegation of the issue to "those immediately concerned." The "pacific and friendly disposition" which could unite the citizens of the new nation would be realized, hopefully become ingrained, in the spirit that grows from many specific co-operations and compromises, from gratitude for those who have served the common good—the heroes of the community, like Washington—and from taking a long perspective of mutual security. It is at this pragmatic level of mutual adjustments of need and power that fraternity will begin to be realized as a habitual commitment limiting the expected adjustments and competitions. Praying for "friendly disposition," Washington asks little more than that his fellow citizens choose longer-term rather than immediate interests, with willingness to sacrifice for the larger community. Moments when such sacrifices must be made will arise issue by issue, in a constant balance of prudent generosity toward the whole with service to local needs. Washington does not say the heritage will deepen, but that is what he asks "those immediately concerned" to accomplish, building on the generosity of past and future sacrifices and long-term common interest. If we take Washington's "Letter" as a guide, the "peaceable spirit" will become civic habit as it builds on reverence for sacrifices and long views of mutual benefit.

Fraternization for mutual help in new settlements and in voluntary associations was easy to establish because necessary, but as the post-revolutionary nation developed, the proper claims of national, state and even local loyalties were contested. When Daniel Webster argued in 1830 against legislation nearly tantamount to secession, he argued (echoing Washington) that exterior powers would pick off the individual states if they were not united. "Liberty and union...inseparable" was his ringing watchword, which was not an appeal to inherited loyalties, for loyalties were in question, but for unity based on the long term need for mutual protection, with liberty the blazing gift to be guarded.

Before the Civil War, American thought about the nation's bonds and socio/economic structures rarely involved sophisticated thought about national culture or the economic structure of society. American images of fraternity had not arisen from the breakage of formal class barriers but from political ideas, from extensive local experience with self-government, from the continual need to support (and profit from) expanding settlements, and of course from the heroic military success of the revolution. Over the next decades, imagination of national bonds was to be complicated by constant internal migration into the lands opened by the Louisiana Purchase and by addition of former Mexican territories, all complicated by division over the spread of slavery. By the end of the Civil War, when the continental scope had been defined and the Southern alliance crushed, new foreign immigration and swelling cities assured that the sort of uniformities that underlay national identities in much of Europe would not apply easily in the U.S.

If we step back a long way from the process of settlement as it shows up in American history, we see a version of an almost timeless, often ruthless process: streams of humans flowing mostly in the same direction, seeking greater prosperity or mere survival—in any case, greater control over their fates, finding places to make their own and cultivate, whether by grant or purchase, conquering, or simply grabbing and holding on, united with fellow migrants by shared perils and a shared doggedness. One of the minor wonders of the Civil War, to this writer at least, was that so many combatants from the Old Southwest and upper Midwest had to be, at most, from the second generation in their locales, without a long heritage to be loyal to. They were defending their claims to a work in progress. Time and again, in pre-Civil War rhetoric in support of expansion, orators suggested that expansion itself—finally, to the Pacific—was a great unifying project[3]. But it must be added that this is a political or ceremonial announcement, the nation congratulating itself for its aggressive policies, but not often a motive among the men and women in the wagon trains or starting their acres after a land rush.

The first energy of migration and claiming one's space did not vanish entirely, but it had swept up many of the footloose, the disengaged, and the local failures of more easterly locales, who might move on to yet another territory or stay where they stopped but as marginal figures in their new world. Twain's Pudd'nhead Wilson, landing in a new riverside town and deciding rather vaguely that it would suit him, is a fair representative of one part of the moving population, heavily male and unattached, that settled or kept drifting by rather random choices. If the collective energy of the frontier areas was that of first possession—or seizure—some of the next generation held its property just as fiercely as the first arrivals and often filled with pride at their plans for further prosperity. But on the other hand, a frequent picture of frontier towns when the first wave had passed is not a scene of bustle and labor driven by the necessities of first arrival but dusty streets where loafers and dogs doze in the shade until the steamboat or the stagecoach comes through to wake them for a few hours.

Uniformity of legal process

Although we have described an inexorable, sometimes ruthless process of "taking hold" by settlers from the first colonial settlements and spreading westward, after national independence territories became states by a process that gave equivalent federal status to all states. Federal action appointed a territorial governor, approved first steps toward a legislature and independent courts, authorized a federal court and marshals, assured land records and rail or canal concessions, and especially after the Civil War controlled gradual opening of parcels for irrigation and settlement. Internal migrants to new territories generally drifted westward along their originating latitudes—southerners wending toward southern lands and northerners to northern regions—so that leading up to the Civil War opinions in the Old Southwest (which were slaveholding states) conformed to southern views of states' rights while the northern spread was unionist and like the northern seaboard increasingly held slavery in distaste. But the sense of their own territory's work-in-progress and its promise of equal legal status with older states was surely central to the developing styles of national fraternity: despite nostalgias and some family connections, the Eastern seaboard was not homeland or heartland of the expanded nation.

To point out the importance of the uniform territorial and political structuring is not to understate the strenuousness of western settling nor to exaggerate the law-abidingness of the expansion, for opportunism was the rule: settlers flowed into Mexican lands and eventually revolted; they regularly ignored Indian rights under treaty but insisted on army protection, when the invaded tribes threatened. But the Americans knew the territorial process ahead and the political structures involved were those in which they were proficient. The uniformity of territorial expansion made federal and local governance in replicated forms the usual political issue for settlers. This uniformity of legal processes arguably allowed writers and artists greater space for emphasis on domestic values as a unifying American ethic.

We say of some games and of team projects that participants "take ownership" or "buy in," as when betting at Poker. "Buying in" in this use is a metaphor for investment of emotion and energy in a sustained cooperative project, a fundamental human capacity that we see with special clarity when new organizations are being created. On the frontiers, what settlers "bought into" would be their own hopes and the bonds developed locally to achieve them, colored with principles they carried from a home region or foreign nation but supplanting the old loyalties. Heroic portraits of pioneers, reflecting admiration for those who carried out exploration and settlement, have been a source of pride and a topic of art and literature for Americans, but they do not tell much about the loyalties that grew out of their energetic seizing and first developments. However, pride in being "American," implying independence and pursuit of prosperity, plus an assumed right to self-govern in the familiar ways, were surely all part of the mindset.

In the works of art that we discuss below, notions of heritage that apply mainly to the Eastern seaboard populace are combined with that of providential *reception* of the land, with hints that the settlers' possession was predestined. This claim of destiny before occupation and continued dependence on Providence afterward is posed as a reminder of the need for civic virtue, as if sustaining the claim to the land.

The notion of "buying in" as a primitive source of American fraternity is useful because in life choices, if not in card games, the "buy-in" turns into a longer, deeper story than that of the possibly impulsive first choices, perhaps a story of long-sustained effort that defines a whole life. Because the Americans opted out of many traditions and changed regions so often, the notion that citizens "bought in" to their collective lives, affirming new social contracts conditionally, is truer of the American imagination of community than is typical of many other nations. That conditionality about "buying in" implied that "cashing out" was possible as the next region or prospect gleamed. The Americans moved on due to failures in one place, or for greater opportunities, or out of sheer Yankee restlessness: they might see the nation as heritage but mainly as a space to advance themselves.

The optimistic sense that options are always open to the industrious was challenged in late nineteenth century realistic fiction about families that succeeded in settling but were permanently caught in hardscrabble poverty; journalism documented the same desolation in cities. In both settings, individuals and families did not have the presumed freedom to affirm or adjust their commitments to the land, the community, or each other. Still, the imagery of frontier independence and of freedom to uproot remained powerful. Part of the impact of Steinbeck's *The Grapes of Wrath* and of the great pictorial and journalistic documentations of the Dust

Bowl and the Depression was that the degree of misery and the public resentment of internal migrants and job seekers others caught in misery did not fit the optimistic ideology.

It is of course relevant to the fraternity motif in the U.S. that until the mid-nineteenth century many regions of settlement were not clearly defined territories nor even U.S. possessions. Settlers moved to territories disputed with Britain, to Mexican territories including Texas and California, and into lands guaranteed by treaty to Native Americans, whose rights were ignored. In all these cases, the Americans might hold to a sense of identity as holders r of typical American views but could not connect that identity to territory or local traditions. That made the question even more relevant: what collective values would mark the inhabitants? Some of the poets mentioned here took on the question, expanding the history of personal and collective investment in migration and settlement into a more sublime heritage based on the heroism of political founders and wilderness pioneers, the grandeur of the land, and noble ghosts including Pilgrims and somewhat mythical Native Americans. The models of morality and of community entailed—the morality that made the Americans worthy of their land—were those of economically modest domestic lives, the political values echoing home and village. Thus, Emerson's 1844 essay "Politics":

> When the church is social worth,
> When the state-house is the hearth,
> Then the perfect state is come.... [4]

While not contradictory, the values that Emerson sees pervading the political realm—religion producing moral "worth" in society, and the state-house nurturing like family—are sharply different concerns from the creation of checks and balances that marked the founders' arguments, and of course quite far from the raucous actual politics of Emerson's day.

The context of expansion and independence highlighted personality types who may not have been typical of the population but were central to the projects that became new states or raised great new fortunes. The explorer Fremont, whose fame in his era supports the idea that westward expansion was a unifying national project, described one of the settlers whom he met in California in 1845, when the American settlers enlisted his aid as they declared independence from Mexico so that California could be annexed to the United States:

> This gentleman...possessed intelligence and character, with the moral and intellectual stamina, as well as the enterprise, which give solidity and respectability to the foundation of colonies. [5]

The gentleman described cannot be typical of any group: not a pure individualist like the Mountain Man or that later stereotype of individualism, the cowboy, for he has the moral and intellectual stamina to create a society of respectability. Fremont's is a knowing assessment: the settler he describes as a "colonist" has been an apparently thriving subject of Mexico but in spirit is a colonist for American control, which he supports with "enterprise" when the chance arrives.

At the same time as the enlarged expanses of land were beginning to be claimed as heritage, the American egalitarian political ideology was understood as necessarily linked, so powerfully so that the Americans were distinctive and yet prophetic for the world. Kindred conceptions, nowadays called American exceptionalism, have periodically flowered in political rhetoric up to the present: the nation described as a "melting pot" for immigrants of various nations[6] was called upon to "make the world safe for democracy" by Wilson and gleamed as a "City on a Hill" for Reagan, echoing the Puritan Winthrop. Whether the world has subscribed is a question with variable answers, but there have been times, including that of Revolutionary France and Perestroika-era Eastern Europe, when the American experiment was deeply admired. For our purpose, the Americans' celebration of their distinctiveness was an appeal for national fraternity and at the same time a reminder that the principles involved were not tribal but universal.

We must add, finally, that the ethic of equality itself alternately supports and undermines the immediate sense of fraternity. Imperfect political equality implies flawed community; reform will always be divisive while the battle is joined, even though the outcome might strengthen community when the issue is resolved. Expectation of conflicting interests is built into the American system as noted, and the egalitarian spirit has time and again created a ferment of reform and resistance. Arguments on each side have appealed to familiar community principles; that ferment of reforming or reaffirming values is at the heart of fraternity in our sort of polity.

Modest Heroics

The post-revolutionary period almost immediately saw efforts to define shared cultural ideals, with calls throughout the nineteenth century for distinctive national arts, literature, and philosophies, an impulse that the Americans often echoed even as they generally imitated European and especially English examples. The poets whom I will discuss in this chapter were household names in their era but are now largely unread; I hope that the reader will pardon my summarizing once-famous works, for the stories are skillfully told and deserve pleasurable attention. Most of the poets are among the so-called "Fireside poets" (Bryant, Lowell, Holmes,

Longfellow, and Whittier). These have been dismissed as pallid Victorians imitative of English contemporaries, but that view misses an important aspect of their work. While offering romantic or patriotic tales, they developed a mainstream popular narrative of liberty with equality as the defining thread of national values, and the modestly prosperous, literate household as the national archetype. They modeled values around which they urged the culture to cohere, which in general were already the genteel aspirational values of their audience. They took extreme views for their day on certain causes, especially slavery, but unlike many modern writers they espoused reform from within the political and cultural establishment, rather than as outsiders. Like the English Victorians, they offered ideals of private virtue—Longfellow saw his heroine Evangeline as the type of "woman's fidelity"—but they also modeled democratic communities. Their difference in this respect from English contemporaries is often merely an added nuance, but they did not hesitate to emphasize this nuance. Thus, in "The Courtship of Miles Standish," a comic romance about miscommunication, Longfellow insists that the lovers' courage and sincerity are prophetic of the nation's future: they represent a founding community "winnowed" by exile and the horrible first winter on Massachusetts Bay:

> God had sifted three kingdoms to find the wheat for this planting,
> Then had sifted the wheat, as being the seed of a nation!
> So say the chronicles old, and such is the faith of the people![7]

The Fireside poets are relevant to our theme because questions of fraternity eventually turn to the question of how cultures embody and continually interpret human ties. Post-revolution, American folkways and social manners continued to derive from England but had to be adjusted for the new conditions, especially the absence of formal ranks (the handshake replaced the bow and curtsey, and the terms "ladies and gentlemen" came to include everyone). Further, the population was so mobile (with frequent separation of elders from the young) that successive generations as well as new foreign immigrants might not be instructed in conventions. As a result, literature as well as formal schooling strove to inculcate distinctively "American" traits and manners beyond political principles. Respectable readers wanted to read stories drawn from their earlier history and/or the exciting frontier, as from the fashionable realms of romance, but also wanted to know how peers were living and what genteel fashions of life they might emulate. As optimistically foreseen by the writers whom we will discuss, the Americans would be democratic in world as well as national principles, commercially vigorous, literate, and courteous but not artificial. Tocqueville, who insisted in the 1830's that there was only one class in America, and that at most there could ever be only two, the rich and the poor, also remarked that at the frontier "society has no existence". He did not mean that there were no settlements but there was yet no collective process respecting higher cultural interests or dialogue reflecting refinement of the community. Defining "society" in that sense was part of what Longfellow and others aimed to accomplish, and what their audiences wanted.

Defining the American community involved a search for key events, heroes, cultural heritages, and significant geography but with reservations as suggested above. When Romantic or Victorian-era European writers offer visions of brotherhood fired by the dawning era of revolution, the humans whom they see with fresh eyes are the common people, but those are often as it were in costume. If the celebration is that of a people, it discovers the historical and cultural roots rising from long use of the native landscape; for Romantics the land was also the sublime presence of Nature, its divine impulse heightening national loyalty:

> Breathes there the man with soul so dead
> He never to himself hath said
> "This is my own, my native land!"
> Walter Scott[8]

Out of their long relation to the land grew the inhabitants' songs, traditions, and perhaps prototypical images of national character, the sturdy English yeoman or the independent shepherd of Transylvania or the tough Danube fisherman of Hungary. If the rural folk of the nation are peasants, they are seen amidst long-valued folkways preserved despite oppression. If they are small landholders their villages may be rich in traditions of self-governance. If urban dwellers are the newly discovered brothers, even the poorest and most abused, including the new class of industrial workers, suffer in venerable cities that carry the people's history in artworks, state buildings, and cathedrals that stand as emblems of the nation's heroism and wisdom even as they may stand for reformers as mementoes of past or present oppression. In any of these cases, the sense of fraternity within the nation and to a degree the distinctiveness of the people is heavily dependent on typical figures, longstanding land use, common language and religious observances along with costumes, music, and family histories—the whole range that signifies a people's endurance. This is "belonging to the land" in the deeper sense implied in Robert Frost's line, "The land was ours before we were the land's." In Europe, it seemed natural to speak of motherland or fatherland, as the *Marseillaise* calls upon *les enfants de la patrie*. But images of childhood under the parenthood of the nation is not one that the Americans adopted.

In the era of revolutions, fraternal enthusiasm expressed in literature was especially sympathetic to peoples rising in revolutions that also re-asserted cultural or ethnic identity, e.g. Greek or Italian liberty within unification. In the American instance, however, national bonds could not be strengthened by physical or cultural heritages without stories, poems, and oratory emphasizing national character as it entered the lands, not as it grew out of them. When Longfellow's god-hero Hiawatha journeys to the Pacific coast or Evangeline seeks her lover up the Mississippi, there is an appropriation of the physical territory to the story, mystical in the former story, but prophetic rather than historical.

One of the most charming and amusing of the early poetic efforts to assimilate the land to the culture, and those to political ideals, was Joel Barlow's mock-epic, "Hasty Pudding" (1796). The importance of his poem starts with the moment and place where it was written. Barlow was in France in the early years of the French Revolution, carrying out diplomatic missions and supporting both that revolution and democratic agitation in England. "Hasty-Pudding" starts with praise of how "gallic flags... unfurled/Bear death to kings and freedom to the world." (ll. 3-4)[9]. Barlow says that he wrote his poem after being overcome by a wave of sentimental nostalgia when he was presented with a version of Connecticut's homely staple, corn meal mush, known as "hasty pudding." In its historic context, "Hasty Pudding" is a celebration of the fullness of democratic life—literal fullness, for everyone is fed, whereas the French Revolution had been preceded by bread riots. The poem becomes a paean to the American hemisphere as well as to the cooperative, egalitarian democracy of the new United States. Maize, he tells us, was a gift of the divine Sun to the Western hemisphere's natives, who taught the European settlers to grow and use it. Every part of the new American nation thenceforth used corn meal as a staple, variously cooked as mush, johnny cake, hoe cake, grits, and so on. (The greatest contribution of the American South to gastronomy, the cornmeal-based hush puppy, was apparently not known to Barlow.) Moreover, the humblest people of the world now grow it, e.g. as the Italian's polenta, spreading like democratic ideas.

As "Hasty Pudding" progresses, good humor as well as the humor of mock-epic infuse the scenes: we see the whole community participating in aspects of the harvest, shucking and grinding and celebrating with music, dances, and flirting among the young. The poet likes to eat his mush with milk, but considers solemnly whether cream, butter or molasses are desirable adornments. Instead of the epic hero's selection of a sword, we are advised what spoon to use (shallow is best because mush is so gooey). By the end, readers see the American alternative to hierarchical society: there are neither courtiers nor peasants but a community that is cooperative, productive, peaceful and well fed.

From the first years of the republic, the historical vision of writers and orators involved three elements in combination: providential guidance, spacious lands in which to expand, and an energetic spirit of community. These ideas are open-ended: the nation could include whatever land and to a certain extent whatever peoples Providence supplied (other than the Native Americans, who wanted to hold on to their lands). As noted earlier, national fraternity would be based on virtuous occupation, not initially on racial or geographic birthright: for the devout poets, brotherhood was a gift to be prayed for. The patriotic hymn that asks God's grace to "crown thy good/ With brotherhood/ From sea to shining sea"[10] was written in 1893 but echoes the earlier literary project exactly. Indeed, in addition to summing up the three aspects of the vision (the vast land, the people's spirit, and Providential guidance), the original verses of that hymn display the same caution that characterized the Fireside poets as they described what God gave or will give to the nation, for its prospering must always depend on industry and moderation, accompanied by suspicion of excessive wealth and the pretensions of class that wealth confers. Thus, the hymn asks that brotherhood crown "thy good" (not the greedy) and that God sustain freedom but within civil order ("crown...thy liberty with law").

This sense of compact is reflected in arguments the great orators made, and which I quoted earlier: Webster's "Liberty *and* Union," Lincoln's "dedicated to [a] proposition." This typically American insistence on the intentionality of the national bond does not explain the strengths of character or the habits of life of the populace; traits and emotional connections constituting the brotherhood that grows within life under a compact are what the Fireside writers help us to see. Celebration of the continent and its landscape as heritage is the easiest of the standard themes of national inheritance to see in literature and art because the landscapes of North American involved so many extraordinary and novel grandeurs, discovered in successive stages. Throughout the post-revolutionary century art and literature were building, in effect, an American version of the sense of nationhood found in other places, based on reverence for the geography and for the specific locales in which one's ancestors toiled or fought their battles.

> "Listen, my children, and you shall hear
> Of the midnight ride of Paul Revere....
> Through every Middlesex village and town ...[11]

Eventually, but mainly in the twentieth century and up to the present, parks, historic battlefields, and other preserves that citizens could visit and even study became widespread, from Valley Forge to Gettysburg to a plethora of Civil War battle sites and including presidents' houses and many other relics of the national past.

Just at and after the end of the nineteenth century, the visionaries who introduced an ethic of conservation and the first federal parks, Muir, Pinchot, and Theodore Roosevelt, were explicitly devoted to creation of a natural lands heritage for generations to come, making wilderness a permanent and positive ground of national self-imagination. It is arguably at this point in the national history, when the continental adventure was closing and the shape of the lower forty-eight states was clear, that something like the conventional and pious mysticism of the land was taking firmer root, even as anxiety over ethnic, racial, linguistic and religious uniformity began to be more central to political life, including debates about whether immigrants "mongrelized" the nation.

The grandeur and mystery of the continent had been foci of the national literature from early on, as seen in Cooper's frontier novels and in the visual arts, e.g. in the Hudson Valley School of painting. The Civil War destroyed one regional version of inheritance of the land by destroying the plantation model, but it arguably expanded the average citizen's sense of the whole continent. Sherman noted in his *Memoirs* that hundreds of thousands of men who had been moved across the country by train and waterway had acquired a new vision of the nation's vast opportunities:

> ...[A] million strong, vigorous men who had imbibed the somewhat erratic habits of the soldier...on regaining their homes, found their places occupied by others, that their friends and neighbors were different, or that they themselves had changed. They naturally looked for new homes to the great West.... These men flocked to the plains, and were rather stimulated than retarded by the danger of an indian war.[12]

The war re-ignited the old Yankee restlessness and the old habit of leaving behind still-raw communities as soon as there were other new challenges to pursue.

In effect, writers like Longfellow and Whittier often were posing a version of the same challenge, that of balancing old and new national virtues, that the historian F.J. Turner was to identify in his famous 1892 lecture on the closing of the frontier. Turner's question was, how would the nation sustain national characteristics that arose amid frontier challenges, such as self-reliance? The Fireside writers aimed to define the ideals to which that frontier, not as it was explored but as it was settled, aspired. Women and domestic life, as well as patriotic adventurers, were crucial for the literary shapers from the first; this reflected both prevalent aesthetics and the facts on the American ground, for women represented higher cultural aspirations as well as familial stability. It was clear from the first and shows up whenever women became part of the historical story that the frontier was a moving edge that settlers pushed further on as quickly as they could, a temporary and self-dissolving state preceding "society" in a truer sense of the word. The first waves of expansion consisted mostly of men, then of families with meager belongings arriving in wagons, steamboats, locomotive-drawn trains, and (in the last wave) in jalopies. None of them imagined that the bareness of their arrival would be permanent. Including migration into Canadian grain lands and Depression-era California, western migrations went on into the 1930's with many of the same characteristics as frontier settlement a half century earlier. In many respects the escape from the Dust Bowl that occurred in the 1920's and 30's is a useful image of the sometimes desperate aspect of the process. As a young man in the 1920's the essayist Eric Hoffer was a young migrant worker in California when the desperately poor farm families called Okies migrated from their dead farms to California. They were widely despised by locals as dirty, dishonest, and ignorant. In the scale of prejudice prevailing at the time, they rated even below the Negro and the Mexican. Hoffer liked to ask old-timers what the pioneer families in California's central valley had been like. The answers were: hardy, stubborn, independent, making do with little, never giving up.

> Finally I asked: "What group of people in present-day California most resembles the pioneers?" The answer, usually after some hesitation, was invariably the same: "The Okies and the fruit tramps." [13]

After sometimes romantic but often harrowing beginnings, the long story of the frontier is that of the filling-in, a surprisingly uniform process across vast areas despite the various ways in which settlers arrived. The process was often locally shaped by railroads, mining interests or land speculators rather than by distant lawmakers or the opinions of the still-raw communities. In a typical case a small settlement grew around a rail depot or crossroads soon featuring a store, a tavern with lodgings, stables, and so on. Churches rose early, often more ambitious edifices than the wealth of the community would have predicted because churches were central to the social life of the well-established inhabitants; support of a relatively impressive church represented the social prominence of better-off citizens. In many houses and farmhouses modest chromolithographic pictures, lace embroideries, or a few valued books (always including a bible) spoke of desire for more cultural refinement These marks of domestic decency were generally located in the female realms but understood as signs of society's advancement.

As for the locales that became cities, they were unlike Old World cities except in some cultured citizens' aspirations (which are not irrelevant for our theme, of course). Most Old

World cities had been ancient cultural, political and economic hubs, older and more stable political organisms than the nations that eventually contained them. With a few seaboard exceptions, the burgeoning cities of the U.S. were raw mercantile hubs, politically subordinate to the state or territory that they served and only gradually and imitatively developing an enduring urban populace and features of urban culture such as a concentrated business district, opera house, lecture hall, hospital, and library. When Andrew Carnegie, in the late nineteenth century, began to donate library buildings to hundreds of American cities large and small, the gifts often marked a moment of cultural conquest, rough beginnings left behind for advancing democratic education and community gentility.

The first wave of the frontier often included people with whom the later waves of settlers were at odds. Typical first arrivals, if they did not thrive as large landowners or as merchants whose establishments served later arrivals, were often stuck with their families in hardscrabble conditions, bypassed by the prosperous growth of the region as the next waves of settlers came with more capital. The footloose individual who arrived early became one of the loafers who waited for each steamboat to arrive at a sleepy river town or the solitary trapper who showed up from the woods from time to time. Along trade or cattle routes, rough workers came by riverboat, railroad or cattle trail, bringing business and carousing before moving on. They embodied the frontier's continued seething movement and imparted color to the scene but although their toughness might have been admired, they were not the citizenry, and their moving on after they blew their pay was a blessing. The great social divide that slowly emerged, raw frontier vs. new gentility, is a knowingly drawn source of comedy in Mark Twain's reconstructions of the pre-Civil War middle South. Thus, in *Huckleberry Finn*, Judge Thatcher and Widow Douglas stand on one side, the redneck drunkard Pap Finn who beats his son for learning to read on the other. Both are satirized: Thatcher and Douglas are decent and conventionally "sivilized" albeit practical and tough-minded; they supply the morality that convinces Huck he will go to Hell (like the abolitionists) if he saves his friend and protector Jim. The gentility to which the Judge and Widow aspire is amusing because so provincial and because it is mystifying to Huck. When Huck visits the prosperous Grangerfords further down the river he sees the drawings of Emmeline, a young daughter who was prompt to arrive after a neighbor's death with a memorial poem and funerary pictures, favorite genres of the period. She has died recently herself, leaving a sketch of a grieving woman unfinished with the upraised arms at different angles. The result, says Huck, who is innocent of funerary and indeed of all aesthetics, is "spidery." On the other hand, the mixture of frontier savagery in the men and contrasting civility in their women is underlined when her brother and father are killed in an endless blood feud with a neighbor clan.

As the long story of the frontier's filling in went on, the same dynamics of life on rural farms and in small towns could often be observed in the eastern states as well as in western territories. The static life and slow decay of many eastern small towns over the nineteenth and well into the twentieth century left them indistinguishable in sterility, if not in primitive settings, from the more recently settled west. As the lonely and embittered characters in works like E.A. Robinson's poetical Tilbury Town (*The Town Down the River*, 1898) suggest, many towns and farms across the nation were permanently caught in a post-frontier stage from which the brightest young people tried to flee. If there were some residents for whom the small town offered a secure existence among neighbors and family, there were others, especially among the young adults, for whom it offered only somnolent decay. This situation set in as soon as the first energies of settlement were exhausted. Eastern towns were being abandoned for better land westward from the first, while southern towns saw economic stagnation and outmigration for generations after the Civil War. By the end of the nineteenth century rural areas had lost population proportionally (and sometimes absolutely) so that for the first time most Americans lived in urban areas, and further migrations enlarged the disproportion, including the Great Migration of blacks from the South to the industrial North and Midwest beginning in the early twentieth century. Depopulation of rural areas has continued to the present day, but small towns and modestly prosperous family farms have remained American paradigms of ideal community.

The Fireside Poets, depicting rural or small town life (in which most had grown up), and mining the humor of country naivete and dialects, explored moral and democratic values in settings universally familiar to their audience. By late in the 19th century and into the 20th, writers like Hamlin Garland and Willa Cather were increasingly documenting the desolation of post-frontier farm life and the stultifying conventionality of the town's leading citizens, in many respects undermining the old idealization but drawing highly recognizable societies that in their work often retain an acknowledgment of the heroism initially required to settle and survive. The two versions coexisted in art and literature, the innocent boys celebrated by Twain in *Tom Sawyer* and by Booth Tarkington in *Penrod* gambol alongside the bitter ghosts of Masters' *Spoon River Anthology* (1915) and the neurotic descendants of pioneers in Faulkner's Yoknapatawpha County.

Images of happy or, alternatively, bleak small towns remain powerful even though they are not now typical memories for most Americans. I suspect that one reason for the endurance of the idea is that for many residents of well-populated suburbs and urban residential neighborhoods their locale is socially a small town. The children, teens, and in fact most adult citizens of great cities pass through the locales of high culture, high finance or concentrated governmental centers unengaged with those institutions. Especially if they have families, they may live with long-familiar neighbors and (in youth) interact with local school or playground peers so regularly that the traditional small town of media or fiction is a useful convention, a rustic version of their home locales. In fiction and movies, stable suburbs and ethnic urban neighborhoods embody the same virtues as fictional small towns: neighbors know each other, and most are portrayed as mutually helpful. It may be revealing that thousands of high school drama societies recycle Thornton Wilder's *Our Town* from time to time, in which the conditions that the characters face—dreams of youth, death in the family, friendship among neighbors—seem authentically universal. The street of modest houses set so close together that teens can talk from window to window on a summer evening, and from which everyone rushes to get kids to school in the Fall mornings, represents the most secure imaginable spot in the culture. The town is old-fashioned, but its essence is recognizable to residents of a quiet street in densely settled South Philadelphia or the suburban ring around Boston. The difference that a passing century has made is that Wilder's small town is an image of values for personal life but not a political standard.

On a different note, basic political and class equality, which has been real enough among most white males throughout the nineteenth and twentieth centuries in America, brings a certain factuality with it that shapes what participants might say of their fraternal relations: a directness, with open-eyed judgment of others' gifts or flaws, easily seen in stories of small town relations or in rough-and-ready frontier conditions. The first establishment of equality after oppression is exhilarating, for it opens hearts that were guarded from each other and creates a new sense of community. This is the widened social embrace that the cry of *fraternite'* represented in revolutionary France and that many Americans felt in the 1960's at successes of the Civil Rights Movement. However, over time equality once established is matter-of fact and often rather cold-eyed about relations with different neighbors. Equality neither romanticizes nor dismisses others who differ in reputation, education or wealth, but individuals in an egalitarian community have considerable leeway to decide whom they want to work with, play with, live near, or marry children to. Tocqueville noticed early that Americans of different social strata did not use condescending manners when they encountered each other in public: the informal but powerful class divisions created by wealth and reflected in prestigious home neighborhoods or "better" clubs or schools generally did not shape day to day manners on the street, and indeed even later in the nineteenth century genteel manners generally forbade crude expressions of superiority of race or wealth. Even face-to-face expressions of prejudice to blacks, women, foreigners, Jews, Catholics, etc., when these prejudices were conventionally acceptable, were considered low breeding: in the Jim Crow South, courteous manners often prevailed between well-mannered whites and blacks, tacitly assuring that caste included due respect and that the lines were not being challenged.

The private/public tensions involved in class distinctions have often been subjects for satire and admonition, especially as to wealth-based distinctions, for in literature as in life the man on the street knows which prosperous neighbor is a blowhard, which struggling neighbor more worthy. The Fireside poets, themselves members of an urbane and well-recognized cultural elite, understood class issues as a threat: they did not confuse class with civility, and celebrated the Americans' history of plain beginnings in order to counsel against class hostility. They celebrated hard work and universal education, understood that social divisions perennially arise but insisted on the error involved if differences became class superiority. They celebrated the lost innocence of the frontier and rural settings, where these resentments were few, as offering models of values to be sustained. Thus, Longfellow in *Evangeline* echoes a political commonplace when he praises the life of the Acadians as "...free from/Fear, that reigns with the tyrant, and envy, the vice of republics."[14]

In the same vein, Whittier's most famous lines come from his poem "Maud Muller," about a young lawyer who has a brief, brilliant perception of a barefoot farm girl's beauty and good heart but passes her by because he is, and will be, of a more elevated class. A vision of her charm keeps returning to unsettle him throughout life while she moves on to a country life of drudgery. The lawyer's wistful recollections indicate that class assumptions are a kind if self-imprisonment, closing off the fullness of life. Whittier knows, as he sympathizes with the lawyer, that Maud would have had a much less dreary life if he had pursued her:

> For of all sad words of tongue or pen
> The saddest are these, "It might have been."[15]

On the other hand, Oliver Wendell Holmes Sr., writing as the "Autocrat of the Breakfast Table," holding forth among the genteel but by no means elite residents of his boarding house (a symposium on multiple topics over tea rather than wine) confesses that he admires the self-made man who has carved success "with his own pen knife," but for companionship enjoys those who have had more opportunity for self-cultivation. The observation is offered with a hint of discomfort: the issue is not wealth but the personal culture that some wealth can bring to individuals and to social fraternity.

Holmes' issue was real and plain at many levels of society. Some of the millionaires of the last half of the nineteenth century derived from modest roots and often had a meagre formal education; some of these undertook enormously expensive efforts to demonstrate their high culture credentials. Carnegie, the most ambitious in this respect and with talents beyond finance, went out of his way to insist that great wealth alone would not have admitted him to the New York circle of authors and artists who welcomed his conversation [16]. On the other hand, some of the robber barons were crude men who invested in grand houses and art as what Veblen called "conspicuous consumption" to signal their superiority.

The frequency with which we encounter this tension—what deference if any is due to wealth, and what to personal virtues? —is more revealing than any of its particular examples. Snobbery and social exclusion clearly always occurred but prevailing mores conditioned how these might be expressed, and the verdict of literature, at least, is all on the democratic side. Yet there were shifts in opinion, including popular fascination with the tycoons of the day; Tocqueville noticed in 1832 that the rich displayed luxury inside their homes but with less external show, whereas the tycoons of the late nineteenth century, like those of the present, were publicly lavish.

Differences in status, if not in formal rank, were expected to arise in communities—the desire to set oneself apart seems to be as ingrained in human nature as anxiety to belong—but story after story insists that participation in action for common good reinforces equality. This was a lesson of experience as well of theory, a perennial discovery in communal responses to emergencies. It has also been one of the perennial lessons of military service in a relatively democratic army; it occurs wherever persons of differing status who are open to egalitarian views cooperate.

Representing discomfort with social stratification, a considerable number of stories from the early American republic onward have involved the comedies of misperception or miscommunication that arise when individuals first learn to work across class lines, with democratic mutual appreciation as a usual resolution. One common plot is the aristocrat or city slicker who must strive furiously to match the qualities of the rough sailor or cowboy but becomes immensely proud of being admitted to their fraternity, a fantasy that Theodore Roosevelt played out in real life and retold repeatedly. For Roosevelt, Kipling, and other writers of the late nineteenth century, the ability to work with and respect men of any class is the mark of achieved and authentic manhood. For these writers it was a deeply male-oriented ideal with imperialistic overtones, making capacity for practical fraternity a capstone value: the fully matured man identifies the truly authentic and admirable characters around him regardless of status differences. While ability to mix with the world was an ideal for men, genteel separation of ladies from the rough world of the lower classes had to be preserved; yet even here, there are stories and poems suggesting that sisterhood could be universal[17].

The Fireside writers and their northern contemporaries created the Plymouth Rock narrative of American history. The story sometimes starts with Columbus, seen as proto-American for his independent vision, who providentially opened a hemisphere that could break free of the old ideas. The most crucial prophetic moment was the founding of the Plymouth colony, which wrote the first American compact, risking all for religious liberty and willingly struggling for modest prosperity. Reading Plymouth as prophecy, the political narrative tiptoes past the Massachusetts Puritans, whose violation of religious freedom was a monitory aberration, and tracks the Plymouth spirit to the Boston Tea Party, Paul Revere's ride and "the shot/ Heard 'round the world" at Concord. There were alternate narratives: the counterpart southern myth involved settlers whose aristocracy derived from hard work and possession of land, endowing the chivalric Old South with an elegant, gallant and resilient plantation class who combined with fiercely independent rural small farmers, and not-too-unhappy slaves. The Northern themes are all present in Lowell's perfervid 1845 poem "The Present Crisis" in which those who take no stand on the expansion of slavery are compared to bystanders at the crucifixion of Christ; they fail the one great moral challenge of their era, though universal mankind appeals to them:

> For mankind are one in spirit....
> In the gain or loss of one race all the rest have equal claim. (ll.16-20)[18]

Instead, let them summon up the courage of the Pilgrim Fathers: "Was the Mayflower launched by cowards, steered by men behind their time? (1.74)[19] In truth, the Mayflower pilgrims were not in the least interested in whether they were behind their times, for they sought to recover primitive Christianity in their communal life, but the poet assumes his audience understands them as a vanguard of human rights.

In addition to the nationally flavored discoveries of *fraternite'*, international classes of "brothers" emerged from the 18th century onward: slave, peasant, and industrial worker were international categories and often on the move. The last, workers, included many emigrants from farms to crowded industrializing cities; their loss of connection to the land was loss of old expectations about social interaction. Those losses afflicted many foreign immigrants who arrived in the United States in double measure if they had been country folk with different languages or customs. One can read at least some of the works of the Fireside poets as efforts to sift and reaffirm the aspects of rural life that could endure as images of moral value and reverence for their increasingly industrial and complex land. The urban poor are nearly invisible in the pre-Civil War literary images of America; their misery may have seemed transitional. After the Civil War, however, immigrant slums and the worst of rural poverty both began to seem longstanding conditions: Tocqueville's two possible classes, the poor and the rich, had come into existence. The division of classes (middle-to-rich as one class, and extremely poor the other) is reflected in the title of Jacob Riis's groundbreaking 1890 book about life in the slums of New York City: *How the Other Half Lives*. It is instructive of enduring assumptions about the American norm (a middle class encompassing almost everyone) and the tendency not to see poverty as an enduring status, that Patrick Harrington's 1962 study of poverty, *The Other America: Poverty in the United States*[20], which helped to galvanize anti-poverty action in the 1960's, explicitly echoed Riis's title.

The most famous of the Fireside Poets was Longfellow. His works represent in themes and content a rich and tolerant vision of human civility and human brotherhood. After recognition in his own century (the only American memorialized among the British poets in Westminster Abbey), Longfellow is largely forgotten except by specialists; he wrote in many forms but was most remembered for long narratives, for much of his audience could read his work aloud in the family parlor just as they read the serialized chapters of the latest Dickens novel. Longfellow's choice of topics for his most ambitious work is often touched with political and nationalistic nuances. Thus, *Evangeline* is the story of a victim of what we would call ethnic cleansing: she was an Acadian, from a population of French settlers whom the British rounded up and deported from Canada after what Americans call the French and Indian War. Their Canadian region was resettled by loyal Scotsmen; many of Evangeline's compatriots ended up in Louisiana, where descendants call themselves 'Cajuns. In the poem, Evangeline searches for the betrothed from whom she was separated in the evacuation; she searches the colonies and the frontier wilderness, at last finding him on his deathbed in Philadelphia where she is nursing the sick during a famous epidemic. It is a quintessential story of exile and of the New World as refuge, hostile to the tyranny of the Old World. Evangeline's former neighbor, settled in Louisiana, says

> "Welcome to a home, that is better perhaps than the old one!....
> No King George of England shall drive you away from your homesteads,
> Burning your dwellings and barns, and stealing your lands and your cattle. "[21]

Longfellow's most famous work was *The Song of Hiawatha*, with metrics echoing Norse sagas for it was intended as an epic for the continent. Based on Native American sources recorded by early settlers along with a few European folk elements, it conflated a mythical Iroquois hero who battled monsters with the historical Hiawatha who created the Iroquois Confederacy. The whole occurs under the eye of the Gitchee Manitou, the great god who possibly was an invention of missionaries translating their idea of one supreme God into native terms. The work is both a mystical celebration of North America and of the Native Americans as noble forerunners, brave but wise in ways of peace. The Iroquois Confederacy itself was a distinctly American and therefore prophetic precedent used rhetorically in writings of several of the Founding Fathers. Unfortunately, Longfellow accepts the end of the red men because each age gives way to the next, while in fact those peoples were still being ravaged and resisting. The immensely popular poem gave rise to clubs and pageants celebrating fictional Indians while real tribes were being eradicated, so that hokiness floats over the very name of the hero. Given the tragic truth of Native American conquest, the brilliant mythic fantasy, though mixed with accurate materials, appear today to be less the tribute that the poet intended than a falsification of the heritage. (We who read today do so in an era that has good reasons to suspect inauthentic histories of any tribe or race, even when well meant.) For our purpose, one of the ways in which the *Song* is important is that it praises the geography in which the American nation was being founded, an ennobling heritage but not separable from a peaceable notion of heroism, proposed as a mythic foreground to the nation's development. In these respects it is akin to Barlow's and Whitman's portraits of the visionary Columbus. The *Song* praises wisdom, courage, lawmaking, and domestic love with reverence for the land, conferring an archaic blessing on the newest people of the continent and proposing that the Americans should respond to Hiawatha's spirit as the spirit of their land.

In the one longer work that might be resuscitated for current readers, "The Courtship of Miles Standish," the Plimouth Plantation's military leader is tongue-tied and shy in romantic matters, and so asks his lawyer friend John Alden to convey his proposal to lovely Priscilla. When she says, "Speak for yourself, John," because she already loves Alden, she chooses a man of peaceful civil arts over Standish and a military ideal. For Longfellow the story is at the heart of the Pilgrim myth as a prophecy of reigning American values. As the poem ends, the bride Priscilla is riding her white milk cow to her cottage, a pastoral scene explicitly compared to European idyllic paintings. However, pastoral innocence is only a sweet association: the couple has already been portrayed as serious, hard-working, and resilient against the bitter losses of the first winter; they will labor toward modest prosperity amid the religious liberty for which they sailed.

The highest amount paid by a magazine for a single poem up to 1870 (no magazine would pay nearly as much today) was paid by *The Atlantic* for Longfellow's longish poem on a newly-married couple moving into their new house, "The Hanging of the Crane." The crane was a device for swinging a kettle over the fireplace; placing its kettle was a ceremonial last step in taking possession of a new home. In the poem the hanging has been the occasion for a housewarming party, and the guests have just left. In the many pictures and prints that followed this popular poem, the couple is formally dressed in a handsome living room or kitchen. The poem is an epithalamium, a celebration of a marriage; however, it presents not the wedding but the establishment of the household in the ideal middle class urban or suburban mode. The newlyweds will soon start a family; the children to come are imagined, starting with a too-predictably golden-haired "angel." Of interest for our theme, the children when grown to adulthood will not necessarily stay close by the parental home when grown. There will be anxiety when one grown son is traveling far away in "Zanzibar" (presumably as a merchant in the New England tradition), and again when a son is called to war. The possible opponent is not imagined, but Longfellow's audience well remembered the depths of family anxiety at sending sons to the Civil War. As the poem ends, the grown children and grandchildren hold a reunion for the parents' Golden Anniversary. The poem reflects an already familiar pattern in which family ties are central values, but the nuclear couple rather than an extended household is the crucial social unit. Family ties are preserved at a distance, at least in the family's hearts, but children and grandchildren are geographically mobile and must return for the parents' celebration. The picture is striking because it is so familiar today, both in the centrality of home ownership and in the assumption of generational mobility. Clearly, although the nation was still primarily rural, these aspects represented an expected pattern and an accepted ideal, no doubt also reflecting the relatively heavy urban readership of *The Atlantic*.

The most frequently anthologized of the Fireside Poets' works today is, I believe, Whittier's "Snowbound," (1866) an elegaic remembrance of snowstorm on the Massachusetts farm on which he grew up. The poem portrays the community as the farmers dig out themselves and their neighbors; it portrays family members and two boarders, the local schoolteacher and a psychologically disturbed young woman. The narrative is leisurely: one of the advantages of long narratives as Whittier and contemporaries practiced it is that it allows illuminating balances and shadings in social or personal portraiture. Whittier was raised as a traditional Quaker and his recollection ends in devout hope of meeting his lost parents and siblings in heaven, but the hope is so clearly personal that like the memories themselves they are a touching personal profession rather than preaching.

The poem begins with one of the many beautiful evocations of snowfall that the Fireside Poets created. The children of the story, safe in a warm farmhouse, are thrilled by the storm's noise; when the morning clears the father is brisk and full of good cheer: "Boys, a path!" As they clear paths a team is harnessed to head off to help neighbors, whose teams will join to help still others, all in good humor and (for the boys) youthful energy.

> From every barn a team afoot,
> At every house a new recruit.[22]

Later, as the family rests in the quiet of snow cover, the parents and an uncle exchange tales. Eventually the latest newspaper arrives with news of the Creek War and patriotic revolution in Greece. Each member of the household is sketched in turn. The male boarder, who in winters is the local schoolteacher, in the summer is an itinerant peddler, a sign of his energy and quick wits. He is the type, Whittier interjects, who are heading south to teach former slaves to read, and will

> The cruel lie of Caste refute
> ...and substitute
> For slavery's lash the freeman's will,
> A schoolhouse plant on every hill....[23]

Another boarder, a girl whose angry emotionality was frightening, later in life toured sultanates in the Near East to complain about their treatment of women and to preach the Second Coming of Christ. (She was regarded as crazy and not harmed by those on whom she descended.) Whittier, once a radical voice against slavery, understands that in this character there was something excessive and pities her as part of the broad human spectrum visible even in a small household. The poem is touched with his sense of the family life lost but the historic storm echoes with that of civil war, now ended. His sketch offers a version of the small town ideal: the outstanding features—the ready mutual help, the enthusiasm for learning, with awareness of the large world, and the old simple morality—imply that these were prototypes of the citizens who finally stood firm against slavery and marched to save the Union[24].

Chapter 10. Walt Whitman Re-starts Himself

The old comedian Will Rogers had a signature line, "I never met a man I didn't like." It's a charming fib, deeply democratic in that it announces—welcomes!—a possible bond with any person, regardless of type or status. It softens satire (*Just in fun, folks!*); in the end, it probably means something closer to: "I never met a man I wasn't ready to like on principle" or even "I never met a man I couldn't persuade to like *me.*" In any case it flatters the audience, all likeable in the eyes of this likeable guy and eager to feel the same good will that he claims to feel. In that good humor they can laugh even if he skewers their favorite cause or candidate. Something parallel to this occurs for readers of Walt Whitman, especially if they first encounter him through "Song of Myself," the sprawling masterpiece of self-advertisement found in his first edition (1855) of *Leaves of Grass.* The presentation of his persona as a man of the people, a "rough" but also a universal soul (a "kosmos") and his celebration of the common people in their freedom, equality, hard work and health proposes a tacitly flattering bond with readers. The reader who enjoys the poet's spread-eagled and generous-hearted egotism is also a healthy democratic individual with aspirations, happy to learn that he or she is generally right by instinct and on track to a great individual spiritual destiny, helped by identification with Walt. We readers admire and want to share the enthusiasm and a bit of the limelight.

There are several ironies, or perhaps they are paradoxes, in this appeal, which is certainly fraternal—Whitman might say comradely—in a large sense. The first irony is historical: the national vision of America in the *Leaves of Grass* of 1855 is deeply political in the sense that it pictures a poet and a people formed in the gifts of their national political character: energy for progress, egalitarianism, individualism, and freedom from limiting traditions. However, this unqualified optimistic vision appeared at the nadir of American political history. Bitter sectional conflict over slavery (with bloody guerilla warfare underway in Kansas and Missouri), a succession of weak leaders, and rising voices for division of the nation culminated in one of the most savage civil wars in history. Whitman personally demonstrated his compassion as a nurse and scribe for wounded soldiers during that war and wrote moving poems on their suffering; at the war's end he wrote the greatest elegy in the language on the death of Lincoln. The war should have contradicted his prophetic vision of America on its face. The poetry written soon after it ended would show his reconsideration of certain qualities of the people and clarification of the role of the national Poet that he had assumed, re-establishing his grand project of celebrating and thereby shaping the American destiny—which, as he increasingly emphasized, would ultimately also be that of all humanity.

If the eruption of the Civil War was the first paradox to be faced, a second and more general set of paradoxes is present in his work as in any system that preaches universal love, world brotherhood, or limitless love of Nature and humanity together. We who hear the preaching eventually want to know how the preacher would handle obvious pragmatic difficulties (war, police, competition for lovers, competition for money, education of children). The issues are so familiar, having been perennially addressed by great minds over centuries, that we do not ask a poet whose gift is to create hymns to comradeship or songs of shared sorrow to give us theories, whether of evil and conflict on one hand, or of natural or divine interconnections on the other. If he or she can create a conviction of community, that may be gift enough. And one must add that a part of Whitman's great appeal is the unstinted warmth of his welcome to all, his joy in his fellows.

The great religions offer examples of holy and/or mystical characters who proclaim universal love but generally their love doesn't imply *approval* of Everyman/Everywoman and may not imply liking him or her either. Whitman on the other hand is remarkably fresh because he embraces democratic man and woman without concern for what the more conservative would call sinfulness and the cultured would call crudeness. As a "rough," a man of the people and watcher of the popular life, he likes his American comrades well; more than that, he sees them as already more perfect than other peoples in the ways that he considers authentic. His exhortations to greater spiritual and material progress never upbraid the average man and woman but affirm their unprecedented native splendor and sure progress along the path that will eventually lead the rest of mankind to the same state.

Whitman was mystical though not denominationally religious; as with philosophic and religious teachers who preach universal love from the more familiar stance of a religious faith or an ethical system, some of his ideals conflict with each other at first glance: one example examined below is the familiar strain between creating American community and the goal of perfected individualism. For the preacher or philosopher, certain aspects of love usually require distinction, e.g. among sexual, friendly, local, and universal loyalties. For Whitman, who applies concrete reality to unities that are abstract in Emerson's transcendentalism, the philosophy he largely adopted, loves are always intermixed, not fundamentally different. We never see loves in conflict: for Whitman, love of one's fellows embraces the dead and the unborn as well as the living and citizens of every land around the globe. These loves are not distinct from the bodily life and physical immediacy of individuals but flower from universal currents of sexuality and sensuality. They include both fleshly and spiritual interconnection with Nature. Currents of affection—"currents" probably the right word for the poet of "The Body Electric"—are constantly the center of his focus: he reaches out to brothers, friends, companions, comrades, lovers, amigos, *intimes*, and so on. The list of terms for human bonds is long and is used to widen his rhetorical embrace, not draw distinctions. All loves are effusions of one spiritual and fleshly current, at once ideal and organic.

> Yet underneath Socrates clearly I see, and underneath Christ the divine I see,
> The dear love of man for his comrade, the attraction of friend to friend,
> Of the well-married husband and wife, of children and parents,
> Of city for city and land for land.
> "The Base of All Metaphysics" (p. 166)[1]

As this quotation suggests, readers can assume that whatever paradoxicality lies in Jesus' or Socrates' view of brotherly love or justice is repeated in Whitman without anxiety about the logic: these are old questions and for the most part we can admire his exuberant affirmations of democratic man and woman without reopening them. However, ignoring them does lead to some paradoxes that the poet struggles to overleap.

In the pages that follow I do not aim to present a new critical understanding of Whitman but to place him in the context of the arguments about fraternity sketched earlier. He is the greatest voice of brotherhood themes in American literature, perhaps in world poetry under the direct heading of brotherhood, and yet the very blending of loves that we see in his work makes it difficult to place him in context with thinkers outside his immediate sources. I will focus on his effort to re-start his grand project of speaking as the prophetic bard of America's democracy after the Civil War ended. The problem he faced was not that he had ignored ample evidence of human evil and impending political failure before the Civil War era offered, for hymns of hope often shrug off that sort of perennial counter-evidence. The Gilded Age that followed the war would offer further evidence of greed, corruption, and poor leadership that he also ignored. Rather, the challenge was that the people's response to the War was a profound expression both of their potential for violence and of the importance of complex institutions and systems. It implied a more militant dimension in the Poet's role if he would be shaper of the popular spirit.

If Whitman were a preacher of universal love in a more standard genre for that theme, e.g. a theologian or inspirational lecturer, we would expect to find a traditional dialectic that makes the sexual and the fraternal, the pragmatic and the mystical, the collective and the individualistic work together with some hierarchy among them. We do not find distinctions of that sort in Whitman. However, we do find some long poems and sequences that affirm the ideals as complementary and blend them in dramatic visions of national and human connection.

Love as the Medium

We can almost say that love, conceived as a universal continuum of comradeships, friendships, sexual attractions, and so on, is the medium in which the poet works rather than simply his great theme. Many of Whitman's great longer poems are verbal ceremonies that weave images and topics together to establish a widening sense of community. The ceremonial or (to use another analogy) symphonic interweaving of motifs into an ever-more inclusive vision occurs in "Crossing Brooklyn Ferry" in a series of greetings to all souls, first the living passengers and nearby Manhattanites, then the dead and then those not yet living. In

"When Lilacs Last in Dooryard Bloomed" the almost liturgical progress of the poem, which speaks for the grieving community, is an unusually clear example of Whitman's method.

Funeral ceremonies in general attempt to acknowledge loss while affirming a community of shared feeling, and then to return survivors to lives that grief has halted while assuring them that the lost loved ones will not be forgotten, indeed may live on in other than bodily form. Lincoln's funeral train, not mentioned explicitly, is a symbol both of universally shared grief and of the moving on. In addition, and certainly in Western cultures, funeral rituals remind mourners of their own mortality: this is true of Whitman's ceremony, for "knowledge of death" and "thought of death" become his allegorical "companions," and he inserts an aria in praise of death as a state of peace. He further expands the ceremonial community by recalling the immense recent sorrow for all the war dead (Lincoln was a late casualty of the war). Finally, the western star shines as eternal reminder, completing the poet's tribute to "the sweetest, wisest soul of all my days and lands"—one of only two lines that describe Lincoln himself, a previous line having called him "the large sweet soul that has gone." The taciturnity of the poem about Lincoln as a personality is part of the poem's genius, for it assumes the enormity of the nation's loss and is about the breadth and depth of its sorrowing.

Somewhat comparable longer poems that involve a widening sense of human connection include "The Sleepers," "The Song of the Open Road," "The Dream of Columbus" and "Passage to India." The last section of several of these poems, as in "Lilacs," returns from a widened sweep of inclusion to Whitman himself, and sometimes also to an address to the single reader as an intimate. Thus, the "Song of the Open Road" ends:

Camerado, I give you my hand!...

I give you my love more precious than money,...
Will you give me yourself? Will you come travel with me?

The poems that I call ceremonial are enactments of what is preached almost everywhere in Whitman. The best of this sort are focused as to the kinds of love they address, while others, like the sprawling "Song of Myself," introduce or hint at all loves. Whitman's philosophic debt was to Transcendentalism, a system that also blurred distinctions, but the range of sexual and physical awareness that he invokes recalls other models such as the classical notion of *eros*, the yearning divinity that imbues every level of human action.

As his poetic career developed, and as Whitman took up different aspects of love, adding to and re-organizing *Leaves of Grass,* a progression of types of love appeared, an artifact of his reorganizations rather than a progress of new revelations. However, even as he focuses on one theme, as with heterosexual sexuality in "Children of Adam" his terminology refuses distinctions. Thus, in the following "Calamus," his readers are lovers, his secret favorite is a friend and lover, husbands and wives are comrades, and so on. The poet's resistance to the conventional distinctions is clear-cut and unchanging:

Underneath all is the Expression of love for men and women
(I swear I have seen enough of mean and impotent modes of expressing love for men and women,
After this day I take my own modes of expressing love for men and women.)
    ("By Blue Ontario's Shore," p. 441)

Whitman was fully aware of the broad generality of his vision and of his purpose as a poet, a generality that the historian or philosopher (or nowadays the social scientist) would achieve by theoretical terms. He is so down-to-earth in terms used and passing observations, e.g. lists of occupations or references to nations around the world, that a reader can easily miss the generality of the relationships he affirms in lines like "Whatever I shall assume you shall assume..." ("Song of Myself"). A great deal of this abstractness, sometimes remarkable and sometimes bloviating, is found in the post-war sequence "By Blue Ontario's Shore," which I discuss in more detail below: "We are beautiful or sinful in ourselves only" (p. 426), "only health puts you rapport with the universe" (p. 426), or "Fear grace, elegance, civilization...." (p.428).

Prophet/Bard/Commoner

To understand the problem of re-starting the prophetic career, it is necessary to recognize how Whitman's adoption of the prophetic role was distinctive. Walter Whitman was a bumptious newspaper editor, an anti-slavery Free Soiler and a not very successful public lecturer and anti-alcohol novelist before he appeared in his persona of Walt Whitman, bard of the new American common man. In the latter role, a "rough," he scorned institutions, priesthoods, and privilege of any kind, celebrating the democratic self-reliant individual without reserve or suspicion. Two familiar conceptions of the Poet were brilliantly combined in this persona, each with wide implications for his explorations of fraternity. Neither of the two stances was original but in combination they unleashed a remarkable poetic energy. In time, the man increasingly became his persona, which allowed his art to flower but now and then limited his ability to acknowledge (in poetry, at least) the power and limits of institutions in American life, as well as the existence of people whom even Will Rogers should not have liked.

The older of the poetical stances is that of the prophetic bard, by Whitman's time a romantic cliché. The figure of the bard is of course ancient, with Homer as the greatest example. In the late eighteenth century the examples included the fraudulent Celtic bard Ossian, invented by the Scots writer James MacPherson, who helped to popularize the bard as embodying the essential primitive spirit of the Folk. A true bard, like the still-existing Nigerian *griot,* is a tribal story-teller, linking the communal past to the present, transmitting history and sustaining the tribal self-imagination. MacPherson imitated, and pretended to translate, old Celtic tales; his impact on his era came partly from the heroic melodrama of his works but also from the fact that Ossian prophesied a triumphant British future. (Ossian astoundingly predicts the union of the British Isles, with implications for British politics in his day that brought him lucrative patronage[2].) Older prophetic versifiers speaking for the national essence were familiar from the Old Testament, in poetry also marked by repetitive elaboration. In 1855, Whitman took on the bardic role with its prolixity, identifying himself as an embodiment of the people, prophesying an ever more brilliant American future, casting his eyes on his times as the Hebrew prophets did but rather to rhapsodize over the common man than to damn excesses as those forerunners did.

The most important element largely missing from Whitman's bardic role, at least at the outset, was the past. Especially in *Leaves* of 1855, Whitman celebrates a folk whom he urges to remain free of institutions, hierarchies, priesthoods, and any other limiting heritage. History is not permanently absent: Whitman tells us that the Americans culminate the experiments in other eras, but in general great names and eras are evoked rather than used in any detail.

The absence of a limiting past is central to the second conception of the Poet that Whitman realizes, that his *persona* is the quintessential man of the people, one of the commons, self-reliant and exuberantly healthy in his instincts. The stance as common American gives us Whitman's revolutionary directness of style, but it also transforms the bardic persona. The life details and aspirations of ordinary persons are transformed into prophetic elements of national epic. Humble daily work, migrations across the continent, railroad- and shipbuilding, and breeding families—every human thing that the Americans do—are infused with heroic destiny.

The Civil War was at first glance an inescapable contradiction to Whitman's bardic vision. At first, his compassion for wounded soldiers and anxiety for the Union took his art in another direction. The wartime poems gathered in the *Drum Taps* section of *Leaves of Grass*, are marked by simplicity and directness, a wonderful record of a nurturing soul. They are a poetic *tour de force* in the sense that most of them lack internal complexity or devices of "craft": the poet's compassion with suffering and the plain telling make them powerful. At the war's end, however, and despite his great threnody on Lincoln, Whitman struggled to regain his grand project—in a way, his vocation. The triumph of the Union powerfully confirmed his faith in democratic man but showed a capacity for organization and collective sacrifice, but also for legalisms and administrative actions, that he had not imagined as centrally important. He had recognized even during the war the magnificence of the national effort, speaking to the Union of its transformation, but seeing it as a revelation of what powers—we would call them capacity for heroic fraternity, among other qualities—lay undiscovered but intuited by him:

> [E]ven and peaceful you learn'd from joys and prosperity only,
> But now....grappling with direst fate and recoiling not,

[S]how to the world what your children en-masse really are,
(For who except myself has conceiv'd what your children en-masse really are?)
"Long. Too Long America" (p.393)

Whitman's most profound poems of the wartime are meditations on the soldiers, yet he believes that the bard's voice *should* call to war:

More than I have charged myself...to compose a march for these States,
For a battle-call, rousing to arms if need be, years, centuries hence.
"Not the Pilot" (p. 288)

In fact, he never did create a "march," but as the war ended, he turned with an almost desperate energy to his original vision, hoping to transmute the military fury into a poetic one. The war's end threatened a period of national exhaustion that he wished to counteract, leading him to plead that it become even more strenuous in peace. In 1865, he addresses the "spirit" of the war years just ended:

Spirit of hours I knew, all hectic red one day, but pale as death next day,...
Leave me your pulses of rage—bequeath them to me...,
Let them scorch and blister out of my chants when you are gone....
"Spirit Whose Work is Done "(p. 406)

The poetic series "By Blue Ontario's Shore" revisits notions of the poet, the national character and individualism that were announced or implied in 1855 with additional elements and implied clarifications of how the poet creates and embodies the national brotherhood. In Whitman's usual fashion, the sequence does not make arguments but affirms complementary ideas in turn. In this re-vision Whitman must take passing notice—it is not much more than that—of those Americans who have stood or will stand against the grand destiny, including artists and thinkers unlike him who are too dependent on tradition. Alert readers would recall the ineffectuality and corruption of national leaders before the war and during it as well, but Whitman dismisses their significance: "The Union always swarming with blatherers and always sure and Impregnable.... " (p. 431)

Historic eruptions of fraternal feeling often have occurred at the beginning and ends of war: Whitman in several places celebrates the quick response of the northern states to the declaration of war, and although he would like a bucolic life in the countryside and "a sweet-breathed woman of whom I should never tire" ("Give me the Splendid Silent Sun." p. 393) he admits that he loves the city and even the sight of armies marching through it: "Give me Broadway, with the soldiers marching " (p. 394). It is only at the end of "Blue Ontario" that the poet, having redefined his role, cries out in the voice of the crowd, "The war is over! The war is over!"

In "Blue Ontario" patriotic sacrifices for the Union are highlighted early; the real topic is how the national Poet must not only celebrate the Union's triumph but somehow embody its power. Whitman offers a grandiose description of the Poet, for the enormity of the War's glory and its losses demand "bards" more obviously than ever: "By them alone can these States be fused into the compact organism of a nation." (p. 433). Whitman follows with a description of the poetic role that the nation deserves. The poet speaks during peacetime in the spirit of peace and indeed is an active booster of economic development, railroads and agriculture but

> In war he is the best backer of the war, he fetches artillery as good as the engineer's, he can make every word he speaks draw blood. (p. 434)

Above all, the poet will embody and defend the "great Idea," "...perfect and free individuals.... O my brethren, this the mission of poets." (p. 435). The ideal of liberty ("Liberdad") is both a national birth endowment and a means of perfecting individuals. A section recalls the Civil War's battles ("the cannons ope their rosy-flashing muzzles") as violent defenses of that great Idea, but then follows a picture of what the Poet should be like, addressed to a would-be poet:

> Have you learn'd the physiology, phrenology, politics, geography, pride, freedom, friendship of the land? Its substratums and objects?
> Have you considered the organic compact of the first day of the first year of Independence....
> Do you teach what the land and sea, the bodies of men, womanhood, amativeness, heroic angers, teach? (p. 436)

The qualifications of the Poet continue for several pages and finally include his or her transcendence of the treacherous and the nay-sayers, "each temporizer, patcher, outsider, partialist, alarmist, infidel..." (p. 438)

This list of the poet's qualifications might fit the graduation address of an Academy of American Bards. The recommended immersion in physiology, phrenology, and so on mirrors Whitman's enthusiasm for new sciences and for progress in general, while the boosterism is sheer blindness to the recent decades of history. Prominent poets and other literary figures, far from being "first backers," had opposed the Mexican War and national policies (such as the Fugitive Slave Lw) before the Civil War; nor were they out of the mainstream of politics, for major figures like the historians Bancroft and Motley, Lowell the poet and Hawthorne the novelist served as ambassadors late in their careers. Nothing like Whitman's ecstatic dream of the poet's role as national booster emerged nor should it have.

Although Whitman's Poet is an illusion reflecting his desperation to re-start his persona, we can turn the equation upside down: the qualifications of the Poet describe the character of the people and their unity as he sees it. Their community is not to be defined by cultural, racial or even geographic heritage, but by an implicit, in fact mystical, compact embodied in the founding political decisions, "the organic compact of the first day." The vision is utopian, but a vision of collective personality rather than of desirable institutions or re-ordered social relations. Whitman's poet embodies the native, inchoate and still emerging common wisdom of the people.

No single term describes what Whitman was trying to imagine: What Whitman was trying to portray includes high culture (the poet's work) but without derivativeness from tradition; it includes political stability rooted in the great documents and first actions of the Founding Fathers but without legalism; it includes respect for daily work and family life, implying equality and domestic virtues, but without the genteel conventionality that he calls "delicatesse." Whitman's poet, taken as an embodiment of social vision, represents unqualified enthusiasm for science and the progress of technology, without overall doubt about the beneficiaries, for the joint labor required is glorious and the benefits assumed to be widespread.

The populace of sturdy individuals embodied by the Poet is serenely confident for the long term. Classical critiques of democracies pictured the dangerous tyranny of the majority, but the people that that the Poet embodies have collectively a generous-minded, self-governed personality. They share a serene confidence that they will work together and value each other as a trait integral to their individualism. What they share is not "culture" in any ordinary sense but traits that infuse and transcend what a sociologist might observe. The Civil War had elicited depths of determination but also organizational dimensions that Whitman had barely intuited, elements of collective character that became visible only under the stress of dire action.

Any society depends on some systematic accommodation between collective and individualistic values. Instilling the culture's ideal balance is central to its schemes for educating youth and is embodied in mores, manners, and the rhetoric of leaders. Whitman's poet is in some respects an educator, an inspirer and creator of models: the synthesis of collective loyalties with individual self-regard that he represents lies entirely on the side of perfection of the individual, who in America will be guided by innately healthy instincts.

The distinctly American aspect of Whitman's vision of the poet, taken as a vision of the poet's *community*, is the extreme degree to which the shaping of persons relies not at all on received heritages or institutions. The logical question we might ask about sources of social unity are not asked because fellowship follows from the essential compact, while brother- or sisterhood are created in shared pursuit of the perfection of the individual.

Taken as a vision of the sustaining wisdom of a society devoted to individual development, Whitman's vision involves a recognition that for communal spirit to be reconciled with individualism requires a shared conviction about the nature of the compact that governs both ideals:

> To hold men together by paper and seal or by
> compulsion is no account,
> That only holds men together which aggregates all
> in a living principle....
> (p. 433)

Following the description of the Poet's qualifications "By Blue Ontario's Shore" turns only briefly to the Individual as center of value, a turn that is logical but startling in its sweep to this reader as apparently it was ("flashing"!) to the poet:

> O I see flashing that this America is only you and me,
> Its power, weapons testimony...,
> Its crimes lies thefts defections....
> Its Congress...
> Endless gestations of new states....
> The war, (that war so bloody and grim, the war I will
> henceforth forget)... (p.442)

While the poet here takes into himself all the crimes and errors along with the strengths of the nation, "I will henceforth forget" suggests that parts of the sorrow and error will be put behind. Nations do tend to forget despite memorials of victories and losses; Whitman as embodiment of the national personality is as eager to do so as the returning veterans. Yet "henceforth forget" reveals again Whitman's unease at representing the corporate nation, the structure that did and can wage wars.

In the scheme of brotherhood ideas that I introduced earlier in this book to understand eruptions of fraternal emotion amidst revolutions and other "enthusiasms," I suggested that the collective and individual are momentarily exalted together. The individual may feel realized, freed of limitations when swept up in the moment. At the same time, the crowd feels powerful and jubilant, confident of its success and uninterested in patient means or crawling institutions: it floats in its own charisma. In "Blue Ontario" Whitman proposes a vision in which the exultant community of the victorious Union and the mystical spirit of American democracy are combined. The liberated American individual is the secret of the collective democratic future, which the Poet embodies and furthers.

Whitman stands at the head of those who acclaim the wisdom of the commons: his version is mystical and prophetic, delighting in the occupations, the independence, and the lusts of the common people. However, Whitman has little interest in details of civic, commercial, or domestic life. This claim may seem odd in light of his celebrations of the breeding families, the projects that build great canals and railroads, the hard work of the frontier and so on. Yet there is little about how households or civil communities function, a usual part of political thought: it is the mainly the bright stream of passing life that he loves.

To be fair, ordinary domestic and civic interaction are not the great subjects of poetry generally, and certainly not of bards, so that we can hardly be surprised at the meagerness of material about such interactions. However, if we compare Whitman with contemporaries who presented tales of town or frontier daily life, Whitman's lack of interest in that level of experience is notable. He does not take the domestic peace of the small rural community as a central paradigm, but rather the urban bustle, which expands to the invisible city of past and future souls and all the crowded cultures of the globe.

Whitman's disinterest in the civic or middle levels of communal interaction is sometimes revealing. In one late poem, "To a Pupil," he addresses an imaginary youngster who wishes to be a "reformer." One of the odd implications of Whitman's confidence in instinct and the inevitably improving future is that reformers, who are unhappy with their society and confront it to fix broken mechanisms, are an uncomfortable presence; they imply that the American advance is not inevitable nor the people "healthy." The reformers' issues might be labor conditions, slums, expansion of schools or ending political corruption—a list even longer in the Gilded Age than at present—and the struggle over them had little to do with perfection of the Individual, except that grinding poverty and cruel labor conditions destroy that potential, a fact that Whitman was unwilling to address. In the poetry of the wartime nursing and observation, we see Whitman in close sympathy with dire suffering, and not terrified or shaken but only deeply saddened; but after the war, the bardic program hides the imperfections and miseries of the moment. "To a Pupil" proposes that the student develop "Personality": not only to become well-rounded individually but to become charismatic, a magnet for followers for whom institutions would be secondary if important at all. Whitman interrupts himself to affirm that vision of charisma as based in the body:

> Do you not see how it would serve to have such a body and soul that when you enter the crowd an atmosphere of desire and command enters with you, and everyone is impressed with your Personality?
> O the magnet! the flesh over and over! (p. 486)

Given Whitman's powerful sense of the body as the gift held in common by humans—health, sexuality, robustness announce themselves in all of his work starting with the "barbaric yawp" of "Song of Myself"—it is not surprising that he distracts himself in this poem to see the body of the charismatic leader. And so we might leave his disinterest in the civic level and in the miseries increasingly obvious as the constraints of vision as a prophet/bard. However, not all those who care for political fraternity find this blindness acceptable. McWilliams' critique of Whitman's idea of fraternity, in *The Idea of Fraternity in America,* represents a cautionary view. For McWilliams, the essence of fraternity is both human and civic, resulting in progressive efforts to govern equitably while recognizing diverse groups, interests, and imperfect answers: it must sharpens, rather than blurring, wisdom about one's fellows. Whitman is a great disappointment in this respect. McWilliams criticizes his fraternal vision as he realizes that Whitman's welcome to comrades would extend to the backslapping pals who join Sinclair Lewis's George Babbitt at the smoking car on the way back from a sales convention:

> Yet what a shabby dream it was, that vision of Whitman's. Sentiment without reference to person, a profusion of superficial contacts without depth or meaning. Whitman's "fraternity" is typified by the "brotherhood" George Babbitt found among salesmen in railway club cars, united by process and not by choice, passively bound by the hearty but meaningless rhetoric of good fellowship.[3] (p.411)

McWilliams' outburst is telling. Whitman did celebrate the human world without exclusions and fellowship without distinctions, urging readers to avoid "delicatesse," the fastidiousness that I suppose might include distaste for the Babbitts of the world. Whitman does indeed shrug off the balancing among loyalties and interests that active political fraternity requires (and which any political action requires). Love of humankind and commitment to specific actions for the community's sake may claim to serve the same ends, but participants need not be in harmony or even like each other.

By the same token, the fraternity of clubs and other comradeships reflects discrimination about individual merit and the worth of those fellowships. For McWilliams, we assume, selection and proper valuation of friends and finding allies in pursuit of just politics is central to the truest fraternity. On the other hand, it is amusing to imagine Whitman joining the boys in the smoking car. Babbitt and his friends might be hostile to Whitman on account of his effete vocation and because as a "rough" he is a little below their status. On the other hand, he is a great talker and "booster," shy with no one, and able to foretell the brilliant prosperity and civic health just ahead for Babbitt's proud cityt of Zenith, Ohio. The boys might love him, and he they. Clearly, fraternity is a river with many deep currents and many shallows.

Chapter 11. *Non decor*: A Note on Modern American Poetry

The next section of this book will focus on a subject that may seem, and in most ways is, sharply different from the immediacy and passionate universality of poetry seen in the last chapters. That next subject will be the Third Sector, the independent or non-profit sector of modern civil societies, a realm of formal or informal clubs, cause organizations, church charities and so forth: rather startling shift in focus. Yet a glance back at the Victorian-era American poets discussed earlier suggests that the shift would not have seemed quite as unusual in their day as it feels today, for Longfellow and his peers ere often amused or satirical but as often respectful in sketching village lives and local democracy. Whitman, too, celebrates parades and such civic and commercial wonders as international expositions. If the contemporary reader has a sense that we deal with wholly unrelated realms in discussing artistic visions of human connection on one hand and daily civil bonds on the other, it is perhaps because we see through the lens of artistic modernism, which distinguished sharply between the processes of art and those of modern bourgeois cultures. For this reason, in the next few pages I offer some brief notes on fraternity-related themes in a few modern American poets from Pound and Eliot onward.

From the early twentieth century on, aesthetic Modernism and the various artistic stances called post-modern freed poetry and other arts from allegiance to the conventional standards of genteel audiences; however, the stances that poets and other artists have taken towards politics and community heritages have varied greatly. The poets I discuss here generally sustained the modernist contempt for bourgeois, capitalist, militarist, and (with increasing recent emphasis) racist and sexist aspects of American society but have had the freedom to avoid or address world or national political issues from either pole of involvement, avoidance or (often radical) espousal of causes. In the last few decades many poets, like other artists, have been recognizing anew the ways in which their art can foster community in specific places, heal divisions over race or sexual issues, and retain life-enhancing traditions. Race, ethnicity, class, gender, sexual preferences and even urban policies affecting neighborhood life are among the wide range of issues that the arts illuminate on the civic stage, while providing education and pleasure. Furthermore, the retreat from bourgeois and middle-class conventionality that the first modernists stood for has been outweighed by the need for voices standing for free thought, free expression, or political reform wherever there has been suppression—civic values for all classes including the most oppressed. I hope it will seem helpful to the reader, therefore, to sketch a few lines of development in the single genre of poetry in America to recognize the defenses of theoretical withdrawal and actual returns to civic interaction that marked that art.

A definitive moment for our purposes occurs just after the end of World War I, with the publication of Ezra Pound's *Hugh Selwyn Mauberly* (1920) and Eliot's more famous *The Wasteland* (1922). Representative of the embittered postwar rejection of the value of western civilization[1] along with the German, British and American nationalistic versions of that tradition, Pound rejected the ancient maxim that death in defense of one's fatherland is "sweet and fitting":

> Died some pro patria, non dulce non est decor...
> believing old men's lies, then unbelieving,
> came home, home to a lie...[2]

Western culture was "an old bitch gone in the teeth,/...a botched civilization[3]."

Eliot's rejection was less focused on the nationalisms that had wasted millions of young lives than on the spiritual emptiness of the era, which lacked the fertility of soul that ancient myths and rites expressed. Modern society, banal and mercantile, lacked the religious depth of Christian, oriental, and ancient pagan religions; the sterility is pointed up by fragmented allusions to those traditions. Even sexuality in "The Wasteland" is mechanical and routine, while the nationalisms alluded to are confused, involving newly reorganized territories and newly created nations:

> *Bin gar keine Russin, stamm aus Littauen, echt deutsch[4]*
> ("I am no Russian, I'm from Littau [in the newly created nation of Czechoslovakia], a true German.")

The title of "The Wasteland" refers to spiritual bankruptcy but in the context of the time it reminded readers of the devastated stretches of No Man's Land between stymied armies, the primary symbol of the futility of the conflict and of the empty ethical and cultural arguments that each side promoted.

Pound and Eliot were lifelong expatriates from the U.S. who in 1918 were recent entrants to one of the artistic and intellectual capitols of the world, London. Eliot had arrived from Harvard to complete a doctoral dissertation in philosophy at the brilliant Oxbridge of Russell and Whitehead, where literary and academic figures of great brilliance overlapped including the Bloomsbury group (E.M. Foerster, Virginia Woolf, J.M. Keynes, Roger Fry, Litton Strachey and others). Instead of returning to Harvard to defend his completed dissertation, Eliot took a job with a London bank and became an increasingly influential reviewer and critic. Eliot had connected with Pound, who was active in the world of experimental journals and poetry publishing, earning his living by giving lectures that he turned into books on such subjects as Provencal poetry. In 1916, Pound recruited Eliot and friends William Carlos Williams, Marianne Moore, and H.D. (Hilda Doolittle) to submit "free verse" poetry to Amy Lowell's new magazine *Poetry,* signaling the advent of stylistic modernism in that genre in the U.S. Pound became a crucial mentor and sometime editor of Eliot's work, slicing pieces off the draft "Wasteland" so that it became more radically fragmentary, symbolizing a disjointed era.

In the post-war works just mentioned, Pound and Eliot followed the usual model of modernism as created in Paris more than in any other center over the previous half century. Their French influences (with many exceptions for each value listed) were anti-bourgeois, anti-clerical, anti-chauvinist, anti-capitalist, anti-imperialist, pro-proletarian, experimental in techniques, and "bohemian." The term reflects the fact that many artists and political exiles of the late nineteenth century had settled into a quarter of Paris inhabited by numerous immigrants from what is now the Czech Republic. The area was inexpensive and thus attractive to experimental or less commercially successful artists who could not easily sell their works. Over time "bohemian" became the term for a cosmopolitan counterculture. Alongside the artists and the working poor flowed an exotic and usually mutually tolerant mixture of political exiles, voluntary expatriates, university students on meagre budgets, visionaries and crackpots of various inspiration. "Bohemian" life in any of the great capitols implied tolerance of sexual freedom and non-conventionality. In the arts, bohemia became the expected birthplace of successive new artistic movements, *avante gardes* that imagined art as advancing by collective attack on old themes and shopworn techniques. (This was not the implicit notion of older and more official art, for which beauty and taste were immutable, so that artists searched for fresher or more refined expressions of settled aesthetic values. However, one might live in a bohemian style and come to be revered by the Academy.)

The use of new methods or subjects implied critical controversy; bohemia supplied the small first audiences for experimental work, *cognoscenti* who would discount the puzzlement or hostility of conventional critics and of the general public. In the aesthetic that Pound assumed and that Eliot later propounded as the century's leading literary critic, literature was not to be explicitly didactic (though its high purpose was exploration of moral truth) and not conventionally political (though it could be savagely satiric): the modernist aesthetic saw the work of art as essentially autonomous from the usual discourses of community life and from conventional civic or religious loyalties.

It is useful in some respects to imagine the bohemias of the great cities as islands in an archipelago housing a somewhat migratory brotherhood of those who had a creative passion and wished to shrug off the conventions of their society. The great capital of this archipelago for pilgrim Americans through the 1930's was Paris with London close behind, though Berlin, Munich, Vienna and Budapest were important. In the U.S., New York, Chicago, and San Francisco were lesser and later emerging islands, rising volcanically from the featureless sea of the general culture: the Harlem Renaissance in the 1920's, the New York School after World War II, and Beatnik San Francisco in the 50's involved artistic movements that were admired and imitated in other islands, including the major cities of Europe. Writers, artists and aspirants flowed from one island to another, and the denizens of each island were continually attentive to new talents or fashions emerging in sister locales. Eliot, whose connections with British society became increasingly conservative and increasingly identified with Anglican Christianity, moved in more elite academic and social circles than Pound, who remained a classic instance of the bohemian, rarely in funds and scornful of conventional thought and values.

The insulation of aesthetic works from external social or ethical judgment was not an invention of modernism (*ars gratia artis* is an old phrase) but was crucial to its power as a grand declaration of independence. The true artist was he (or more rarely she) who pursued the techniques and subject matter that fit his vision, alongside the most daring practitioners of his or her time, regardless of adverse audience reactions or societal disapproval. Master of his craft's traditions but not enslaved by them, he or she assumed a freedom to experiment that was almost scientific in its aloofness from expectations of profit or even of intelligibility to general audiences.

Taken thus far, asserting the autonomy of the work of art is simply a special case of claiming intellectual freedom: the work must be judged on its merits, if judged at all, without regard to the personal morality of its creator or the conventional social acceptability of the message, and usually on the terms that the artist proposes: for example, with attention to color blocks but not figural accuracy in a painting. The modernist work of art is a new intellectual product, possibly reflecting theoretic innovation in the discipline. A difference between art and science, of course, is that even in many highly experimental works the modernist artist intends to be eloquent in some respect, revealing a truth or pattern that will engage the audience once the aesthetic conventions that he has assumed are understood. It is true that in some visual arts and some experimental writing the meaning or structure consists almost entirely of interplay among the artist's materials, e.g. the interplay of shape and color in abstract painting, but other works aim to present an actual commentary or new perception of reality. Certainly, Pound and Eliot had ambitious social and moral intentions in their works.

Nothing comes without its price, however. An indication of the price of the modernist assumption of radical autonomy, an episode clearly related to our theme of brotherhood, occurred in 1948 when Pound's new volume *The Pisan Cantos* was nominated for the Bollingen Prize. Pound had moved to Rapallo, Italy in 1924 to begin his interminable epic *The Cantos*, publishing installments every few years. Over the next two decades, he became increasingly obsessed with an esoteric economic theory, ever more furiously scornful of American culture and politicians, and virulently anti-Semitic. When allied troops invaded Italy, Pound was still an American citizen but gave radio broadcasts aimed at American troops in which he criticized the American government, Roosevelt, and Jews. This was treason, a hanging offense. Pound surrendered to American forces when Italy fell and was held for a while in Pisa, where he wrote a new set of cantos, touched with self-pity and unrepentant. After literary friends interceded to save his life, the poet was committed to St. Elizabeth's Hospital for the Criminally Insane where he remained until 1956.

Newly established in 1948, the Bollingen Prize for Poetry was to be administered by the Library of Congress and awarded to the best single book of poetry published that year by an American. When the panel of judges assembled, Eliot appeared before them to insist that no other work than *The Pisan Cantos* could possibly merit selection. Eliot was the most famous poet then writing in English and the unmatched colossus of literary criticism. The young poet Karl Shapiro walked out, but the committee caved, selecting Pound's work. Congress angrily cancelled the Library's participation in the competition. This famous incident is impossible to imagine without the influence of that underlying modernist assumption that the work of art is unaccountable to ethics, loyalties, or even questions of fact beyond the terms it sets itself.

The two Americans of 1920 and their contemporary modernists shared and declared artistic independence, high seriousness, and little concern for conventional audience tastes. The freedoms of that stance have remained available to successors even when their techniques, their intended relation to audiences and their relation to the politics of the day have differed. The general history of artistic movements and experiments in new styles in the U.S. has been that older fashions are not replaced: rather, the different aesthetic traditions, newer and older, radical and more conventional, exist together so that artists of high ability choose traditions that fit them, often respecting the best in other current traditions and sometimes shifting among styles, as some musicians do who play both classical symphonies and modern jazz.

In the 1920's and 30's in the U.S., even among poets influenced by modernism as to style, a rich variety of writers celebrated regional or ethnic heritages and along the way continued the nineteenth century appropriation of American landscapes. They often tried to catch the spirit of a city or technological wonders (like Hart Crane's epic song to the Brooklyn Bridge) rather than a rural landscape. In some cases, the poetry paralleled the experiments of visual artists in celebrating industrial life and labor, as with many works by Sandburg. African-American life was celebrated in both traditional and vernacular forms by Cullen and Hughes among others, while a Southern tradition was elaborated by the "Agrarian" movement led by Tate and Ransom. Stephen Benet tackled the epic of the Civil War in *John Brown's Body* while Robert Frost continued to mine New England settings with an irony that was deeply modernistic even as the verse forms he used were traditional. Free-verse pioneer William Carlos Williams celebrated decidedly unheroic Paterson, New Jersey[5].

Especially after World War Two—to generalize breezily about a complex and widening scene—awareness of international literature and international issues along with parallel ethical and political issues in the U.S. undermined any notion that the artist stands aloof. Resistance to fascism before the war had engaged many artists in all genres; after the war, topics with some relevance to fraternity included condemnation of oppression of artists and thinkers in totalitarian societies, opposition to colonialism, and espousal of sexual liberation, all infused with a new post-Holocaust sobriety about human capacity for evil. American and South African racism, the nuclear race, and American materialism and conformism came in for attack. There was a dawning recognition that the old raw but vibrant dream of American destiny, always tinged with bucolic innocence, had ended. Thus, Lewis Simpson's significantly titled *The End of the Open Road* (1963) addresses the statue of Walt Whitman that faces the Pacific from Bear Mountain above Berkeley, California:

> Where are you, Walt?
> The Open Road goes to the used-car lot.
> Where is the nation you promised?[6]

Like other artists, the poets retained the option of modernistic autonomy, but either in the work itself or in personal activism the attitude toward civic and political engagement changed. The Beats, especially Allen Ginsburg's "Howl" (1956) represented a complete rejection of the modernistic distance while embracing both bohemianism and whitmanesque freedom and directness of style. From the early Cold War to the Civil Rights Movement and then on to the anti-Vietnam War movement, feminism, and recently gay rights and the rise of Latino voices, poets along with other artists displayed an increasing awareness of the connection of local, national and international political themes. The movements of the 60's and early 70's increasingly confirmed political advocacy and/or community engagement as an acceptable, potentially well integrated facet of any artist's vocation without undermining modernist and postmodern independence as to subjects treated or techniques adopted.

In the American scene as in some other nations, complementary changes in audiences were occurring, especially due to the widespread expansion of universities. By the 1960's, American universities were teaching modern and contemporary poetry in literature classes and often presented readings by current poets, augmenting the readings that might already have been occurring in nearby coffeehouses. The universities also hired creative writers to teach that art along with literature, and modern free verse poetry was infiltrating pre-college curricula including programs to encourage schoolchildren to write as well as to read poetry in free forms or in simple forms like haiku. (This was a small part of the massive expansion of encouragement of creativity as a goal of learning that has marked the American school systems from top to bottom.) Writers of great formal elegance like Elizabeth Bishop already offered surface clarity in deep meditations; in fact the canon of major contemporary poets expanded to include as many superb women writers as men, offering at least as much attention to political and social issues including women's rights and social condition: Adrienne Rich, Maxine Kumin, May Swenson, Gwendolyn Brooks and Sylvia Plath among the important voices that emerged. Sustaining some of the regional color, James Dickey wrote with amazing energy but accessibility about the South as well as about his combat experiences. The tight and subtly nuanced lyric poetry of the academic New Critics flowered as well but was hard to follow in oral readings; some writers shifted to more accessible forms and the felt need to address a wider range of experience by telling accessible stories. This was exemplified by Robert

Lowell's shift in style from the dense allusions and metaphorical intensity of *Lord Weary's Castle* (1946) to relatively relaxed narratives in *Life Studies* (1959). By the late 60's, Poets who were addressing anti-war issues and/or racial issues, like Ginsburg and Amiri Baraka, began to be recognized as partners in international movements[7], representing by their very existence defense of freedom of expression.

There has long been an implicit but widespread popular perception that the poet's gift in essence is speaking truth as the poet freshly sees it, not in an officially authorized or pre-screened fashion, so that against repression he/she embodies truths that may be known to the multitude but impossible to express as freely as he or she can and dares to do. Sometimes the simple fact that the poet's speech is not authorized has been the important thing, a key to the international power of the arts, especially literature, against oppression even when the work is not explicitly in opposition. This sort of unauthorized and puzzling freedom made western rock music and related forms important signals of disaffection among Eastern European youth before the Eastern bloc broke up. In similar fashion, in Beijing in the late 1970's and early 80's poets like Bao Dai and Yi Ping attracted thousands to unauthorized readings of poetry in city parks: their poems were obscure and indirect in the modern mode, which authorities could not clearly identify as critical of the regime. Their subversiveness lay in use of contemporary style itself, ignoring officially approved styles and messages, although alert listeners connected the imagery to critiques of the regime. Both poets mentioned wound up in exile after Tiananmen Square, about which they would have tried to speak frankly as official silence was imposed.

When oppression has lifted, as in most of the former Iron Curtain countries, poets who drew intense and occasionally very large audiences under communism because they were uncensored voices lost part of their audience, for speaking one's heart was not so dangerous anymore. Over the last couple of decades, enthusiasm for authentic unauthorized speech and resistance to injustice supported the rise of "slams," which in the U.S. started with the ghetto-inspired protest poetry of the Neuyorican poets.

Writers of many persuasions had often used organizations like international P.E.N. to advocate for foreign writers under political oppression, e.g. under fascism or communism. From the 60's onward the emphasis on rights and international rescue of artists and intellectuals has increased and additional new "third sector" organizations have emerged to join the defenders of artists, scholars, and journalists[8].

Jumping ahead to the present, the admittedly small corner of the arts in which poetry occurs has flowered in the U.S. along with more popular arts. This has occurred not only because of wider formal education among potential readers but also because so many modes of poetry writing and performance have been acceptable, fitting different capacities and tastes among aspiring writers. There is essentially no commercial market for poetry, but online and in small magazines, in slams and in school rooms, writing and enjoying poetry are probably more widespread than ever. Many communities use the arts, primarily music and drama but with some inclusion of literature, to attract "cultural tourism," while others use the arts including storytelling and poetic performances to enhance the citizens' sense of local history or to address community stresses, healing division or expressing grief. Writers' conferences and literary festivals abound across the nation, hardly a mass phenomenon but representing a widespread participatory interest. Creative arts for the aging has been an expanding field as well, as senior centers and assisted living facilities engage a growing population that is better educated than ever and generally healthier, eager for engagement in creative leisure. The U.S. government itself has established a rotating position of national Poet Laureate, an enhancement of the longstanding "Consultant in Poetry" position at the Library of Congress. A typical holder of that office does not attempt celebratory occasional poems in the old British mode of Coronation Odes and such, but generally designs a public service project, perhaps free performances around the nation or a communal activity like collecting and publicizing citizens' favorite poems. The laureateship has served to identify and promote the art of poetry as an expression of civic vibrancy without discomfort at hearing the unfamiliar ideas and uncomfortable truths that the poets present.

SECTION III: The Twin Themes of the American "Third Sector"

Chapter 12. *Bowling Alone* in Romania

Robert Putnam's 1997 book *Bowling Alone* argued with extensive statistical evidence that Americans were becoming less involved in their communities in almost every way—membership in volunteer organizations from PTA to NAACP was down, social organizations like bridge clubs and bowling leagues had dwindled, church memberships had decreased, and even informal socializing such as dinners with the neighbors had decreased. The likely causes were many, including TV, dual-career marriages, and increased urbanization, which produces many isolated individuals. Whatever the causes, the decline threatened civic culture, the web of connections (mostly non-political) which form citizens' skills at community action and express their involvement in community life and local self-governance. I happened to be teaching college freshmen from time to time after Putnam's work came out and assigned it to classes to engage students in discussion and writing on civic participation, drawing on their personal experiences as well as readings. I wanted them to think about citizenship after college, but more immediately to think about citizenship within the college community, where opportunities to contribute and explore causes would be less restricted by employment and family duties than after graduation. Although the theoretical and statistical side of the subject was new to most students, a great number had experience volunteering in their communities and/or participating in athletic teams, student government, scouting, and church or charity events. In many of these activities, democratic styles of leading and following were emphasized. In 2011-12, when I had the privilege of serving as a Fulbright Scholar teaching American Studies in Romania, I proposed a course on a topic largely neglected in humanistic cultural studies, "The Third Sector in American Culture." As the course developed, the Romanian students needed a review of standard topics in American history for upcoming examinations, so that I wound up highlighting familiar historical moments as illustrative of how the third sector works rather than focusing on the extent and structural intricacies of the sector. The following pages arise from that experience, offering not an analysis of the third sector as part of American culture but a set of reflections on moments in the American historical experience that are illuminated by viewing them from the third sector: my goal in repeating the process here is to argue that the Third Sector involves two great themes for fraternity: first, creation of citizens "capacity to act," and ever more complex organizational networks to channel that capacity.

The topic I address here reflects once again the notion that we can understand many aspects of political fraternity by examining purpose-driven organizations, whether humdrum organizations for local service or ecstatic movements striving for salvation. The shrunken world and the new recognizability of mankind that nineteenth century poets struggled to express in its glory and terrors is pragmatically reflected today in a vast network of organizations that work in partnership for commerce, world health, environmental actions, human rights, and sometimes peace keeping. It is a patchwork of quasi-independent governmental structures (IGOs) and non-governmental organizations (NGOs), overlapping actors with limited powers but constantly lobbying or allying with the others, raising voluntary funds and mixing them with state funds in a highly fluid, usually expert-driven process. The whole complex of organizations and partnerships is hard for an ordinary citizen to follow because many of the issues addressed are arcane except to specialists in their realm, from regional diseases to banking and currency. Although the basic IGO/NGO world was largely created by the victorious allies after the Second World War, the proliferation of organizations and issues addressed mirrors the crowded bazaar of the American third sector more than any other nation's model, so that it seems reasonable to consider American history with the third sector to explore some issues that will be critical for world fraternity. The "spirit of brotherhood" on a world scale must be expressed in widely held attitudes and principles of human rights supported in law, but often must be concretely implemented through limited purpose organizations acting in neighborly fashion in an ever-shrinking but still vast and complicated world.

For me, the opportunity to present American history from the perspective of the Third Sector to Romanian students was especially interesting because so many thematic conjunctions and contrasts were possible. The Romanians are an ancient people, but a Romanian nation was created only in the 1860's and did not include Transylvania until 1920, doubling the size of the national territory. Transylvania's population at that time was nearly half Hungarian (percentages are disputed) and Hungary has bitterly resented the lost territory. During my teaching stint, which took place in Transylvania, my Romanian friends were fascinated by the recent American election of Barack Obama; the joke I heard several times was that while it was *almost* unbelievable that the Americans would elect a black man, the truly miraculous thing would be for Romanians to elect an ethnic Hungarian as their President.

The major cities of Transylvania were historically dominated by ethnic Germans ("Saxons," descendants of immigrants invited to build walled cities in the 1100s). Many of the descendant "Germans" living in these ancient cities and still speaking German were sent to work camps by the Russians after World War Two; camp survivors and most of the remaining "Saxons" eventually emigrated to West Germany, many ransomed with funds paid to the Ceaucescu government by West Germany. As a result, few Germans remained but the character of the cities has retained their influence as more cosmopolitan and more invested in interethnic tolerance than the rest of the nation. Romania also had had a significant Jewish population (American vaudeville theatre had roots in Romanian Jewish theatre); about half of Romanian Jews survived the Holocaust despite the nation's powerful tradition of anti-Semitism, but almost all survivors and descendants have migrated—many ransomed with funds from Israel. Romanian villages, representing the last true peasant culture in Europe, are either ethnically Romanian or Hungarian with an admixture of Roma (Gypsy) settlements. Romania had been under the highly repressive (and paranoid) communist rule of Ceaucescu until his 1989 assassination, so that the whole range of issues we might lump under the heading of civic fraternity was either shaped by Party control or carried on half under the surface alongside ethnic and regional tensions until the last decades. Religions, mainly the Romanian Orthodox Church, Roman Catholicism, and (in the "Saxon" cities) Lutheranism, were objects of deep loyalty but politically quiescent.

Nowadays, even as old competing ethnic and national loyalties remain alive, Romania is part of the European Union and of NATO, eager to identify with the West and to prosper economically as western and European. A tenth of the young adult generation leaves for employment in other nations each year; the drain among the most educated is especially problematic. My students in American Studies, a few of whom had visited the U.S. and all of whom had followed American movies and TV, were quite sure that America is pretty much what the movies show it to be, offering opportunity and glamor. They were typically proud of family, hometowns and heritage, but not committed to their parents' ways nor to their old locales.

Romania was developing a third sector, yet its political culture two-plus decades after the fall of Ceaucescu was highly corrupt and the young people were uniformly cynical. There was a lively tradition of literature and love of the arts that historic disasters had not suppressed; my university was named for a great poet, Lucian Blaga (d. 1961), who celebrated the peasant as the heart of Romanian identity, but that peasant culture is fading away. The long American experience at creating fraternity and civic culture amid mobility and ethnic change (and sometimes failing to do so) seemed particularly relevant. That is the part of American history that is most easily observed from the third sector because cultural and sentimental bonds are largely addressed outside the realm of government, as the voluntarily organizations that Tocqueville called "associations" push and pull the political realm.

The term "third sector" denotes the many and complex organizations in American and world society that have some public purpose and are neither commercial businesses nor parts of government: they are a "sector" of the political economy by exclusion from the other parts. Defined positively it is a large group of splinter sectors that includes charities like the Red Cross, civic clubs like the League of Women Voters, advocacy organizations like the NAACP, "private" schools and colleges, lodges, amateur sports leagues, national sports associations like Ducks Unlimited, and international "NGO's" like Amnesty International. Churches belong to the sector partly for reasons of legal and tax status, but as devotional communities they may integrate with almost the whole life of some members, unlike most other third sector affiliations which tend to be ancillary to home and work life. Setting devotional aspects aside, the churches are among the most active charities, although large denominations often have spun off non-profits like Catholic Charities or B'nai B'rith to avoid violating church/state separation.

The characteristic that the third sector splinters have in common is that they once utilized or still utilize voluntary contributions of time or money following individual decisions to support or donate. In the U.S., the third sector is largely identified by federal registration and tax exemption, commonly 501c(3) designation, which require that the organization have an unpaid board and an educational, charitable, scientific, or religious mission. The various public benefits served is enormously wide and ranges from disaster relief to providing educational messages—i.e. propaganda— for a favored governmental policy. In recent years, political advocacy organizations that are mere shells for large donors' gifts to a favorite political cause have arisen as an important splinter: political candidates court this support because the funds spent for advocacy of their favored position is in effect support for their election.

In the United States, the level of citizen participation in the third sector has long been seen as an index of civic vitality, and the same view has been extended to democracies throughout the world. Putnam introduces "social capital," as his index of civic vitality. His definition of social capital includes informal interactions such as neighbors inviting neighbors to dinner, but as noted earlier the solution most often proposed to remedy the decline in civic culture is not more neighborhood barbecues but increased volunteer action for the public good, opportunities for which arise mostly in the third sector.

Books and articles about the third sector are often illumined with enthusiasm for the idealism that moves so many of the participants. The enthusiasm of those who describe the sector often comes from the belief that, in Peter Drucker's phrase, its mission is neither control (government's role) nor profits (business' role) but to "change human beings"[1]. The non-profits heal, educate, or involve us with each other, changing either clients or members in ways that each organization believes are for the better. Some of the most recent works on the third sector, including Putnam's work in *Bowling Alone* and later volumes, evince a pervasive concern that the processes of democratic government are failing, but that the information and active commitment that citizens acquire in the third sector offer hope for rejuvenation. This view sees the ferment and diversity of the sector as a civic benefit by itself, accepting the cacophony of voices and even the rise of organizations that some would call destructive as costs of the freedom being exercised.

In the pages that follow, I discuss individuals and events of American history that have been massively studied by scholars. I do not offer new information but take each as the starting point for reflection on two principal and complementary aspects of the third sector: its culture of individual civic engagement and its evolving organizational networks. Each aspect is sometimes quite distinctly visible; a useful example is the large charitable foundation that at the outset reflected one wealthy individual's engagement with a civic need but over time came to operate as part of the organizational network. Considered together, they illuminate the most pragmatic elements of the American experience of fraternity. Individual civic engagement shapes what I call the individual's "capacity to act" in his or her immediate setting. "Capacity to act" is expressed when the actor finds or creates an organizational context, a fraternity to amplify his or her voice and efforts. The other half of the picture, the organizational structures and their networks of partnership, have often pursued pragmatic "brotherhood" goals on a national or world stage and have done so with vision, although their bureaucratic apparatus and their locales of action have often been distant from the scenes of cooperative citizen action that Putnam and others worry about.

Fraternity and Social Capital

Putnam understands "social capital" as the sum of relationships and interactions that individuals have with relatives, co-workers, co-religionists, fellow members in clubs, and so on, seen as a reservoir of connections that can be used for many purposes, from general social comfort to political organization to job seeking. That potential convertibility into action—expenditure, often to build more interdependence in return—is why the metaphor of capital is useful, although as noted briefly in the Introduction, the statistical measure cannot gauge the social instinct nor underlying ideals involved, matters which we periodically urge each other to imagine as well as practice. The relations included in social capital represent workaday loyalties and civic expressions that from time to time flower remarkably and surprisingly into action, eloquence, and sacrifice.

To repeat the distinction introduced in an earlier chapter, "fraternity" is commonly used (in English) for the bond of members in organizations that have defined and somewhat limited purposes and are neither the family nor the church at its devotions. Fraternity in this sense is the standard model for bonds created in third sector organizations although fraternities that wish to assert militancy or to pledge loyalty against opposition often call themselves "brotherhoods" to emphasize that the electricians or carpenters will stick together on strike through thick and thin, or that the college housemates brothers will remain loyal after their parties have ended. "Social capital" encompasses both the fraternities of purposeful cooperation and the whole thick web of neighborly contacts, friendships, colleagueship at work, and so on that characterize a much-connected community.

If "social capital" is in decline, the participation that seems most valuable for repairing it, for Putnam and many others, is that which is personally involving, ideally involving a physical presence with colleagues rather than donation of money or submission of opinions on social media. I have asked classes of American college freshmen about it and they, natives of the digital culture, distinguish limits and drawbacks connected with the media-mediated connections: they know peers who shy from in-person social contact or play out alternate identities, having only on-line friends or fellow gamers. On the other hand, e-mail, cell phones, Facebook, blogs and tweets keep old connections alive for students who have gone away to college, contact with hometown friends and family (in fact administrators talk about "helicopter parents" who monitor or are consulted by students at every turn, hovering.). Social media allow instant dissemination of news or invitations to a party: the same remarkable speed has been observed in the spread of revolutions and organization of protests in various nations across the globe, including the Arab Spring.

In political upheavals as in campus calls to party, quick communication often leads to face-to-face interaction, but where physical presence is missing the accidental benefits of mutual observation using all the senses, patience in communicating, and perhaps friendship are less often present. Moreover, participants can restrict their attention to those with whom they already agree, so that in politics or indeed any matter of dispute one need not encounter debate or arguments for compromise. Real politics in a democracy and real workplaces do involve these adjustments, so that as noted in the earlier discussion of digital "crowds," social capital expressed only through electronic media may contribute only marginally to social capital.

Being a member of a national or international organization that one might support on-line (like ACLU) likely involves much less social capital than membership in a local party. In fact, the increase in numbers of such cause organizations that marked the past decades may mask the declining social capital of our communities. On the other hand, members in such organization are more informed about favorite national or international issues than the average citizen, so that they arguably enhance the intelligence of the citizenry. They are specialized publics within the larger public. The enormous growth of social media surely broadens the meaning of "participation," and the individualization of my interaction through media means that what I choose to be my charity or service, sport or cause, is emphatically *mine*.

Despite the doubts that Putnam and others harbor about long-distance affiliations that do not build social capital very perceptibly, it is mostly the non-volunteer driven international NGO's like Ford or Gates foundations, which have no membership, and small but expert advocacy organizations like Human Rights Watch, all members of the "organizational web," that best express the *international* "spirit of brotherhood" in action. For this reason, one might conclude that the visions of fraternity just described—civic social capital vs. universal humanity—are not closely connected, but in practice it is surprising how often the third sector attempts to bring the poles together, to sustain both the local and the far-extended commitments. One reason is that subsectors, especially the religions, preach universal brotherhood. While giving to the local or parish needy, the church, synagogue or mosque may also gather foodstuffs for victims of a disaster abroad or support a mission church in a poor country. Similarly, the PTA may support foreign student exchanges by housing students in volunteer parents' homes while the local Rotary welcomes foreign members' visits to affirm international fellowship. These activities are symbolic but that is precisely their purpose: they declare a universal value by performing a modest service. Organizations that have little or no citizen participation in the U.S. but work on international health or food issues often emphasize building civic culture in the locales of their projects to assure that the irrigation network or farm cooperative that the NGO has initiated will be sustained. That local buy-in by communities, praised by exemplary locals, is what the large organizations most often highlight in publicity. Thus, the Third Sector is permeated with awareness of local and universal fraternities as interrelated.

Seen as a vast bazaar of competing and cooperating purposes, all enlisting voluntary support of some sort, the third sector has a close kinship to that imaginary space of constant debate and dialogue that Hannah Arendt called the "public space."[2] The underlying image is the Greek *agora*, the central plaza in which citizens talked constantly about politics in the largest sense, i.e. anything to do with the life of their city. Arendt's "public space," imagined concretely, includes formal and cloakroom debate in legislatures, political campaign speeches, town hall meetings, the blogosphere, press and TV debate, and sometimes argument over the kitchen table. The third sector overlaps with the "public space" because it offers an immense number of venues in which citizens argue about community values and in effect about fraternal obligation, for the organizations are always recruiting, fund raising, advocating for recognition of a community need, or delivering help. In great crises and war, when civic loyalties without limits are awakened and sacrificed for, the "public space" may involve quieter voices for a while as the crisis is addressed; the harmony of that moment, that coming together to face the crisis, becomes a bright memory for some participants. But in ordinary times the mix is chaotic. Within that mix the third sector organizations strive to define and re-define our brother-and-sisterhoods to practical effect.

It is important to repeat that, as with any of the great political ideals—liberty, equality, fraternity—the advocate of the ideal accepts the certainty of abuses, though we might disagree on which uses of the rights asserted are the destructive ones. The third sector offers many proofs of civic vitality and examples of human good nature, but it is also the "space" in which we define our divisions most sharply: your view on race, mine on the death penalty, your stance on Israel, mine on animal rights, and so on. We may be said to affirm our interconnections by entering the public space, even if on opposite sides, but the result is that the *agora* or commons is a crowded and noisy, more a marketplace than a forum moving toward consensus. The activity is central to how democracies set priorities, yet (to complete the metaphor) the cry of our greatest needs may be drowned by other cries.

To return for a moment to my adventures teaching this topic in Romania, one of the pleasures of teaching undergraduates in the humanities is dialogue about familiar things that students have not seen as significant. The third sector offers several challenges for class discussion, but a reward is that the students recognize factors already active in their own environment. The third sector is hard to imagine because of its many splinters, but those splinters offer different narratives about the world, often raising issues that students had not heard of. Third sector organizations hew close to their specific issue: racism, hunger, African elephants, folk arts, youth soccer—the list is endless—so that learning about the sector involves recognizing what a variety of passions distinguishes fellow citizens. The social "normal" turns out to be complex, a rather exotic mix of national and world themes.

Assuring that obscurity and familiarity will be intermixed in an introduction to the third sector is the fact that so much its activity occurs at the margin, using fractional surpluses of money or energy. A charitable giver is usually donating from surplus funds while the volunteer is donating a margin of leisure time. In the U.S., a national average for the half of the adult populations that claims to volunteer is about four hours per week. A corporation's charity rises and falls and will be a small percentage of profits in any case, often a marketing gesture. Even non-profits receiving regular governmental contracts or subventions, as museums and city symphonies often do, still need to raise private donations so that their fiscal stability depends on a voluntary fraction. Working at margins is hardly unique to the third sector—business profits are a margin of income—but non-profits may seem even more contingent than commercial enterprises because they can't often liquidate inventory or assets nor, usually, borrow against expected revenues. When small and new businesses fail we expect that a competitor will fill their market niche if it is potentially profitable, but the collapse of a non-profit is not an opportunity for a new entrepreneur. Rather, a social need that may be of some of some urgency goes unmet if the non-profit that served the need collapses.: Many non-profits tend to have purposes that are abstruse to average citizens (like world carbon reduction) or they serve clients who are relatively invisible to typical donors, i.e. convicts or threatened bird species or victims of a far-off epidemic. The marketing challenge for the non-profit is to attract donors so that those issues become the priorities that their surplus time or money will address. And finally, the fact that Third Sector actors work with marginal income and human resources means that partnering relationships with other agencies and governments are often extremely important, a necessary complexity that also puzzles students at first.

Despite the complexity just explained, basic patterns including partnering among allied non-profits, government, and business, are easily recognizable. In Romania, it was easy to present the Third Sector as part of a complicated interweaving of organizations and personal interests because the students knew well that their ambitions might involve making allies and contacts in a still-emerging economy. Their parents and older adults had survived under communism, where the official system worked poorly and personal security often depended on alliances with relatives or friends, favors given and received, and gray or black market activities. When our semester was starting, the central plazas of Sibiu were filled with tents: a "volunteer fair" was traveling from one university town to the next. Its purpose was to recruit students and passersby for environmental organizations, child protection organizations, art guilds and so on, inviting young adults to participate in the still badly underdeveloped volunteer organizations of the country. Late in the day, the fair mounted a free rock concert with dancing that went on late into the night. I asked the students to consider the list of sponsors posted for this event, a considerable number because Sibiu is a vibrant cultural capital. This list included national and provincial government agencies, banks, stores and restaurants, non-profit arts councils and specific non-profit organizers, a typical mix for the U.S., Britain, and other nations where the Third Sector is well developed. The motives of each partner were easily figured, and the networking and management required to mount the event easily imagined.

In the next two chapters, I trace a series of moments and figures in American history representing either "capacity to act" developing in the third sector, or the organizational networks of the third sector as they influenced events, or the themes overlapping. No facts new to the historians are offered, but rather a perspective on how the third sector has influenced the American story.

Chapter 13. American History from the Third Sector I: Forming "Capacity to Act"

1. Franklin and his friends

Benjamin Franklin is an unavoidable figure for our theme. He presents himself in his *Autobiography* as an increasingly shrewd young student of how to persuade people to act together, creating social capital for himself, his friends, his city and colony. His principle discussion of that topic arises as he describes founding the Junto, a club of working-class friends who agreed to improve their general education and enhance their skills in writing and debate while proposing projects of public benefit. The combined emphasis on self-improvement and social good is a secularized version of the Puritan ideal amid which Franklin was raised: for the Puritans, self-discipline and learning led to prosperity followed by public service and acts of charity; the combination of success and service reflected the likelihood of predestined salvation. The fact that Franklin's was a secularized model rather than pursued out of desire for evidence of salvation makes service to humanity for its own sake a deeper motive, and indeed one of the questions that the young members of the Junto answered in the affirmative at each meeting was ""Do you love mankind in general…?"[1] The basic self-portrait offered in the *Autobiography*—the studious, clever, and disciplined young man who becomes prosperous and respected, then turns his talent and wealth to public good—is that which many of the leading philanthropists from Franklin to the present have presented as their own. Franklin differs in that he is extraordinarily useful to his society from the moment he establishes his career, furthering his own success but genuinely industrious and public-spirited.

Given the humble class status of its members, the Junto expressed the social equality and individual freedom to improve one's lot that was emerging in the new American setting. The fact that it was a secret society suggests an avoidance of class issues and unwanted public scrutiny, which might be both jealous and embarrassing as the members acquired their skills. Secrecy also strengthened the bond of friendship among members. Franklin clearly had identified the personal gifts required of leading men, including networking, writing, public speaking, dependability and engagement in public-spirited projects. He and his friends acquired those gifts because eminence was not to be inherited but could be awarded by the community. Many elements of the future "voluntary sector" are visible in the Junto, starting with the fact that the projects proposed were for public benefit, not self-aggrandizing, and that they were voluntarily supported, which made the Junto members relatively immune to obstruction by those who would defend official prerogatives.

Franklin's report allows us to highlight several elements of "capacity to act." One aspect is legal freedom: Franklin and his peers were not prevented from meeting or acting, and most of the proposals they brought forth were no official's prerogative to approve. Many projects once underway were later supported by government; acting privately to alleviate a social problem even while hoping for eventual support or a change in government policy has been a constant facet of Third Sector activity in the U.S. In addition to legal freedom, the Junto's members had what might be called tacit permission: in the *de facto* egalitarianism of the American colonies, no one else in the city was deferred to as the proper leader in "projects" due to his social rank. (Franklin admits with pride, however, that in time, when any new voluntary project was proposed in Philadelphia, potential backers would ask "What does Franklin think?") If the Junto members had been female or free blacks they might have had a degree of liberty under law but would not have had tacit permission, though the Quakers had wider views on women than most in that era. "Capacity to act" must include training in needed skills and the information necessary to proceed realistically, which the Junto members encouraged in each other while sharing as well their knowledge of the city and its key people.

Franklin was the leader: leaders often recall the fraternity of an intense group differently than do their followers, partly because sustaining the group and focusing efforts is their role. They discriminate among personalities whom they manage or restrain, and in a purposeful club like the Junto, as in many voluntary service organizations, they find a balance of social pleasure, shared ideology, and work to be accomplished. Franklin's recollections, not atypically for founders, is mostly about successes: what became of the best Junto proposals and the eminence of some members in later life, with only a few words on personalities. When the Junto's existence became partly known, Franklin cloned the model by having the Junto members lead new secret cells. The cell approach was both generous and liberating to Franklin: his aim was not to take on the burden of leading a growing faction but to pursue public good at the same time as his own and his friends' fortunes, rising within rather than displacing the elite of the city. One suspects that former Junto members would have devoted more reflection to the pleasures of their fellowship, and no doubt to their observations of their eventually famous leader.

The Junto is a revealing model of third sector action, energizing the fraternity of the small group within a set of rules and ceremonies and with a defined purpose, but combining that with the pleasure of socialization. Its secrecy is more typical of groups that involve opposition or unconventional beliefs, adherents of a distrusted religious cult. Secrecy is of course bonding in itself, a defense against outsiders and a privilege for members. In American society, where social fraternities and sisterhoods have often offered same-sex comradeship, rituals and secrets (handshakes and initiation rites) have always suggested that brothers or sisters in the lodge were allies in a society of impressive but partly invisible importance.

Franklin admits tongue in cheek that good humor and a conciliatory tone in debate did not come naturally to him. A Quaker friend had informed him, even as he strove to improve his virtues item by item from a list, that he was considered to have too high an opinion of his own views. Franklin says that he learned the manner, if not the substance, of modesty, learning to concede merits in his opponent's view even though he was cocksure of his own. His lesson of persuading others by managing one's own argumentative instinct is elementary, though difficult for most of us to master; like other practitioners of sentimental persuasion—like Shaftesbury, philosopher of "Wit and Humour"—he uses the assumption of the other's good sense and good will to lay the ground for agreement. The anecdote is an urbane and amusing admission, not only of his pride but of the ambition and intellectual voraciousness that he learned to discipline and give a soft appearance.

Franklin also understands several other basic lessons familiar to the Third Sector. One is that people follow the crowd in good as in mischief. When a friend asks for help in raising funds for a charity, Franklin offers seasoned advice: start with those most likely to give, then turn to those who *may* give with the names of the first donors as seconds to your request; finally, do not fail to approach the unlikeliest prospects, who may surprise by following the others. It is a standard formula for a fundraising campaign.

The practical educational function of the Junto places Franklin's narrative in the mainstream of a longstanding national discourse about the style of education proper for an egalitarian society. For "capacity to act" to become widespread, education that encourages it explicitly will be crucial, because the training required to lead that comes to elites through their informal association with each other or through special class-restricted schooling is not offered to the democratic multitude. "Capacity" might be conditioned at any historic moment by unchangeable factors of gender or race but educating for widespread sharing of leadership enhances whatever opportunity there is. The creation of common schools was an immediate priority for early American settlers, especially in New England; a grand theme of American educationists from early in the Republic onward was to prepare all children for citizenship. Horace Mann was the great nineteenth century exponent of the common school as the key to equality; voices in support of the same ideal became numerous and were echoed in literature by figures like Hawthorne and Whittier. The same theme is central to the profoundly influential "progressive" educational philosophy of John Dewey in the 20th century and remains a pervasive value in American educational practice. It is a declared purpose or an important nuance in student governments, group study projects, numerous club and sports activities in schools, and more recently in movements to inculcate independent inquiry rather than rote learning in the academic disciplines. Many high schools require volunteer community projects for graduation, and in many U.S. colleges "service learning" or off-campus internship experiences include explicit emphasis on group participation and leadership skills.

Ben's virtues

The elements listed above as aspects of "capacity to act" that can be expressed in the voluntary sector develop a quality that is hard to measure, the *desire* to act for the community growing alongside the practical skills required. It is clearly an individual characteristic but also one that is contagious, in fact a group standard. In a Franklin it was a powerful personal drive but over time was influenced by others' expectations of his leadership. The characteristic came to mark his friends, for whom (as for most of us) it involved imitation, friendship, a matured sense of responsibility for the community, satisfaction at respect earned, and self-interest, an inextricably fluid mixture. That compound of motives, which do not need to be examined by participants at the moment, is one of the reasons why a club like the Junto works: it gives structure and courage and a sense of common adventure to actors who have not shown the will to fight a problem or innovate. In the Junto, the first of the principles that members swore to was that they did not "disrespect" any member: one would think that a weak expression of brotherhood but it reminds us that the members, all from the "leather apron" class, in fact would be especially sensitive to issues of respect because their society was certainly not classless: perceptions of status were drawn from European traditions and supported by differences in wealth and education. The American difference was that manners were more egalitarian and the classes that existed, based mainly on wealth, were porous for those who climbed to prosperity.

These considerations taken together lead us to ask an old-fashioned question: in what senses was Ben Franklin a figure of *virtue*? I call it an old-fashioned question because we don't talk about virtue (or "the virtues") very often, yet the question would have been common in Ben's era and a century beyond it. It is necessary to step back a bit from the picture that he presents of himself, for he was a moral teacher in many of his writings and a cunningly winsome self-presenter, so that we identify him too easily with the earnest striver whom we see in the *Autobiography* but also with Poor Richard, that frugal modest shrewd old fountain of maxims. Neither *persona* matches the intellectually voracious reader of philosophy and adventurer in science who dabbled in theories from vegetarianism to metempsychosis, nor the rebellious and immodest soul who condemned religious tyranny in Boston as a young man and unseated English tyranny as an old one. For successive eras Americans have celebrated Franklin for the variety and good effect of his virtues, and as we noted above, he is the poster boy of voluntary leadership in the community. Yet it seems worthwhile to reflect on his virtues, not least because he explains in famous section of the *Autobiography* that he tried to systematize and enhance his personal virtues.

The word *virtue* had enormous power for men and women of Franklin's era. It echoed classical ideals, where personal discipline and rectitude were foundations for the Roman republic, which the neoclassical era idealized. Virtue was assumed to be a necessary and central trait of republican citizens: the classical heroes important to republican rhetoric included Cincinnatus and Cato, Scipio and Brutus. Machiavelli in his *Discourses on Livy* had celebrated *vertu* in the Roman republic, which for him was basically strength of will and loyalty to the republic rather than overall morality: a viable republic requires citizens of *vertu* while the successful usurper whom we see in *The Prince* possesses *vertu*—will and cunning—far above his peers. To republican followers of Machiavelli including those who influenced the Founding Fathers, the need for ethical virtue as well as *vertu* was obvious: the republic requires patriotic loyalty and courage but a generous passion for justice and democratic restraint of ambition must be added[2]. One sees the ideal in the political poems of Marvell: the "Horation Ode to Cromwell" praises his powerful spirit but warns with careful tact that overweening ambition attaches to such heroic spirits. By contrast, Marvell's "On Appleton House" praises Cromwell's counterpart Vere who fought with great success and then retired to his estates. Two centuries later Herman Melville picked up the nuance by creating his Captain Vere in *Billy*

Budd, strict in duty yet saddened rather than intoxicated by his authority. In the American pantheon, the great figure of restrained *vertu* is Washington, who declined kingly power. Washington also possessed many ethical virtues, and hagiographers added to the list with the cherry tree story and unlikely pictures of him on his knees in prayer at Valley Forge.

Virtue in the eighteenth century was also considered beautiful and the ultimately dependable source of pleasure in human life, though we don't see much of that explicitly in Franklin's story. An unending series of allegorical paintings, sculptures and pageants from the Renaissance through the nineteenth century present the grace of the virtues, either for the sake of their own loveliness or attending dead statesmen and heroes on memorials. The Statue of Liberty, gifted to the U.S. by France on the revolutionary centennial in 1876, is such a beauty. Extending the charm of virtue even on a practical social level was an aspect of the cultivation of good humor, benevolence, and conversation that arose in the Enlightenment: grace and respect of one's fellows followed from virtues of temperance, industry, friendliness, and charity as well as from acquisition of Taste. When Franklin explains in the *Autobiography* that he set up a table of virtues to monitor his growth in virtue, he is amused by the presumptuousness of his younger self because he knows that human nature is not wholly perfectible and that self-examination reveals much that we did not wish to know, but he tells the story because systematic self-evaluation was widely encouraged and even expected as an aspect of growth in both virtue and social graces. (Washington, the great American exemplar, as a young man kept a journal devoted to perfecting his courteous graces, with items ranging from courteous listening in conversation to not scratching private bodily parts.)

Franklin's search for virtue would have been a highly understandable project to his literary audience because it arose from twin sources, Puritanism and the Enlightenment. He was never a Calvinist or orthodox in any of his varying religious views but his environment and literary predecessors such as Cotton Mather were intensely devoted to self-examination and self-appraisal of one's good works along with one's worldly progress. The result was constant moral interpretation of daily life. For the religious, one might become prosperous but not saved because wealth without proper humility and good works was a snare. As for the Enlightenment's neoclassical perspective on the same issues, happiness was the classical goal of life; but that happiness depended on reason and temperance for withstanding the blows of fate and examination of one's life and character. For the Puritans, happiness from day to day was not necessarily a sign of salvation: a disciplined *desire* to do well and then better was a better indicator of salvation than satisfaction in one's own lot. That desire, of course, implied systematic monitoring of one's virtuous actions and one's lapses but also a concern for the morality of one's community and its displays of vice or indolence—hence the sometimes stern and sober mien of the Puritan. The religious understood as a mystery of Providence that one might have both faith and the virtues that usually lead to a worldly competence and yet fail, but the general sense in Protestant America at least through the nineteenth century was that the prudential virtues Franklin preached would result in worldly security. It is a little hard to recover, now, the overtones involved when a young man (usually a man) was described as having "merit" or as "worthy" because he had qualities of dependability and temperance even if success still awaited him. A person of gifts who failed to succeed for no apparent reason was a conundrum, a slowly developed private tragedy, a version of the mystery of Job on a small scale.

One effect of the close observation of oneself and others that the Calvinists encouraged was that the prudent worldly aphorisms and cynical folk wisdom that Franklin adapted in his almanacs were entirely appropriate to, and existed side by side with, complex intellectual and spiritual idealism. It is a combination of nearly opposite levels of observation and moral aspiration. Melville, who understood the paradoxes of Calvinism because he was raised amidst them, presents an elderly Christian towards the end of *The Confidence Man* (1856) who refuses at first to be duped by the title character because his long experience has taught him to be wary, though he cannot explain how that warinesss fits his faith: he cannot explain the scriptural injunction to be at once wise as the serpent and innocent as the dove. In Franklin, as indeed in many of the New England writers who grew up around rural Congregationalism or other Calvinist creeds, the aphoristic advice to be worldly wise and being innocent-souled at the same time made perfect sense.

My reason for rehearsing these well-known aspects of Franklin's career is to suggest that he is an unusual exemplar, as well as a shrewd teacher, of principles and skills for action in society continually shaping each other. Every society educates youth for some of the virtues it claims to value, but practical ethics in adult life tends to be learned and given nuance by taking on adult responsibilities as mundane as starting a family or holding a job. If we take Franklin as a model, his projects were beneficial to others as to his friends, but he grew within the role himself. To a remarkable degree he made the practically focused spirit of brotherhood a more prevalent community virtue as well as a personal one.

A final prophetic aspect of Franklin's volunteer leadership is this: he not only organized his fellows for mixed service and pleasure, but with them scanned the environment for needs and opportunities that would be most timely to pursue. When we sketch the invention of "scientific" philanthropy in a later chapter, that function of scanning needs and identifying new leaders of talent turns out to be a crucial gift of the third sector.

Franklin's era called a broad charitable impulse the virtue of benevolence. If fraternity is imagined as a virtue, communities possess it as well as individuals and that communal virtue involves not only principles but developed skills and underlying them a collective imagination of the kind of community it aims to be. To call fraternity a "virtue" emphasizes that active practice as well as maturing attitudes are involved. One can measure attitudes up to a point by surveys or other methods; a broad measure of mutual contacts like Putnam's "social capital" can gauge the resources for fraternal action that society possesses. But fraternity seen as a virtue implies characteristic attitudes toward future action rooted in the community's notion of its own values, just as private virtues are rooted in a vison of oneself. Seeing fraternity as a virtue less developed in the society than in many individuals helps us to imagine the best and worst features of the volunteer sector: improvisatory and individualistic creativity on one hand, inconstant priorities and partial successes on the other.

Finally, it may be worth noting that ordinary virtues, including those of fraternity, are often nearly invisible. Many individuals who in fact have value commitments reflected in occasional or part-time action may seem featureless and homogeneous in the mass. Over the years, various figures and movements have striven to awaken or re-awaken what might be called the American *vertu,* with calls like that of Theodore Roosevelt for strenuous life or Kennedy's "Ask...what you can do for your country." The relative strength of the independent sector in the U.S. suggests that the virtue of fraternity, which does involve following a crowd of fellow volunteers but is not necessarily blind or empty conformism, involves a self-possession that is easy for observers to miss.

2. The Mathematics of Democratic Equality in Action

Alexis Tocqueville's visit to the United States in 1832 is not in itself an historic event, but his observations were so acute and so relevant to our topic that it is necessary to examine some of what he said. One of the most widely anthologized passages in *Democracy in America* (1838) is an observation that we have referred to repeatedly, that this new people, the Americans, were extraordinarily active in forming "associations."[3] The Americans formed associations for any number of functions that in Europe would have been carried out by government or initiated by the wealthy or aristocrats, whose expected role was to lead in such matters.

There are arguably two great narratives around which American historical experiences can be grouped, and Tocqueville's analysis of "association," i.e. organizing without waiting for permission beforehand to effect one's ends, relates to both. The first great American narrative has to do with prosperity, the collective and individual "pursuit of happiness," meaning at a minimum freedom from dire want and beyond that owning property, for sustenance and security. "Association," as Tocqueville realized, was a key to the endless creativity of commercial enterprises that he saw among the Americans, where creating new commercial endeavors was frequent and scheming for advancement seemed a national trait. Independence from hampering regulations that might require official permission beforehand was a factor, especially in the Jacksonian era when Tocqueville visited, but in fact the associations that he observed often involved partnerships or sponsorships by political bodies helping to open the way for canals, railroads, and so on. The behavior was fundamentally in the same style in commerce, politics, and what we now call the third sector, with its charities and clubs.

The second great narrative of American history is that of rights, starting with ideals of liberty and equality. The young French visitor was convinced that the idea of equality would irresistibly sweep all nations: this American ferment of associating offered a multi-sided revelation about how equality, as the central principle of democracies, could work. It suggested a fundamental, almost mathematical algorithm by which an egalitarian society might direct itself successfully, the possibility that classical commentators on democracy had dismissed because *hoi polloi* were inherently a mob, without well-prepared leaders (i.e. a king or aristocracy) or the capacity to sustain a course of action. In the American democracy, no one citizen had the social weight to initiate change alone, and no one had been anointed to leadership by law or class status. Almost as a matter of arithmetic, the individual must multiply his social weight by enlisting others in "association." That was what Tocqueville had seen to a degree in England, but on every side among the Americans. Among the Americans, it also became obvious that associations could *counterbalance* each other and even resist the majority. Small groups of ordinary citizens could display something like the classical republican hero's capacity to resist the multitude: indeed, a minority could associate to resist and eventually win over the majority. Tocqueville saw that even in politics, associations and parties did not aim to tyrannize over the rest and eradicate opposition as he thought European parties did: he thought this was because in fact all were of the same middle class and open to compromise. The American party differences, he says at one point, are differences "in hue." They could temper the tyranny of majorities, which was the greatest danger facing a democracy. Moreover, in America an immense number of new undertakings, appropriate to a commercial economy but also expressing exuberant liberty, were under experiment because of this trait of association.

Tocqueville was finding an answer to the problem of how to manage a society in which hierarchies have vanished; his answer has implications for imagination of fraternity as well. As we noted earlier in glancing at late medieval Europe, class hierarchies can offer many dimensions of functionality and stability, and several kinds of brotherhood. They seemed to echo spiritual and natural order, designating each class for leadership in some important function in a system of expected mutual reliance validated by the gods and tradition. They imply solidarity among the different classes as they carry out their assigned roles, and fraternities of equals arise within each level. They offer a status, inferior to the highest but for many groups superior to the lowest: we know from the history of racism that members of relatively low classes are often the fiercest defenders of their superiority to those ranked further below them. Traditional hierarchies give the comfort of visible stability, supporting the sense of law and order.

The French revolution's *fraternite!* was the exultant cry of a new discovery, the fervent brotherhood discovered at affirmation of equality. It is the polar opposite of the resentment and fear that sulks when inferior classes rise to threaten status or order, and of course the revolutionary period saw waves of both emotions. Tocqueville's view of the French Revolution, published in a later book, was that the French aristocracy had once been functional, providing management of wealth (which consisted entirely of land), trained military leadership, and administration of justice. All these functions the emerging middle class took over, developing commercial wealth (i.e. not based on estates), infiltrating the officer ranks of the military, and supplying learned magistrates and officials for civil administration. American efforts to establish a formal aristocracy had already failed; what he saw (discounting the slaves) was one vast middle class.

Although American thinkers came to be concerned with explicit training for democratic citizenship, Tocqueville suggests that the middle class from which America grew was capable as soon as the assumption of leadership by aristocratic authority was removed. He praises the establishment of Connecticut, where educated men of "the middle rank" developed laws and a functioning government before the crown had a chance to authorize them. Classical views of democracy and the reactionary writers on the French Revolution tended to see the *demos* as subject to mob hysterias. Tocqueville does not directly address that issue, which suggests his penetration because he visited in a raucous period. Rather, he describes what happens inside American political parties as he observed them: the American had such long experience that they expected partial successes rather than seeing their causes as a war of principles of which no compromise is possible. They all possessed roughly the same class status though competing for different interests: interests, unlike status, are always somewhat negotiable. (A few decades later the non-negotiable interest, linked to an absolute difference in status, would be slavery.)

Tocqueville made other corollary observations relevant here: he discerned that the climate for commerce, as well as for social initiatives, was sure to be faster-moving and more diverse than any bureaucratic authorities could approve beforehand even if that was desired. In effect, he dismissed the feasibility of a successful command economy; the ferment of a modern commercial economy the political flexibilities. His recognition of the limits of bureaucracy has sometimes been oversimplified as a warning against governmental restrictions on business practice; what one sees time and again is his amazement at the fertility of democracies—he does not think it a purely American trait but as a function of egalitarian conditions. In effect, he understood the chaos of democracy and its "associations" as a condition of creativity, not a terrifying disorder.

A closely related observation was Tocqueville's surprise at learning that thousands of men had taken a pledge not to drink alcohol. Why not simply stop, if that was their intent? Why a public pledge? What he came to realize was that the force of ten thousand men's opinions created a moral force, in effect revealing that the same democratic algorithm (a few individuals enlisting others and those others) might even change *mores*. One can also read the brief passage as forecasting the immense weight of conventionality, counterbalancing the individualism that the culture professed; however, Tocqueville's surprise at the temperance pledge also foreshadows the way in which many attitudes and behaviors that define "culture," including relation to the land, religion, family structures, and traditional arts may be challenged by initiatives from any level of society that engages in "association." Americans would have to enlist each other to re-affirm, change, or abandon common aspects of their culture, for neither class hierarchies nor traditional institutions would assure continuity.

One morning while teaching in Romania I asked my graduate students in a literature class, most of them young women who were already teachers of English in small villages and towns near the university, "What would you like American students to know about you?" They answered, "Our traditions." This was not a surprising answer, though it surprised me at the time simply because an American class would never have given that answer. I understood it to mean that they felt fervently close to their land, their families, and often to each other; the "traditions" were symbols of that loving identification. The Romanians are an ancient people, but Romania as a nation had a relatively brief and much-troubled history and we were meeting in historically contested Transylvania. The traditions of which my students spoke were church holidays, celebratory holiday customs within the home, and the distinctive songs, costumes and festivals of the different rural districts. These were rich in spiritual recollection and family renewal, islands of love and familiar connection embodied in old songs and traditional foods.

A little later in the semester I tried to suggest that many of the students would face the American dilemma: their culture was already heavily influenced by international commerce and media and their lives would be shaped by professional and physical mobility. Each of them would choose which traditions to preserve and what those meant to them. This does not destroy the value of the traditions, but it does change their relation to those who preserve them: they become consciously chosen and are individually adjusted continuations of the inherited culture. Such choices are a world phenomenon, but because of the diversity of American immigrants, the vast areas the American settled and the absence of strong institutions the Americans explicitly faced that need to sustain, re-invent, or abandon ancestral heritages for several centuries. Commentators over the years have sometimes observed that in comparison with European or other old cultures American culture is "thin": the Americans individually sustain (or invent) selected traditions and their communities may seem to have none in common; further, traditions that do exist are not necessarily sustained through generations. This is troubling because traditions express both personal and communal ideas of the meaning of life, including brother- or sisterhood, neighborliness, and shared identity. "Tradition" in the living sense is the heritage of the past awakened to new life in the present, not shreds of the dead past affixed to the living; but for this reason, tradition in the modern situation is not the enduring reservoir of shared values that commentators on the old Europe or on tribal life sometimes describe with admiration and nostalgia. Transmission or revival becomes a matter of conscious reinvention and explicit education of successors amidst competing ideas, with decisions to be made along the way concerning who is (or is not) within the cultural community. In the traditional tribal or peasant village, elders or women's circles or perhaps the village curate oversee continuation of traditions season after season. However, the dialectic of new vs. old, of cultural reinforcement or abandonment, is sustained in an urbanized modern democracy by formal recognition of traditions in schools and governmental proclamations and but also, intensively, in the third sector where churches and synagogues, cultural heritage clubs, museums and arts organizations revive, interpret, or abandon aspects of the past. In changing democracies and in globalizing societies the task of sustaining or changing traditions, which always implies refreshing community bonds, has become a main function of the third sector.

3. The "Burnt-over District"

In Tocqueville's America, burgeoning "associations" were almost inevitable aside from the mathematics of combination that he saw as the key to feasible democracy: channels of ordinary cooperation for meeting life's needs that were customary in Europe were just developing, and in many cases were improvised by early settlers with as little of officialdom as possible. There was an ingrained resistance to taxation (typical of farm- and land-based economies everywhere), while the aggressive merchant classes aimed to maximize profits with *caveat emptor* as ruling creed and no governmental interference; many foreign immigrants arriving were suspicious of all governments based on experience, and when Tocqueville visited the Jacksonians were in power. Taking all these factors together, was clear that organized activity for public benefit would be carried out by non-governmental organizations or, in matters like canal-building, in state-supported or state-approved partnerships with private companies. Many public-benefit organizations, if created, had to be in the voluntary sector even if partly supported by meager local taxes. At the same time legal conditions favoring what we call the third sector had strengthened: the Bill of Rights assured freedoms of assembly and speech, and since federal establishment of religion was forbidden, sects were in lively competition even in the few states that for a few decades after the revolution still had official religions. The Supreme Court decision in the Dartmouth College case (1819) insulated charities, privately founded colleges, and religious foundations still further from official control; the 1830's and 40's saw the establishment of educational institutions that explicitly contravened majority views, including racially integrated colleges and others where women (shockingly!) studied beside men.

Tocqueville's Americans had a further characteristic that he recognized and that has arguably endured to a degree: an exuberant optimism, from time to time almost a capacity for social fantasy that convinced some of the populace that experiments in utopian communities and/or changing society could succeed. New communities and movements enlisted the most enthusiastic. Not all the ideas that fired communities were new, for a great part of the "burning over" was waves of revival, social but also devotional and even confessional assemblies of families from isolated farm as the old time religion blazed again to awaken work-weary communities. The revivals crossed the region from county to county like the fires that leave scorched farm field even more fertile for the next season. Despite the conviction of sin and possible doom that marked the revivals, they always ended in hope for salvation and exultation in grace, a revival of that kind of optimism. The early American optimism was marked by exotic diversity, arguably prophetic of the modern proliferation of third sector associations. The historical pattern history is most dramatic in the "Burnt-over District," the expanse of upstate New York and western New England so called because it was swept again and again by religious revivals, reform movements and utopian experiments from the Great Awakening (1730) to the late nineteenth century. Movements whose fires lit the region included abolitionism, temperance, and women's rights (The Declaration of Women's Rights was drafted in Geneva, New York in 1848). Utopian experiments included the serially polygamous Oneida Community, while religious movements in addition to the revivals included the asexual religious community of Shakers and the founding of at least one major new religion: Joseph Smith, founder of the Latter Day Saints, had his first vision of the angel Moroni near Palmyra, New York in 1823. The same region fed many recruits to the Millerites, who sold their possessions and mounted rooftops in white garments for the Second Coming in 1844. After the Great Disappointment, as it was called, a faction of believers established the Seventh Day Adventist Church, which by late in the century sponsored health sanitaria in several parts of the nation offering fresh air, exercise and health foods; today the sect sponsors a network of hospitals and colleges[4]. Without question, the availability of land for experimental communities, the habit of "awakening" to moral and political crises, and the general tolerance of new causes[5] made enlistment in utopias and reforms logical.

To amplify a point made in an earlier chapter, for a historian of fraternity the frontier is of interest less for its brave and bare first settlements than for the decades of filling-in behind. In the case of the "Burnt-Over District" even the geography, improved by canals and railroads, tells much. The region was filling up with farms and prosperous towns and cities; until the railroads reached Chicago and could ship from the deep-soiled wheat lands of the Midwest, upstate New York and northern Ohio were the breadbasket for the Eastern cities, taking advantage of waterways, canals and short line railroads. It was both the target and the conduit for continuous migration, sometimes adding its residents to the numbers moving further on. The fact that mobility was so commonplace and that so many dreamers came through must have made dissatisfaction with one's life in one locale or one's current "associations" easier to act on, supporting the conviction in adventurous souls that amazing things— amazing to the world!—might as well begin right *here*!

Although the "associations" and movements that we illustrate by this glance at the "Burnt Over District" are distinctly American in focus, from the first many of the movements saw themselves in a world or a biblical-historical perspective. Thus, the *Book of Mormon* settled a number of conundrums of the day including the origin of Indian mounds, the fate of the Twelve Lost Tribes of Israel (they came to North America) and how the Pentecostal command to preach the Gospel to the whole world could have been obeyed when the New World was not yet known (the resurrected Jesus appeared to deliver the Good News). Women's rights and anti-slavery were international issues, as was temperance. In retrospect it is easy to dismiss some of the movements and experiments as exotic, but it is also true that the "Burnt-Over District" offers an accurate glimpse into the anarchic diversity of the third sector wherever it thrives.

4. Reconstruction(s)

Peter Drucker called the Third Sector "the most authentic counterculture"[6]: it is the sector of the political economy that counterbalances government, opens new questions or refuses to close debate on unresolved questions, propagandizes against a majority prejudice, or experiments with new policy models. Among many possible examples, the long multi-sided history of black progress during and after Reconstruction and extending for generations after is the most powerful example of third sector leverage for social and political change in American history.

The story of post-Civil War Reconstruction by the federal government and its aftermaths is too complex to detail except to make the main point, which is that coincided with a widespread and continually growing pattern of local associations against official power and majority prejudice. Even as we remind ourselves that the term "third sector" is anachronistic, reflecting a modern desire to divide voluntary action for others from commerce and government, the term applies particularly well to the long history of civil rights because the forces on the side of discrimination were so long dominant in government and in control of wealth. The recurring effort of civil rights proponents at every stage was to imbed Negro civil rights in law because the powers of law were being used to deny these rights, but since both legal action and social prejudice so often went against the Negro, the persistence of non-governmental actors was crucial.

Because of the large populations involved and because the Civil War and decades of sporadic later violence marked the depth of the conflicts involved, the case of black communities pursuing rights is unique in American history, yet the strategies by which institutions developed and prosperity was pursued have been repeated throughout American history by immigrant groups and religious sects that wished to protect themselves from the majority or to preserve their cultural distinction. In many of these parallel instances as in black history, the training of leaders and networking for mutual interest bequeathed leaders or created alliances for other causes and for political office.

When the Union imposed military occupation on the Confederate States at the end of the Civil War, it began as well to establish schools for primary education of the former slaves, for whom literacy had been forbidden.

Enfranchisement of black voters began as well, and since white leaders who had served with Confederate governments or as Confederate officers were excluded from office, some rebel states had majority black legislatures and many black officials until official Reconstruction ended in 1876. In the retelling of the story of this period that prevailed until around the 1960s, historians and popular writers echoed Southern white opinion in characterizing this as a period as one in which "carpetbaggers" (corrupt Northerners) and "scalawags" (corrupt Southerners) took over state governments and exploited the naïve (and easily corrupted) new citizens. By 1876, the former Confederate states had been readmitted to the Union on terms that offered some protection to the rights of Negroes under anti-slavery amendments to the Constitution, but in the contested election of that year Southern Democrats agreed to support the election of Republican Rutherford B. Hayes as President in return for an end to Reconstruction. Relieved of the federal power, the former rebel states swiftly removed black state legislators (several were murdered) and began the legal formalization of the segregated system known as Jim Crow. Over the next decades, the conservative U.S. Supreme Court steadily supported the laws and procedures by which the former Confederate states reduced black voter registration and exercise of the franchise.

For our purpose here, what is significant in this history is the meagerly financed, half-invisible but sweepingly widespread seedtime of negro non-governmental institutions. Churches were at the heart of the change, for African Americans had become deeply committed to Christianity and their participation had usually been fostered and respected by slave masters. The many small congregations on plantations had been informally monitored to assure that the church taught obedience and submission; in some instances, as in the spread of Methodism among blacks, abandonment of that sect's traditional opposition to slavery was the price of permission to make slave converts. The rural black churches had always been allowed latitude for self-government and slave leadership, e.g. by elders and deacons, so that they were poised to emerge to independence. Before the Civil War, some southern cities held white congregations that included black members; further, churches started and led by free blacks such as the African Methodist Episcopal had developed both northern and southern congregations, with a history of quiet mutual support. When the Civil War ended, racially mixed congregations in the South split, but despite great poverty and widespread illiteracy the black churches flowered as the center of black community life. From early in Reconstruction, northern white churches and religious synods provided charitable support and assisted with the founding of colleges and midwifery programs, and dedicated northerners, white and black, arrived to staff the schools of the federally supported Freedman's Bureau. As rudimentary as some of the institutions were, the churches and first colleges immediately found regional leadership and developed affiliations that would prove resilient even amidst the growth of Jim Crow.

Although the prevailing white view of Reconstruction for many years was that it had been an excessively punitive, humiliating period of white subjugation to control by ignorant ex-slaves and white con men, the alternative argument was made by WEB DuBois in 1910, and the consensus of academic historians began to shift after the 1960s, partly as the accomplishments of black legislators and some measures of former slaves' advancement were reconsidered. DuBois' argument highlights how the network of rising institutions expanded what we have called the "capacity to act":

> Three agencies undertook the solution.... (a) the Negro church, (b) the Negro school, and (c) the Freedmen's bureau. After the war the white churches

of the south got rid of their Negro members and the Negro church organizations of the North invaded the South. The 20,000 members of the A.M.E. in 1856 leaped to 75,000 in 1866 and 200,000 in 1876, while their property increased sevenfold. The Negro Baptists with 150,000 members in 1850 had fully a half million in 1870. There were, before the end of reconstruction, perhaps 10,000 local bodies touching the majority of the free population, centering almost the whole of their social life, and teaching them social organization and autonomy. [7]

As for educational beginnings, DuBois continued, "within five years a dozen colleges and normal schools started; by 1877, 571, 506 negro children were in school." When the badly underfunded Freedmen's Bureau began to establish schools, its leaders discovered that grass-roots efforts had already begun the task in many places, and rather than attempting to supplant these it learned to collaborate[8]. Political scientist Jeremi Suri has argued that the lesson learned, that of encouraging independent local leadership combined with government institutions, was carried on in later American ventures in the Philippines and under the Marshall Plan.

An issue rarely addressed because so diffuse, and yet in its way obvious, is that formalization of color lines in social relations such as membership in clubs and membership in professional associations occurred in both the North and the South for the century after Reconstruction; social mixing across race lines had been unthinkable in the slave South and was rare elsewhere, but now that legal equality had been promulgated, rules for restriction or admittance in private settings became more explicit. This thread of post-Reconstruction history is embodied in a myriad of personal reminiscences and no doubt in the archives of many clubs; the whole story probably is untraceable by statistics but the black citizens' answer included development of black fraternal orders, service clubs, and professional societies serving the small but growing black middle class. Part of the history of civil rights in the twentieth century was the gradual assault on exclusions and quotas in white clubs, neighborhood associations, schools, and so on, restrictions that had often extended as well to Jews, Catholics, and (on different grounds) to women. In typical cases the restrictions were changed due to either agitation from within or after publicity embarrassed the organization[9]. Informal exclusions were at the heart of racial as well as ethnic exclusion in the North; in the South, the racial barriers were confirmed in law while other exclusions, e.g. of Jews or recent immigrants, was usually less official. Even two and three generations after slavery ended, when white leaders like Eleanor Roosevelt violated the informal barriers, the genteel South as well as what might be called the redneck South seethed in resentment[10].

As indicated above, development of a separate non-governmental sector, partly in response to exclusions, was not unique to the black community: Roman Catholics developed a massive system of parochial schools and Catholic universities, while concentrated immigrant communities from specific regions (German, Irish, Hungarian, Ukrainian, Chinese, and so on) created their own clubs, mutual aid organizations, and sports leagues. These institutions often declined when new immigration from that nation slowed; assimilated successor generations lost interest in being other than American. An evidence of the enduring functionality of third sector associations for mutual support has been that so many ethnicities, religions, immigrant cadres and religious movements have followed the same organizational track to foster group coherence and defend their distinctive values. The new associations and institutions have been largely left alone under American law, so that the energy of each group has channeled fully into these fraternities as far as they seemed useful. The African American version of this history is remarkable mainly because the extensive populace was under such continuously hostile pressure and started with so few resources.

To give the Reconstruction story as it related to non-profits a more concrete illustration, I told my Romanian students two anecdotes of my own. Charleston, South Carolina, was the greatest American center of slave importation; the city and region became wealthy and in nurtured a glamorous planter/mercantile elite using slave labor. In the mid-1980's I bought a house in the city, close to the College of Charleston, which dates its founding to just before the Revolutionary War. The house had several Queen Anne architectural elements that were a bit unusual for Charleston but would have been common in the North during the 1890's when it was built. Professor Lee Drago of the College explained its history to me. Before the Civil War, the Circular Congregational Church (founded 1689) had a mixed congregation: black parishioners, slave and free, sat in an outer ring while whites sat in the central circle of the nave. Both sides had their own deacons and treated each other with respect, although as 1860 approached they differed strongly over secession, the whites for and the blacks against. Just before the Civil War broke out the church was destroyed by a great fire that also took the hall next door, where the state's representatives had voted for secession. After the War, the white congregation invited their black co-religionists to rejoin and help to rebuild. (Eventually, a beautiful Romanesque church in the style of H.H. Richardson was erected.) The black congregation declined and instead created the significantly named Plymouth Congregational Church, housed in a large plain wooden building that would look perfectly in place in a New England village. By the 1890's, Plymouth Congregational sponsored a newspaper distributed to churches around the South and an encyclopedia of Negro life focused on prominent churches, clergy, and educators. To attract a new pastor from Connecticut who had the literary skills and education to oversee these enterprises, the congregation built a fine house for him with currently fashionable Queen Anne features, a photo of which soon appeared in their encyclopedia. That was the house I happened to purchase. The network of churches receiving the newspaper, the encyclopedia, and the northern links represent an almost invisible but sophisticated growth in civic life for blacks under Jim Crow, a life necessarily embodied in third sector institutions.

Further down the same street, as I told the students, stands a monument to another local story that tells another hidden part of a national story. In 1865, northern donors established a normal school to train Negro teachers for the enormous challenge of educating former slaves. The Avery Normal School was named for a Connecticut clergyman; it was housed in a handsome but unadorned red brick building that would be immediately recognizable as a school building of the era in any northern city. Eventually functioning as a private high school, Avery sent many graduates on to colleges and produced many leaders of the local black community. In 1945, the entire graduating senior class (without telling most of their teachers) applied for admission to the nearby College of Charleston, which had become a municipal (and therefore public) institution. The city fathers did not wish to integrate the college, but Charleston was a Navy town and they saw that national pressure for integration was rising. The Avery students' applications were ignored, and the college transferred to private status, protecting it from integration. However, by the 1960's the small institution was in financial difficulty because it was not eligible for federal student aid funds. An alumnus, L. Mendel Rivers, was Chair of the Armed Services Committee of the House of Representatives in Washington, and he did not wish to see his *alma mater* disappear[11]. Armed with enormous power to affect the state (the state had numerous military installations, and the economic importance of the Marines' Parris Island and the Charleston Navy Yard was enormous) he easily persuaded state legislators to make the College a state institution. A newly appointed President, Theodore Stern, swiftly admitted the first black student. He later appointed as affirmative action officer Ms. Lucille Whipper, a local educator who had been one of the 1945 Avery seniors.

By the early 1980's the Avery building was a state property for which demolition or sale to a developer was under discussion. Ms. Whipper organized the Avery Society for African-American History with the goal of making the building a museum. Although Charleston had been the greatest landing-place of slaves and the home of secession, it had no museum devoted to slavery or slave life. (As of 2015, a remarkable Mayor of Charleston, Joseph Riley, proposed creation of a museum and the project is underway.) With support from black state legislators, the Avery building was taken over by the College and restored as The Avery Research Center on African American History, part of a public institution but with the non-profit membership organization customary for many museums. Retiring from the College, Ms. Whipper stood successfully for election to the state legislature, where she led the fight that opened the state's military college, the Citadel, to female cadets. I mentioned this story to my Romanian students and share them here not as typical but as revealing: whether post-Reconstruction or after the peak of the Civil Right Movement, the push for equal rights has continued less dramatically, and (as Ms. Whipper's case suggests) the training and political influence gained in one cause sometimes carries on to leadership in related causes.

In some respects the emergence of black communities to rising commercial and social functionality even in the face of legal oppression is marked by Booker T. Washington's famous speech at the Southern Exposition (1892), which compared the black and white communities to separate fingers on one hand, which must work together. The speech effectively accepted the caste system that supplanted the slave system, but proposed that it be a partnership of mutual dependence and mutual respect. Washington's famous speech was an appeal for both races to concentrate on advancing, for whites to abandon mourning their old economic model and recognize a new interdependence necessary for mutual prosperity. It offered whites an unthreatening collaboration without claiming social equality—the fingers could remain separate. Washington tacitly assumed that negro communities would continue to develop institutions and prosperity in parallel, as they had been doing in business and the third sector:

A final dimension of the Reconstruction story as related to the Third Sector is speculative and tenuous but involves extraordinary long-term effects. Perhaps no other nation that has directed, or attempted to support, large scale "reconstructions" to the degree that is true of the Americans from 1865 until today, especially if we consider the aftermaths of the world wars. Some of these "reconstructions" were tragic: the history of Native American reservations is a national shame; the takeover of the Philippines after the Spanish-American War offers a record of brutal suppression followed by a largely benevolent colonial dominance with enlightened educational initiatives and some power-sharing with Filipino citizens. The intriguing case related to the third sector in U.S. history is Woodrow Wilson's approach to post-World War I peace talks, which eventually shaped much of today's world system and its enormous flowering of independent organizations.

Wilson was a former professor of political science and a leading Progressive Democrat, so that his views came from many and urbane sources, but a view of Reconstruction as too punitive—and of the Civil War as arising from abuses on both sides—surely weighed on the Southern-born politician, who had written a popular history of the U.S. that presented Reconstruction in that light. Wilson's history in fact is quoted in the famously racist movie, *Birth of a Nation* (1916), which romanticized the Ku Klux Klan and suppression of blacks in favor of Anglo-Saxon rule. The movie argues that the United States after the Civil War was truly one nation at last—hence the movie's title. Although he was a theoretical supporter of gradual "advancement of the negro race" who disapproved of lynching, Wilson increased segregation in federal offices and was personally uncomfortable with negro advocates who confronted him demanding swifter progress[12]. However, he also believed in popular sovereignty as a principle for all countries, and he led a Democratic Party of many isolationists, anti-colonialists and pacifists. Many Populists and Progressives shared the same racial prejudices but also favored proposals for disarmament, dispute resolution through the Hague, and were anti-colonialist. Nor were their views politically marginal: even Colonel Roosevelt, who was dismissive of arbitration and world courts but had received the Nobel Peace Prize for mediating peace between Japan and Russia, favored an international league that had power to suppress unjust attacks. Anti-militarist and pro-labor movements had marked the previous half-century, especially in Europe, and William Jennings Bryan, the U.S. Secretary of State until war was imminent, was a pacifist dedicated to arranging treaties for dispute arbitration. In 1916, when Wilson foresaw the likelihood of American entry into the Great War, he assembled an unofficial group of over sixty scholars, lawyers and former statesmen called simply The Inquiry to advise him on a peace that would "have no victors," as he significantly phrased it. Shortly before his request to Congress for a declaration of War, he argued that the United States must remove the old autocracies to make the world "safe for democracies"—a standard of immense significance, co-opting the war aims of the combatants on both sides, whose pre-war alliances aimed to sustain or tilt the "balance of power."

Wilson's summary of the Inquiry's recommendations was his famous "Fourteen Points." As Desmond Morris notes, none of the points were new, but they were new to most of his audience; what was startling was their potential to coopt the nearly exhausted combatants for a vision that reflected many of the aims of many liberal political movements, labor and socialist congresses, and anti-colonial leagues. Wilson's experts, over thirty of whom he later carried with him to Versailles as a "brain trust," arguably represented the best thinking of several generations of intellectuals and activists on achieving a peaceful world order. The British delegation had assembled a team of experts as well. After the Treaty was completed the American "brain trust" eventually became the non-profit Council of Foreign Relations, from whose membership numerous statesmen have been chosen up to the present day.

In Wilson's directive that there be "no victors," idealistic themes that were developed largely among "associations" and reform movements rather than in halls of government dramatically entered the pragmatic considerations of nations. Wilson's world parliament soon revealed its weakness, but the founders of the United Nations revived it, setting the groundwork for an international assembly but also for intergovernmental organizations regulating trade and promoting service to children, agricultural improvements, world health initiatives, cultural preservation, and human rights. Around these agencies the complex world of third sector international actors (NGO's) has crystallized in structures that arguably parallel the third sector/governmental partnerships developing in the U.S. and many other democracies. In these efforts, and in related initiatives such as the post-World War Two Marshal Plan for Europe and Cold War-era foreign aid to "third world" countries, a main strategy has been that there must be reconstruction without victors, i.e. restoration of civic society and promotion of commerce along with rights for non-governmental actors. Suri, as a key example, points out how post-World War II reconstruction recalled the improvisation and use of local leaders that worked in Reconstruction establishment of schools. Just at the end of the war, the western Allies faced the prospect of starvation among the conquered peoples: Herbert Hoover was enlisted to conduct a quick fact-finding visit and returned advising that the German economy be supported in rebuilding with local Germans leadership. Advisers and experts, many associated with the Council of Foreign Relations, found ways to assist the project, which was formalized as the Marshall Plan; the U. S, provided grants rather than loans to speed the work.

In 1917, Woodrow Wilson certainly was not looking toward the expansion of an international third sector, but his advisers drew on ideas long in the air outside of government and his model, restarted after the Second World War and growing up to the present, spawned the modern world of NGO's.

5. Andrew Carnegie scans his environment

Andrew Carnegie is crucial for the history of the third sector in American culture for his ideas on philanthropic use of wealth in a capitalistic economy and for his pioneering practice. He created "scientific" philanthropy, targeted for long term improvement of societal institutions rather than immediate relief of suffering—an imperious adjustment of what charitable brotherhood might mean—and one of his means was founding the first great American foundations. Charitable foundations had existed for support of particular hospitals and similar institutions, but the modern foundation was essentially pioneered by Carnegie, followed in short order by John D. Rockefeller and a variety of other enormously wealthy individuals, some of whom like Carnegie had been the ruthless monopolists of the era. Carnegie's statement of philosophy is briefly examined below, but it is useful to notice at the outset that establishing a foundation or charitable equivalent has become, for many of the wealthy, an enlightened fashion, meeting and sustaining what is almost a class expectation with moral and civic implications. Even those who do not feel much moved to generosity but have a favorite cause or institution use the charitable instruments for tax purposes; Carnegie founded his endowments before the U.S levied income taxes but over the years and especially in the last few decades a remarkable variety of tax-advantaged giving strategies have become commonplace, These include family foundations, charitable remainder trusts, charitable investment funds and other schemes, making reflective charity more feasible for a great number of donors along the lines that Carnegie and his peers pioneered. For those who have sufficient wealth to make the term meaningful, the mechanisms and the process of deciding how to use them are part of the art of "wealth management," along with prudent investments and choice of advisers.

Among the many ways now available for helping one's neighbor the foundation mechanism has influenced how other means are used. There are over 18,000 foundations[13] in the U.S., most of them "family foundations," relatively modest conduits by which individuals or families of established wealth administer their charities. Some of these family foundations contain long term endowments while others are periodically refreshed by new gifts: donors give irrevocable amounts to their own foundation, then disburse over time to a few or many beneficiaries. Many corporate foundations follow the same pattern, refreshing the fund according to the previous year's profits. While only a few hundred foundations among these thousands have major endowments and highly competitive application procedures, the process of establishing such mechanisms declares an intention to donate systematically and sometimes to sustain charitable activity through generations. If one of the satisfactions that wealthy donors seek beyond the impact of their gifts is recognition in one's community, establishing a foundation identifies a long-term role as an exemplar, with credit perhaps to the whole family and an ongoing community stature.

The different strategies in use today reflect a donor's serious consideration of his or her charitable role, which in turn usually creates or expands his or her relationship with a community, college, arts organization, church or synagogue. A professional field, splintered like the Third Sector itself, has grown up to solicit, advise and administer such funds. The great charities, churches and universities offer expert suggestions on how to give to them most conveniently and prudently in terms of the donor's and their own needs. If the donor is happy with the use of his or her gifts the relation will be developed by the assiduous recipient institution to assure that gifts are repeated and that the happy donor's satisfaction and honors inspire his or her peers. Consultants and short courses as well as lawyers and accountants are available to plan one's charities, to learn the best legal and financial mechanisms, and even to train the scions of extreme wealth in the twin arts of preserving family assets and meeting societal needs lest they become wastrels. Carnegie thought that estates should be taxed at confiscatory levels because the descendants of the founder rarely have his capacity to enhance economic productivity, but he granted that some second-generation wealthy had become intelligent philanthropists on lines that he praised. Donors of great wealth who do have children face complex human choices about what to give and what to withhold from them as well as from charities: the need to structure charitable choices and estate strategies together often triggers major endowment gifts and use of the advisers just mentioned.

In the U.S., the category of those who must "manage" wealth or an estate late in life includes not only the recognizably rich but individuals who have accumulated significant assets over a lifetime such as a home in an expensive district or an unusually large retirement account with no heirs. Gifts or bequests to a church, symphony or university by such individuals may involve impressive sums. For many such individuals and for wealthy families, the question of which loyalties are most important arises: it is not unusual for major donors to have experienced several stages of mobility in life so that the list of institutions and communities with which they have been identified may be long but sustained affiliations may be few. Among the possible long-term affiliations, individuals are permanently identified as alumni of a school or college and some have long term commitments to a religious denomination. Once settled in a locale, they may have entered its life by pursuing a lifelong interest such as belonging to and underwriting the city symphony. In general, Americans of low to moderate means are readily generous in giving to their churches and to immediate appeals like those of the Red Cross and the United Fund while individuals of high means are disproportionately courted by, and generous to, major arts organizations, hospital or recreational building projects, and other causes where significant gifts are visible as well as having financial impact. For both the very the well-to-do and those of modest means, donation and volunteering are ways of assuring admittance and welcome to a community, creating networks of peers in the new locale.

Universities, some religious denominations, and cause organizations strive to build cultures of connection both locally and at-a-distance, often highlighting the generosity of major donors but enlisting everyone possible. The universities, among the most sophisticated practitioners and with natural advantages, refresh their community by repeated invitations to class reunions, sports events and tailgate parties and by offering volunteer roles in alumni organizations. Alumni as well as parents of students receive the college magazine and messages from the university web site, sharing self-congratulatory stories of successful teams, scholarly recognition earned by professors, or unusual field studies undertaken by an outstanding student. The stories enhance the perceived prestige of the education formerly received by the alumnus and/or the value of that attained by the young person currently attending. Many alumni once set on the path to their careers are willing to help their institution, in fact are proud to take part; some also seek to sustain networks that benefit them professionally. In these cases, as in much of the Third Sector, it often appears that the invitation to help identifies a sense of marginal emptiness in the donor or volunteer, offering a recovery of lost associations or even of lost idealism that church or school or an old cause once supplied. The volunteer's response to that awakening gives a sense of usefulness that may not be celebrated in the rest of his or her life. When fund raisers are asked why people give money or time (e.g. to a college) there are as many answers in detail as there are donors, but the overall answer is, *they give because they were asked.*

Like political advocacy organizations, and like the many businesses that try to build loyal customers, universities, churches, and arts and cause organizations constantly invite the small active steps that sustain the sense of connection. As in political groups the networking among adherents often builds on friendships, for the alumnus, church member, lodge brother or activist is eager to recruit his friends. Part of the Third Sector's energy derives from constant invention of ways to re-connect and involve, utilizing the arts of modern commercial marketing but drawing on informal past or current networks. In the local arts organization, "friends" organizations and receptions in which donors meet the artists are common; in the university or school case, alumni may be invited to find old schoolmates in a "Where are they now?" section of a web site and to write in to a volunteer class secretary to document a major life changes like retirement or the death of a spouse. Religious congregations usually have fewer options for connection at a distance but milestones in the history of the congregation are celebrated and committees for fundraising, white elephant sales, a food pantry, and so on are available for as much immersion as the congregant desires. It is possible to read these voluntary patterns of affiliation as counterbalances to a formless social state to which Americans can lapse and which especially threatens those isolated by lack of family, geographic isolation, poverty, or illness. In the description I have given here I have emphasized schools and churches heavily because contemporary Americans are mostly high school graduates and approximately half of adults have attended college; they have often passed as well through multiple networks of co-workers as jobs and locales changed. As a result, it is difficult to determine from a distance or even by calculation of current "social capital" how many sentimental or occasionally realized connections offer themselves to the citizen for engagement. The third sector offers those connections but almost always as choices, not (as with traditional religion or kinship networks in other societies) as inheritances.

To return to Carnegie and the invention of the modern foundation: there have always been philanthropists who were systematic in their giving and cautious in their choice of recipients, but Carnegie's endowments were notable in part because they focused on categories of social need that implied long term improvement of the condition of the recipient community—libraries, educational institutions, research and studies on peace—and because his foundations shifted their recipients and projects as time went on according to the state of the field. In other words, his gifts involve scanning of the social horizon for unmet needs (within his criteria) for which a foundation might catalyze a solution. The implied scanning of society was as much an innovation as the "scientific"— meaning evolutionary—rationale of giving for long-term structural progress rather than to meet immediate distress. When John D. Rockefeller created his foundation, he had already been a notable donor to Baptist causes, to Negro education, and to the fledgling University of Chicago; he appointed a minister friend to the task of systematic filtering of causes that applied for support. As his foundation passed to descendants (eventually several Rockefeller foundations were created) staff review of proposals became professionalized and periodic re-assessment of priorities occurred. The much later creation of "public foundations" like the National Endowment of Humanities adopted the same periodic re-assessment and re-setting of priorities within a general charter as their *modus operandi*. The method is "scientific" in the sense that like experimental science, scientific philanthropy seeks to identify and manipulate some variable of a significant problem that is ripe for attack. As noted below, the philanthropic world can serve to sustain economic inequities because philanthropic largesse is greeted with praise and recipients of gifts celebrate their donors regardless of past commercial ruthlessness; those donors, raised in public estimation, usually support the system that made them rich. On the other hand, scientific philanthropy has arguably sometimes sewn elements of the community together by involving wealthy persons who otherwise would be isolated from the social needs of the "other half," and it has certainly clarified by experiment how problems can be addressed. Advocacy of a controversial cause by a respected foundation has often helped confirm its importance to the wide community; moreover, some of the progressive foundations have used their programs to identify and train leaders in marginalized communities, supplying opportunities and networks that allow them to sustain reform. The Kellogg and MacArthur foundations are particularly noted for that development of "human capital."

Carnegie's statement of his philosophy in *The Gospel of Wealth* (magazine publication of the first chapter as "Wealth" occurred in 1889) is worth parsing in detail, for he sets inequality of wealth and of comforts of life as the inevitable modern condition and sustaining brotherhood as the key problem, requiring proper "administration of wealth":

> The problem of our age is the proper administration of wealth, so that the ties of brotherhood may still bind together the rich and poor in harmonious relationship.[14]

A staunch defender of capitalism as a source of long term benefit to humankind, Carnegie argues that accumulation and investment of capital benefits the living standard of all classes in the long term more than socialistic equal distribution would, and that strategic philanthropic disbursement of that wealth, in addition to reducing hostility, offers more benefits than simple gifts drawn on the moment's compassion.

Carnegie's argument is both Darwinian and paternalistic, making no apology for the inequalities of a system which he sees as both inevitable and advantageous to social evolution over the long run. For him, inequality of wealth is an inevitable factor in the industrial age, a result of opportunities created by the most entrepreneurial individuals but slowly raising the conditions of life for all. The end, meaning not the purposes of the individual capitalist but the eventual overall economic result, justifies the means; however, that positive evolutionary result can be amplified by the philanthropist.

More than one earlier writer on American democracy had made the point that the grand palaces, cathedrals and artworks of feudal Europe were not worth the human suffering involved. Taking the other side, implicitly defending what Thorstein Veblen called the "conspicuous consumption" of the era's robber barons, Carnegie says that for the sake of high culture it is better than some have wealth than that none have it, because the arts and higher studies require leisure and surplus.

> It is well, nay, essential for the progress of the race, that the houses of some should be homes for all that is highest and best in literature and the arts, and for all the refinements of civilization, rather than that none should be so. Much better this great irregularity than universal squalor. Without wealth there can be no Mæcenas[15].

In this statement, and in its pragmatic elaboration in a later essay on the best uses of philanthropy, we see the excitement of participation in creation of a higher civilization as a motive supplanting the challenge of building a business empire. Carnegie lists the best fields for great donations: universities, museums, concert halls, libraries and so on, which reform the human condition and ennoble the civilization. They will be especially effective, he insists, if guided in first implementation by the seasoned philanthropist/manager, who is not subject to vagaries of politics. As to the *realpolitik* of the situation: the man of brisk action adds that it's the system we have, and it won't change: "It is a waste of time to criticize the inevitable."

Carnegie is an exemplar of the Protestant ethic in that after hard work, determined self-formation and providential success he began to exercise public leadership and to donate more frequently than before (but with exemplary prudence!) to charities that served the industrious and virtuous. He is untypical of his forbears, and of the religious donor generally, in that he does not value giving for its own sake nor to obtain religious merit; nor is he humbled by others' meager lot compared with his prosperity. At the same time his motivation is ultimately tied to the principles of Christ as he understands them: the reason for his program obviously does not lie in capitalism itself but in a distinctly personal combination of Social Darwinism and a nonsectarian version of the Social Gospel, restoring "ties of brotherhood."

Carnegie's chapter on *how* philanthropists should give, added to the original essay "Wealth," for book publication, gives us a sense of the creative thought and seasoned judgment that he sees as keys to the philanthropic service to "brotherhood." The good effects of philanthropy will reflect the MAN (capitals in the original) who has the proven talent to manage a great business and now turns that wisdom to scientific giving. In idealizing the capitalist who leads his own philanthropy, Carnegie denies praise to donors of bequests in favor of those who give away most of their fortunes in their lifetimes. The argument for managed philanthropy obviously loses some force if society must wait for the old codger to die, hoping that his charities will receive a portion alongside the heirs' remainders. He positively blasts those who give out of simple compassion for a beggar's or pauper's need: the duty of the extremely rich is to improve society systematically, with more splendid monuments than the democratic state will build. As for those who depend on charity because they won't work out of sloth (an ongoing bugbear of defenders of capitalistic charity), or who can't work because of age or infirmity: caring for them is the duty of the state.

Carnegie's delight in his own cleverness reminds us that display of one's talents in managing great expenditures, along with pursuit of praise, seem to be common motives when those whose fiscal empires have become too large for the next million to matter turn to philanthropy. Whether controlling politics or solving insoluble social or health issues, later tycoons who act as Carnegie's spiritual progeny seek to prove themselves in new fields as in the old commercial ones. Whether splendor of estates, effectiveness in philanthropy, shrewdness in art collecting, exerting political influence or developing superior cattle or horses is their new passion, they test themselves against their wealthy peers as well as against their first successes.

One can argue that the philanthropic activity helped to save American capitalism from popular revolt: one recent book on the subject is entitled *How Philanthropy Saved Capitalism*. On the other hand, it would be fair to recognize that individual philanthropists, once they have made their fortunes, have no inherent interest in saving capitalism for later arrivals. Some of the great philanthropic endowments since Carnegie were done out of rivalry with peers, for the rich follow fashion in their giving as in their mansions, and *noblesse* is satisfying; but many deserve credit for reflective generosity, for they did not have to give as they did. At present, a remarkable half-way version of Carnegie's plan to disburse all his fortune is being promoted by some of the world's richest individuals, the "50% pledge," a public determination to join others in giving away at least half of their fortunes[16]. The leaders have been Messrs. Gates, Buffet, and Bloomberg, very much public personalities after they became billionaires, and evincing the same enthusiasm that we see in Carnegie for the application of wealth to effect difficult change. Reflecting the complex contemporary pattern of collaboration including corporations, other NGO's, and governments Gates has worked with U.S. school districts experimenting with small high schools, and with foreign governments, the Clinton Foundation, and the drug industry to fight AIDS in Africa. Buffet, while calling for the very wealthy to pay more taxes, has shifted a large fortune to Gates' foundation as better able to achieve strategic impact than he could design. Bloomberg reputedly asked a public health adviser how to have the most impact on world health and learned that the most preventable diseases were those caused by smoking: he has devoted hundreds of millions to international smoking cessation campaigns while strengthening the anti-smoking regulations in his role as Mayor of New York City. In confidential meetings with possible subscribers to the 50% Pledge (later reported in the major business magazines) a main topic was where to get the best advice and how to identify areas of need where large gifts could have impact; there was clearly a certain pride in being part of the club that could take the pledge. The Irish billionaire Charles Feeney, an admired exemplar who had previously turned almost all of his fortune over to charity without publicity, was reportedly pleased at the turnout: ""the great and the good were there."[17]

The philanthropists mentioned are clearly as serious in their philanthropy as in their financial and political careers, but vivid evidences of the new glamour of philanthropy are widespread. An example is the May, 2015 issue of *Town and Country* magazine, a glossy upscale publication for those who possess large suburban or rural estates (or imagine having them). The "philanthropy issue" features Bill Clinton on the cover and an article highlighting the good works of the Clinton Foundation. Inside, as in a major newspaper society page, the reader finds bright photographs of major philanthropists, many of them couples in formal dress as at the opera. (Major city operas are often among the charities that the most well-off support and attend in formal finery.)

It has long been understood that the great moguls, as they used to be called, at some point pursued wealth less for its purchasing power than to establish their preeminence in the world and among peers. Skillful provision of public benefits offered a measure of that satisfaction, as examples from Benjamin Franklin onward illustrate, and as numerous philanthropists preceding Carnegie demonstrated. Carnegie's listing of exemplary American donors in *The Gospel of Wealth* (Pratt, the Vanderbilts, and Stanford among them) is clearly an invitation to aspire, to join the select circle. The importance of joining and inspiring an elite fraternity is clearly one motivation of Carnegie's insistence on donating during one's lifetime. Today, in addition to the 50% pledge, foundations have been created that must expend all their funds over a limited period instead of sustaining an endowment, on the argument that the needs addressed are urgent while creating an organization as one's monument is less important.

As with so much of the Third Sector, the philanthropic pattern offers rather uniform basic mechanisms and types of organization partly due to legal requirements, yet in the realm of motive and in the notions of human bonds involved there is no consistency and the actors' explanations are mostly *ad hoc*: "I saw such and such a need, and acted." Levels and timing of participation, whether in community volunteering or financial support of charities are extremely individualized, and yet within groups and perhaps economic classes there may be strong expectations to conform. Especially among the wealthy, who tend to know what their neighbors are worth, the fund-raising committee for the prestigious opera company, collegiate alma mater or the new hospital will set a figure that a rich individual should be expected to give and his or her friends are delegated to help make the pitch. The variability of the social interaction involved, the class or club implications, and the recognition offered differ from one situation to the next but there are many cases where donations buy into an honorific circle.

Chapter 14. American History from the Third Sector II: "Networks and Partnerships"

1.Herbert Hoover as Hero and Exemplum

Hoover, as I told my Romanian students, would be regarded as one of the greatest Americans of his century if he had not had the misfortune to be elected President. His great feat was organizing, as a volunteer with no official status, the Belgian Relief Effort in World War I, saving the lives of millions from starvation. He joined the U.S. government to sustain relief efforts on an unsalaried basis when the U.S. entered the war; his project extended to Eastern Europe at the War's end, saving more tens of thousands of lives. During the war he persuaded warring governments and wary neutrals to provide passage for civilian relief across blockades and battle lines, raised funds in the U. S. and elsewhere, developed staff and oversaw great refugee camps and logistical feats. He was a founder of the American Friends Service Committee, a longstanding international peace organization reflecting his Quaker roots. Remaining in public life (he had become wealthy as an international mining engineer before the war) he was appointed to President Harding's cabinet as the first head of the Commerce Department and stayed on under Coolidge where, in response to disastrous flooding of the Mississippi in 1927, he oversaw creation of the system of levees for flood control that was successful until Hurricane Katrina overwhelmed it in 2005. As the Depression unfolded, he devoted governmental resources to massive infrastructure projects that provided some employment, including Hoover Dam, but moved too slowly and without obvious expressions of sympathy with those suffering, a patience so resented that homeless camps were called Hoovervilles. Franklin Roosevelt's New Deal provided greater federal activity, expanding Hoover's initiatives and adding others, and represented a different tone of commitment to addressing popular suffering through government action. Hoover believed that social relief should be supplied through private organizations, though on occasions his administration applied federal funds through non-profits like the Red Cross; after losing office he wrote about the dangers of socialism. Ostracized in politics for years, he was drafted in 1948 by President Truman as volunteer chair of a commission on government-wide re-organization that he led with distinction.

Hoover's career is emblematic of the almost ceaseless ideological debate among American political about the relative roles of the Third Sector, private business, and government in ameliorating social and economic problems. There is no doubt that in the Great Depression private sources such as local and national charities were unequal to the human need: in cities, the numbers of unemployed were overwhelming, while in many rural areas the years of drought had drained the coffers of local donors to charity. Suspicion of government power is an original principle in American politics: calls for limited government, praise for private charity, resistance to taxes, and sometimes class- or race-based disdain for the poor have been inextricably mixed motives. The arguments involved are perennial and in their pure form are bromides because the American system has not offered the simple alternatives implied in the debate for a very long time. At the level of ruling ideas, Hoover stands as a victim of the conviction that government should not meet certain social and economic crises for fear that its role in doing so will become permanent, resulting in dictatorial powers and sapping initiative. If the welfare of the people in the short term is at issue, logical corollaries to his position ought to be that private charity can meet the needs of a populace in distress: this corollary is usually argued in the abstract because examples of concrete unaddressed suffering, such as unemployment in central cities that industry has abandoned, or poverty in rural areas where rural areas where mines have closed, undermine it.

As noted above, the debate is still lively, and riddled with myths. My Romanian class looked at political cartoons and several speeches of candidates in the 2011-12 American presidential primary campaign—all Republicans by necessity of the timing, for President Obama ran unopposed in Democratic primaries. The primary candidates included Mr. Romney, an admirable exemplar of Third Sector activity: he directs a large personally funded foundation that focuses on Mormon charities and he famously rescued a troubled Olympic Games organization in Salt Lake City as volunteer chairman. On the other hand, as governor of Massachusetts he was noted for introducing a scheme of universal health insurance that was the model for Obamacare, suggesting a willingness to use government to solve a great social service problem, a stance that he abandoned while campaigning for President. His stump speech focused on "entitlement" vs. "opportunity" as prevailing social values: "Do I as a citizen want the government to take care of me or do I want to advance myself?" We examined the speech at length, attempting (as with any political speech) to translate code words into proposals and claims of fact. Though trying to be non-partisan, I could not propose a translation that made sense—not a translation into Romanian, but a translation into reality. The "entitled" in the U.S. are mostly children in poverty or elderly retirees on Medicare/Medicaid and Social Security, served by programs that Mr. Romney did not propose to dismantle. My students wanted an Obama speech to analyze and did not get the chance: I could not guarantee that his speech would be free of code words either, but what struck me most, as I told the class, was that the terms of ideological debate had hardly advanced as the nation changed over eighty or so years. The Third Sector in its wide present activity, the vast "military/industrial complex" of corporate and governmental interactions that arose after World War II, globalization of commerce, and the now longstanding "safety net" of Social Security and Medicare—to mention four sweeping changes—have profoundly changed American government, the nature of the economy, and the people's expectations in ways that the old political code words deny.

It turned out none of my Romanian students had ever listened to a whole political speech in their lives. They believed that their system was too corrupt to pay attention to. Later in the semester, two friends from South Carolina, Drs. George and Carol Tempel, visited my classes and discussed American electioneering. George had just stepped down as Democratic Party Chair of Charleston County, and Carol was running for the state legislature. Students were deeply impressed by the analyses of voting patterns and the communication strategies that American campaigns must follow, but were convinced that the politics of Romania would inevitably be so corrupt that parallels were useless. The Tempels exhorted them not to leave the field to the dishonest; Carol, who was also active with the American Association of University Women and with state teacher associations, explained how non-profits are among the actors that can insist on transparency, set agendas, and call political leaders to account, resisting the obscurity that covers corruption. (As this book was being completed the Romanian Parliament voted to decriminalize political corruption, although their President vetoed the bill: my students may have been shrewder judges of the level of corruption that I was.)

Setting aside the ideological debates, in the U.S. today we find innumerable cases of crossover among "sectors": government organizations like state-or city supported museums and universities request charitable donations beyond the tax dollars they receive, while businesses graft charity causes onto marketing ("A dollar of every purchase goes to fight breast cancer"). Non-profits in such fields as the arts seek government grants while marketing merchandise and performances with great commercial skill; the great research universities, both public and private, compete for government and private foundation grants while harboring "incubator" centers for high-tech development of commercial products. That partnering of sectors arguably had its first great model in the Manhattan Project, developing the first atom bombs.

2. The Manhattan Project

One of the first great examples of intersector partnering, hardly an exercise of world brotherliness, was the Manhattan Project, in which government discovered how to use universities (including "private" institutions like Princeton, MIT and Chicago) alongside of industrial corporations. The speed with which the partnership developed the atomic bomb was a revelation. The military, which had long used industrial contractors, learned that universities could be used in a three-way partnership, parceling out research and development tasks among partners, and guided on the science side by high-level researchers who could judge the unsolved technical questions. Since future wars would probably be won by the side with better weapon technology, this was an important discovery.   The discovery of how to manage an aggressive, multi-pronged pursuit of a practically important research field was soon transferred to medical science and other fields. Private foundations, such as the Rockefeller Foundation under Warren Weaver in the 1950's[1], strove to identify areas of science or health that seemed ripe for a major new scientific advance and then brokered parts of the program to different investigators, with the expectation that governmental grants would sooner or later supplement the private foundation initiative. In time, governmental think tanks in high tech fields and more entrepreneurial industrial actors imitated the process, with fluid boundaries between research, development, production, and field use. Weaver is a useful example because, as a pioneer in information science who turned to administration of science, he was aware of interdisciplinary faculty exchanges and technological innovations that would be mutually illuminating in neurology, linguistics, computing, and communications among other fields: theories and technologies that promised great breakthroughs if the different disciplines could be brought together. This campaign model, essentially the Manhattan Project model, sped new discoveries, limited wasteful duplication and sped communication among allied workers on the key problems to be solved.

Something analogous occurred during the post-Sputnik era. For much of the decade before Sputnik went into orbit, a national dialogue featuring widely discussed books and studies addressed weaknesses in American education, especially in science. The groundwork of identifying educational needs and possible remedies had been done in many forums including the much-discussed report of a commission headed by President Conant of Harvard and writings of Admiral Rickover, father of the nuclear submarine program. Popular interest in rockets and space technology was high: Disney television shows proudly (and repeatedly) featured Werner Von Braun and the American rocket program. Sputnik broke the dam. Its flight triggered an enormous flow of government money to universities and schools as well as directly to the military and space programs, the educational needs having been well defined beforehand. This funding addressed all sorts of perceived Cold War needs, primarily in science and engineering but including expansion of foreign language instruction in colleges and ideologically defensible international humanitarian aid like the Peace Corps. In education and medicine foundations provided funding for experimental or specially focused initiatives that government grants might follow up if the results were evaluated as useful, a pattern still occurring. Over the period since, leading foundations and/or collaborating government science agencies have learned to recalibrate shared priorities, dropping one area of science as well pioneered for the moment and identifying another as ripe for coordinated acceleration such as mapping genomes.

It has made little difference whether universities, hospitals, or research centers were, or are, "private" or "public" in these endeavors: the great public research universities and medical institutions were granted great freedom to contract for scientific and health related activities from almost any source, and some public universities, like the University of Wisconsin, had long ago established private foundations to channel grant and patent income. On the "private" side, the most prominent universities including Harvard, Stanford and Johns Hopkins receive more government research funding annually than do any of the nation's public universities; the latter two oversee major federal research facilities in nuclear physics. Public and private institutions enter the same competitions for federal funds in science, approach the same foundations for research funding, and participate in multi-institutional initiatives when these occur. A relatively minor difference in their relation to foundations is that some private foundations that support *educational* programs (as opposed to research projects) will not donate to public institutions, and some private donors do not wish to support public university instruction that tax dollars should provide. For these and other reasons, including no doubt lingering ideological convictions about "public" vs "private," until the last few decades public universities were far behind the privates in their devotion to fund raising, and their efforts often focused heavily on athletic support. Currently, however, major public institutions are active in fund raising, obtaining bequests and scholarships and offering naming opportunities the same as private institutions. Some outstanding public undergraduate institutions, like the University of Vermont and the College of Charleston in South Carolina, receive rather modest annual taxpayer support for operations and in effect are mixed types, "state-assisted" but heavily dependent on tuition and gifts. Like the tax-supported museums and libraries, public higher education has joined the cacophony of gift appeals that nowadays marks the Third Sector.

Federal control has been most complete in research that involves military uses or massive investment, e.g. atomic energy research and space exploration, but even here deep intersections of corporations, universities and government are customary, and transfers of ideas and technology has become a standard goal: thus, the internet was first developed by a military research network, DARPA, for military use and then set free to be developed in the commercial world.

The partnerships described here have involved occasional cultural collisions and over time an elaborate world of regulations and protocols for ownership of information and of inventions. One early collision, minor but revealing, occurred shortly after World War II, when the U.S. Navy, which had discovered the power of university research for its strategic purposes, discovered that no applications for its research contracts were coming from MIT. The reason was that mathematician Norbert Wiener, who was deeply respected and also feared by colleagues, had published a letter in *Harper's* arguing that academicians must now abstain from science in the service of the military as corrupting to the academy. During the war Wiener had developed a mathematical analysis of feedback for improved anti-aircraft targeting that became the basis of his later seminal work in Cybernetics. However, Wiener was a talkative and absent-minded man who had very low security clearance and his manuscript was taken away from him for the duration of the conflict. This convinced him that the wartime marriage of academe and the military, serving what would later be called the military/industrial complex, must not be continued[2]. MIT soon did enter the funded research game as a major player but over time universities have realized, sometimes after painful incidents, that their culture of open discourse and peer review does not mesh with the secretive worlds of military and high-tech corporate development. Nowadays most American universities will not perform secret research; many of the great universities have instead fostered regional institutes and development corporations, "incubators" in which the academic knowhow of the university can be utilized in development of discoveries that are not subject to open review until declassified and/or patented. When patentable devices are developed, complex guidelines attempt to assure academic integrity as well as the commercial interests of the institution.

The highly bureaucratic and often arcane partnerships just described may seem removed from questions of civic participation and fraternal emotion with which we started, and it is reasonable to ask whether some "military/industrial complex" collaborations are not both corrupting and threatening to the common welfare. But they deserve a place in this narrative because they include mechanisms by which political, technical and policy consensus on certain large priorities involving medical or other uses of science is sometimes reached. And occasionally, when partners combine to pursue a "war" on a childhood disease or on dis-functional schools, projects that the public can readily grasp, a long list of collaborators helps in engaging wider support for that campaign.

3. The War on Poverty

The next major step in American three-sector partnering on a large scale was Lyndon Johnson's "War on Poverty," where non-profits operating under contract began to deliver a large portion of the new social services that governments created at all levels. Day care centers, training programs for the unemployed, and other social services were created, in many cases funding older or newly created non-profits to deliver expanded services. The infusion of funds enlarged the mission of the Third Sector partners as well as that of the governments involved. Some religious organizations used their separate non-denominational organizations (like Catholic Charities) to accept government funds within the limits of the First Amendment; commercial operators provided services as well, sometimes as subcontractors to non-profits. All partners negotiated within a complicated web of legalisms and restrictions.

When the "Reagan Revolution" cut War on Poverty programs in 1980, those steps were accurately perceived as withdrawal of services that poor and marginalized people concretely needed, and both clients and providers often fought for at least partial restoration. (In fact, some of the contraction had started in the Carter years for budgetary reasons.) Many of the canceled services continued under the rubric of the "New Federalism," block grants to the states that sustained many of the same sorts of programs at moderately lower funding levels with the same mix of for-profit and nonprofit contractors. A major difference from the New Deal implementation of social relief programs, aside from the wider diversity of the War on Poverty efforts, was that the most famous New Deal programs involved direct governmental hiring and administration. The War on Poverty made heavy use of the familiar mechanisms of grants and contracts to commercial and non-profit contractors alike, as do successor programs. At this writing approximately one third of the income of all charities in the U.S. derives from government grants[3]. These funds may be largely federal in origin but often are mixed with state or regional matching funds for purposes ranging from affordable housing to after-school care for children of low-income working mothers to disability services. The extensive web of both for-profit and non-profit contractors, many of which are awarded funds under competitive mechanisms, allows for limitation of the federal and state employment rolls and sometimes encourages entrepreneurial program development. It also can excuse failure to fund important local needs on the grounds that applications were weak or that program budgets ran out while serving other programs. This can means that communities less polished in their bureaucratic skills or political contacts are further disadvantaged. The governmental funds involved are rarely ample, so that a widespread pattern for sophisticated non–profits is to add fundraising to their budget mix, resulting in a hopefully stable mixture of private and public funding. A glance at the mix of governmental and Third Sector provision of social services in other nations, including Britain and the Scandinavian countries, indicates that a parallel but less extensive mixed model has developed. In some instances, for example in Japan, conservative political leaders have pushed for expansion of the Third Sector as a way of reducing government expenditure on social services[4].

I was a college grants officer for a public university during the "Reagan Revolution" years, 1980 onward. What occurred from my perspective was not that corporations or individuals greatly increased their voluntary support of social services— that hope was always a chimera—but that foundations and sophisticated corporate givers re-focused more narrowly, identifying core project areas or (in social services) seeking projects that could be seen as models for eventual support by governments if the climate changed once again. In fact, patterns of corporate charity were already changing in an opposite direction from Mr. Reagan's assumption. In a previous era, the charity committee of a corporate board might convene and agree rather casually to assist the board members' favored collegiate alma maters and to make modest gifts to a few local charities including the United Fund. Now and then a larger gift for a building campaign would be authorized, with prominent recognition of the donor company as a good neighbor. By 1980, strategic business questions were being asked more often. Local charities were aided—it is hard to back out of the United Way—but gifts beyond that began to support marketing strategies and the corporate mission, e.g. a cancer walk for a health care provider, nursing education for Johnson and Johnson, gerontology programs for insurer MetLife, sports stadium sponsorship for Pepsi-Cola, and so on. In these cases, giving was increasingly market-related and professionalized. In other instances, the focus turned more exclusively to the company's local community and enhancing employee identification with the company. Small gifts paralleling or directly supporting the volunteer interests of employees might be offered: for example, AT&T offered small grants to community organizations in which its employees volunteered. The purpose of such programs was to engage employees in their communities and with each other outside work, improving community relations and creating "social capital" within the workplace.

In large-scale philanthropy, a sharpened strategic focus as described above became the rule and a new breed of entrepreneur-philanthropists emerged as well, often successful individuals who wished to invest in and personally oversee projects such as small business incubators in distressed areas, a challenge that had been mostly abandoned as a federal government priority with the end of the War on Poverty. This last development was arguably a domestic version of the pattern already familiar in international development work by IGO's and NGO's, but it also reflected a newly stylish admiration for entrepreneurship while satisfying the donors' desire to be actively involved.

Arts organizations in the U.S., especially those in fine arts and classical music, are mostly found in the Third Sector: they rarely make much profit and their legal independence avoids disputes over artistic content that might occur if a city or county funded controversial exhibits directly. Non-profit status insulates them to a degree from the anti-intellectual instincts of American society in general while the deductible tax status is helpful to well-heeled patrons. Delicate balances are struck in support of arts by public funders: museums and symphonies are seen as ornaments and educational resources serving the general needs of a locale, but they also offer prestigious occasions for patronage by the wealthy, so that governments fund them with an expectation that donors will meet some needs. The commercial aspects are well understood on all sides; for instance, a great city needs museums, concert halls and theatres as attractors of "cultural tourism" and thus of income to hotels, fashionable stores, and restaurants. A frequent formula is that the concert halls and museums are non-profit while large commercial theatres and popular film houses are for-profit. Impressive marketing efforts are undertaken by all in collaboration with the city. Ironically, concerts in non-profit halls supported by local government are often priced out of range for many local residents but attract tourists and those locals who are well-to-do; discount days or senior's or children's matinees attempt to strike a balance and make the prestigious arts resources more democratically available. Because the fine arts audience in such areas as classical music is so heavily composed of the very well-to-do, there is little concern about the fact that some arts, especially famous presenters of classical music and big-city professional theatre, are priced out of the average citizens' reach. Museums are often not out of the ordinary citizens' range, precisely because there is a public funds contribution.

Many relatively wealthy individuals, including politically conservative business and professional people whose national political spokesmen ritually oppose arts funding, are enthusiastic members of the symphony or the museum so that modest political support for government underwriting of major organizations has been stable in city after city. The wealthy patron and the political partnerships are both crucial because cities in America, unlike European cities, generally have no inherent aesthetic commitments except perhaps in architectural and preservation matters; in the fine arts they are restrained by the longstanding strain of popular anti-intellectualism in the U.S. However, many individual major donors, even if they are politically allied with opponents of public arts funding, enjoy connoisseurship (a privilege of wealth) and visible association with other pillars of their community's high culture.

The result of all this interplay for the arts, which are a deep source of community for those who partake of them, has typically been steady but inadequate public funding of major presenting organizations and museums, with further needs met by memberships or donations in addition to ticket fees. The inadequate governmental funding that *is* provided, especially when given as competitive grants, is often important to donors and advertisers as a warrantor of quality and prudent fiscal management, for regulations come with governmental funding. Each partner's money thus has "leverage" to enhance the other partners' stake. As an example close to this writer, a smallish federal or state grant might be obtained for one major event within an arts festival like the Spoleto Festival in Charleston, South Carolina. This might require larger sums in "match," i.e. gifts from individual patrons and corporate sponsors marketing their name as good citizens. Ticket revenues are factored in, and the application for funds will have included an advertising plan for the event and projections for ad revenue from sale of programs. The public and private grants and donations obtained are attractive to advertisers and sponsors of the overall festival as confirming the quality of its various events. These confident sponsors help to attract the knowledgeable audiences that also buy dinners at local restaurants while staying at local hotels. Over time, pride and pleasure are such that the partners collaborate easily, whatever rationales they may offer for doing so. If official spokespersons talk about these arrangements, they offer ahappy mix of three themes: presentation of quality arts, a delight in itself; celebration of community through enjoyment of the arts; and the wide benefits of "arts tourism."

One further ironic result of both the War on Poverty, the following "Reagan Revolution," and more recent conservative initiatives against funding of social services is that some actors of the Third Sector have taken a more direct role in attempting to sway governmental policies than before. In recent years of anti-government sentiment, some service providers have adopted a new activism, lobbying in their own spheres or dramatizing how clients would be hurt by cutbacks. As an example from 2012, Catholic Charities, which in some regions brokers food distribution to soup kitchens hosted by various religious denominations, lifted its usually apolitical voice when Congress considered curtailing unemployment benefits as the recession lessened in severity: the need of those using unemployment compensation for food would overwhelm the church centers. A more broad-based example, started in the second Bush administration, was the effort to enable faith-based organizations to receive federal funds for social services with less red tape: many beneficiaries would be churches in rural communities, which are the only feasible operators of day care centers, literacy training, and so on but lack the bureaucratic structure to monitor and report on their use of governmental funds.

One important further implication of the "federalization" that followed on the Reagan Revolution, which canceled some services but passed much of the burden of social programs to the states, was that it undermined national discussion of the role of government in meeting social needs, Regular attacks from the right on the federal portion of funding, variation among the states, and arguments about states' autonomy made a coherent national discussion much more difficult. The Obama administration was able to pass a policy for universally available and reasonably priced health care, but at this writing it is hard to say that there has developed a clear national consensus on the right to health care, while states have taken sharply different tacks on implementing affordable insurance.

The marginally increased alertness to policy issues that now characterizes relatively apolitical Third Sector charities is part of a larger and perhaps alarming politicization of the vast sector, which at times seems to be carrying on the deliberative and advocacy roles of the political sphere because the latter is in so many ways paralyzed, unable to engage modern citizens in its old processes of debate and deliberation.

Partly due to U.S. Supreme Court decisions undoing limits on both indirect political campaign contributions, and partly because of the flourishing of social media, political non-profits have become vastly more prominent in recent years, adding to the polarization of the political climate and the expense of elections. Some of the non-profits are mere legal shells through which one or a few major donors funnel money for a preferred cause, such as anti-abortion legislation or against light rail systems. The major political parties use the same mechanisms, but to a degree are hobbled by their need to reflect the broad interests and needs of their constituencies, whereas the ideological or cause-based foundation speaks with unalloyed focus on one issue or one election.

Even with respect to more legitimate civil cause organizations, the question must be raised again about the nature of immersion in civic life that they offer. The relative ideological purity and single-issue focus of the new political organizations, both shell organizations and those with real memberships, allow tremendous pressure for or against one their issue and often one-issue candidates, with breadth of experience and willingness to compromise becoming a handicap for the veteran candidate. The parties, too, even if they offer the traditional alliances among their constituencies, must count the highly financed non-profits among their constituents. When a great deal of political interchange is a competition among media messages including tweets and Facebook pages aimed at citizens who seek no deeper sources of information, the wealthy propagandist outweighs thousands of his fellow-citizens in the volume of his free speech, shouting down debate and obstructing whatever reasonableness flows from talk and argument rumbling through the public space.

4. New Ways to Join or Give

In the current generation of Third Sector activity, and especially over the last decade or so, the constant interplay we sketched earlier, of mechanisms for individual or small-group action and of focused, sometimes arcane mechanism for delivery of social good (as defined by the sponsors) has been expressed in the expansion of methods of giving. The *Chronicle of Philanthropy* publishes an annual "Philanthropy 400" in imitation of the famous Fortune lists of the top 100 and 500 corporations: the 2015 survey recorded that the largest charity, but only by a slight margin, was the United Fund. Present in almost every community, it includes a significant volunteer dimension because employee volunteers solicit their peers in the workplace while local businesses and corporations also give, cheered on by recognition at Rotary or Chamber of Commerce meetings. However, two of the top ten charities were donor-advised funds, the largest being one operated by Fidelity Investments. Essentially a mutual fund categorized as a charity (and operating like a large grantmaking foundation in many respects), a donor-advised fund manages the investment and disbursement of major donors' charitable gifts. The donor chooses where his or her funds will be directed but the fund receives and filters applications for the money, standing between donor and applicants and handling tasks of monitoring and reporting. Additional articles in recent issues of the *Chronicle* recognize the rise of crowdfunding, a new option made possible by the popular technologies of social media, where individuals or groups can assemble online donations from a wide range of small donors. Crowdfunding, which is also used for small business start-ups, allows individuals without capital to start and carry through a brief campaign for a specific cause such as support for the victims of a well-publicized crime or disaster. A handful of businesses have arisen that facilitate crowdfunding appeals. We mentioned entrepreneurial social investment above as in some respects moving into the vacuum created by the end of the War on Poverty: these efforts include foundation portfolio investments in businesses that offer employment or new industries to communities of high unemployment, and potentially profitable entrepreneurial ventures with training programs in such communities. The *Chronicle* sums up the change from the point of view of donors who might consider their options in what I call below the Grand Bazaar of the Third Sector:

> When the Philanthropy 400 debuted (1991), you probably gave money to a non-profit. Today, the range of options has broadened to include impact-investments, for-profit social enterprises, independent

crowd-funded movements, and political social welfare groups—known as 501©(4)s that can pour unlimited dollars into elections.[5]

If some sense of fraternity (or even "social capital") is the issue, the concentrations of political influence in cause organizations, both the 401©(4)s and the older advocacy organizations, heighten the sense of constant confrontation in some parts of the Third Sector, arguably blurring what public consensus does exist on many issues. If the cause organizations are shells for one or a few rich people, they exert undue influence; if they truly represent a cadre of actively involved members, they have arguably both good and bad effects on civic culture. When at-a-distance cause organizations enlist interested citizens in issues such as animal protection or against torture or abortion, the members tend to be informed about their issue, which presumably means wider awareness of laws and leaders in general. As in much of life, it is hard even to be an "informed citizen" without specialization in some favorite issue and an organizational mechanism of immersion. The narrowly focused engagement is surely a plus for politics overall—certainly for international issues like global warming—but it probably tends to move joiners away from local participation in governance. Moreover, it is easily possible to be part of activist and even militant causes without ever participating in the back and forth of local discussion about various issues, so that the specialized engagement-at-distance may contribute to polarization. A decline of participation in ordinary local politics has coincided with the growth of these cause-based, ideologically insistent non-profits. Although the local decline fits the general pattern that Putnam and others described, blaming TV and limited time available to working couples and isolation tied to mobility. My amateur observation is that the split is not among locally focused participants and those with more national or global causes, for the latter have local and regional dimensions, but among those who have some engagement and those who have none and are more susceptible to in their cynicism, misinformation and rumor.

Non-engagement is a self-feeding pattern, just as engagement is. When I surveyed my American freshmen in recent years, admittedly not a scientific sample, a number were well up on national issues if it was a presidential election year, but almost none had ever taken part in local campaigns and few had campaigned even for a national candidate in their home community. Far more had taken part in organizing or assisting a charity event. I conclude that the ability to participate civically is not lacking but immersion in a setting where disagreements must be respectfully understood, and compromises made, was a rare experience.

Montesqieu has a quip somewhere to the effect that to those who do not understand them, republics always appear to be on the brink of chaos. In general, American political thinkers tend to assume that the buzz of civic talk and the competitions among innumerable voluntary associations is a long-term sign of civic health. Nonetheless it seems clear that, as Putnam and others warn, the growth and professionalization of Third Sector organizations does not in fact mean that "social capital" is increasing if that means connection with one's neighbors or what I call "capacity to act." If the Third Sector is a large part of our "public space" it is an *agora* so crowded and so noisy that we do not need to hear our neighbors or shop for ideas different from those we already hold. The new style of Third Sector political actors makes politics more strident and ever more dependent on sophisticated fundraising, while social-service and cultural organizations operate as mutually competitive arms of the system.

Chapter 15. The Grand Bazaar and the Public of Many Publics

To return to the simple distinction underlying these chapters, the easiest aspect of the third sector to imagine is of course the involvement of individuals or small groups exercising their "capacity to act," while the organizational networks and partnerships, like complex ecosystems, tend to be well understood only by experts in their special niches. Sometimes (as is true in any bureaucracy) they know only their specialty within their type of organization: professionals in one area such as international health may not know much more than the average citizen about how organizations in the arts or children's sports work except that gifts, grants, contracts and fundraising would be generally familiar. However, the broad commonalities in motives and in patterns of support lead to the hope that participants, whether volunteers or professionals, share an underlying, perhaps inchoate, humanistic ideology. While it is common in many societies for individuals who are deeply loyal to family or tribe to be indifferent to outsiders, third sector associations in modern civic societies almost always involve persuasion to act across social barriers. In many cases their rationale includes an explicit view of human community and/or human rights. While it is rarely possible to measure how widely or deeply those announced values penetrate the general public, one reason for our fascination with outbreaks of popular elation or sorrow that erase social divisions is that they suggest what power for solidarity lay unexpressed until that moment. The next few pages do not suggest a way to measure how the universal "spirit of brotherhood" resides within near-at-hand organizations for neighborliness, but it identifies a few common clues.

To begin with an elemental fact, stories are important across the spectrum, from local third sector charities to world human rights organizations. Picturing those who are aided by third sector activity and stories of people who took exemplary action make values concrete. Stories of need being served highlight the broad principle of generosity or justice at work; stories of individual involvement in providing that generosity or justice lie at the heart of claims for the importance of the third sector to civic culture. The two types of story taken together—that of the need and that of generous responders— are the immediately imaginable aspects of the fraternity motif that the third sector embodies, often embodying donors' or volunteers' ideal of their own relations to other humans.

Stories are especially relevant to the question of whether the needs of brothers and sisters at a distance arouse our determination to act. Although that arousal may be grounded in religious or ethical principles, it is given flesh and blood by imaginative sympathy reaching across the distance and is given practical expression by work with an association. For some participants this motive is sustained by intimate encounter with those who are helped, but for supporters who are less immediately involved stories must cement the sense of connection. In the great outbreaks that astonish or horrify us, participants are swept by the surging energy of a sect, team, or movement armed with myths and storied events, heroes' tales and songs endlessly repeated.

If that is a dramatic, easily imagined part of the fraternity motif in the third sector, the second part—especially as it works in large nations and internationally—is embodied in services and interactions through networks that involve little direct contact among donors, supporters or the clients served. These networks tend to reflect well-articulated ideals of national or international cooperation; supporters tend to be small publics interested in both the guiding principles and the specific issue addressed. Even to these informed audience the complexities of delivery and necessary alliances may be obscure. For this reason, foundations and other NGOs carrying out projects at distance look for ways to tell of heroic, tragic or sympathetic cases addressed by wise organizational activity. Organizations involved in such projects as combatting an eye disease in Africa or labor abuses in South Asia mix governmental with non-governmental actors and navigate bureaucracies, but they also use marketing tools at home and in the target locale to work against lack of public awareness and political apathy or resistance. Like local volunteer agencies in the U.S., the international NGOs that work on esoteric problems or in exotic-seeming places must constantly re-enlist and educate a base that includes individuals and allied organizations and often governments. The appeals are both to principles of humanity and to supporters' sympathetic imagination, but in many cases the professionals involved make the policy case of long term mutual benefits, e.g. in climate policy and infectious disease control.

Among the stories that third sector actors tell, those that picture volunteers and donors are always celebratory. In thanking and recognizing the outstanding volunteer an organization meets several goals at once: it re-enlists its members, for thanks is the coin in which they are paid; it publicizes its mission, for the story of the volunteer is the compelling story of the compassion that sees the need for the soup kitchen or the nobility of the overseas mission. That celebration also characterizes the tribute-giving organization as harmonious and well led. The process of recognition and of publicity through giving thanks is seen at all levels, from the local food bank's Volunteer of the Month to national awards for exemplary individuals and organizations. Thus, President George H.W.Bush established a national recognition ceremony called "A Thousand Points of Light" which has continued annually, a commendable program though it reflected the Reagan-era political preference for delivery of social services by volunteer agencies rather than government. Thanking is part of graceful management and is sometimes jealously expected and valued across the Third Sector; this is especially true at the local level and in relatively restricted communities of supporters, so that the mayor who fails to thank the Rotary volunteers at the annual Rubber Ducky Race or the school principal who forgets to praise the PTA volunteers is soon unpopular. Talk is cheap, as we know, and these conventions most often resonate no further than their moment of delivery, but in them we hear time and again collective affirmation of mutual bonds and of generosity spirit.

The volunteer or individual donor enlisted to a good cause is usually a relatively simple case, whereas an accurate leadership profile is often a good deal more complex because it offers a view of the leader's cause and the attitudinal obstacles he or she faced. In case studies like those of Peter Drucker's *Managing the Non-Profit Enterprise* (1995)[1] the exemplary leader is often a person of dogged perseverance but also of multi-sided talents appropriate to the multiple constituencies that he/she must hold together. A leader who has had to change or update the mission of his or her third sector organization needs strategic vision, as might be true of any leader, but may have to politick with a series of constituencies including clients but also with third sector partners, politicians, government bureaucrats, and long-faithful supporters. The latter must be held in the fold, assured that amidst innovations the best traditions (e.g. of a college or a scout organization) are being preserved for a new era. This politicking within the circles of current and potential supporters blends with efforts at wider publicity to create public welcome for the organization's function; that in turn often involves serving as a public advocate for the religious, educational or artistic social values involved. Thus, a particularly eloquent third sector leader often becomes a recognized spokesperson for the relevant social value as well as for his/her organization. At the level of organizational management, many organizations in the third sector feature thin leadership ranks so that the major symphony maestro, museum director or university president who can both manage and advocate in public takes on special authority: he or she may become the only trusted decision-maker for collaborators from outside the organization and may be something of a dictator within. A few major corporate leaders follow a like pattern, becoming recognized spokespersons for business in general or for their industry, but a difference is that the non-profit leader is constantly engaged in public advocacy for his or her cause as a social value.

A further difference of great importance is that the ordinary volunteer rarely challenges the system that makes soup kitchens or comparable charities necessary[2], so that the climates within third sector service organizations and within those dedicated to reform are quite different. The leader of a service organization, whether for health or service to the homeless or to higher education, might morph into a crusader but because that transformation is sure to alienate some donors and participants, he or she is often unwilling to shift to political critique if it makes the organization seem partisan. In this respect many service charities are liable to the old accusation that philanthropy sustains an unfair system by palliating its damages; the leader who becomes a notable spokesperson for change from within his or her sector is often adept at straddling the opposite sides of the leadership role, delivering services and criticizing social policy at the same time.

Given the constant flow of ideals and needs expressed, one can imagine an innocent citizen discovering the third sector as a tourist discovers the Grand Bazaar of Istanbul or comparable great markets of the world: a sea of hawkers enticing anyone who seeks a satisfying way to be generous. Instead of the tangled streets of rug sellers and lanes of spice merchants, he or she encounters avenues of health advocates and providers, lanes of political reformers, district after district of sports clubs, and so on. To the astonished newcomer the scene would be noisy and chaotic, with offerings too numerous to take in and every sector highly duplicative. On some streets the sales pitches would be aggressive, as hawkers sell not spices but the urgency of the moment; yet once the newcomer grows accustomed, he sees that most of the districts are orderly, with regular customers and a good deal of mutual helpfulness among the merchants. The panoply of the bazaar touches almost every imaginable human activity in some way. Of course, in most citizens' lives the sense of the bazaar's variety is missing because we fall into volunteer or cooperative activities close to our interests, perhaps as friends or neighbors enlist us. Except for the moments of public thanks mentioned above, the cases which we pause to notice are the radical ones when a neighbor leaps headlong into a burning social movement or makes a sudden decision to preach the Gospel in a jungle village.

What the image of the bazaar does not hint at is the regulations and legal powers, the bureaucratic politicking and alliances, and the arcane expert activity that express the networks underlying fraternity in pragmatic action. That complexity is most visible in national advocacy organizations and in international NGO's precisely because there scope is large and enduring; they are not the easy affiliations that citizens drift in and out of.

A considerable academic industry has devoted effort and study to describing and analyzing the multiple splinters of the third sector within and among nations and to gauging the functionality (or malfunctions) of the whole as a locus of civic culture. A useful survey is Jon Van Til's *Growing Civil Society: From Non-Profit Sector to Third Space* (2006). Van Til, who had previously devoted a book to "mapping" the Third Sector, in this work attempted to include third sector activity of other nations in highlighting the sector's centrality to civic participation. When the question of civic health arises, the vast diversity of associations needs to be considered because that world includes far more than the formally registered non-profits. The identifier "non-profit" is helpful for research purposes but that tax law related designation does not tell much about levels of citizen involvement and misses more associations than it includes. Van Til notes[3] that there were 1.5 million non-profits in the U.S. at the time of his writing but that this number, large as it is, is far smaller than the total of over nine million grass-roots organizations that are estimated to fulfill comparable functions in communities. A great number of charitable or civic organizations including neighborhood associations, sports clubs and youth teams are not registered as non-profits, and many organizations come under other tax designations, such as cooperatives, credit unions and mutual benefit societies that do not exist mainly for profit and often involve unpaid citizen boards. Again, many local and regional governmental organizations such as public schools use volunteer advisory boards and unpaid governing boards, along with booster clubs.

In some realms of social service, research, and cultural engagement it makes little difference whether an organization is a non-profit, commercial, or governmental. Thus, hospitals are organized and run as businesses and/or research centers in about the same way regardless of their governance and support mechanisms because regulations and professional standards demand the same procedures. Public and private universities, too, are almost identical in organization and functions; and many arts organizations and museums operate with comparable structures and donor and volunteer relations regardless of tax status. The fact that the associational sector includes so many organizations that are not registered non-profits highlights the surprisingly fluid and sometimes improvisatory nature of the organizations and their activity. Van Til suggests the usage "third space" for the non-commercial non-governmental associational world, including registered non-profits and the heterogenous others. He also notes that European usage for the mixture of governmental social and cultural services along with voluntary associations acting in the same realms is the "social economy." The term is more sensible than "third sector" but uncomfortable for American usage because it suggests a consensus on ways to meet citizens' needs that has been contested. Moreover, the oppositional power of the third sector has been highlighted in American thought for its sheltering of fringe religions, utopian movements, unpopular reforms and unpopular opinions reaching beyond or changing the social "economy."

In a recent article on Mark Zuckerberg's entry into large scale philanthropy, James Surowiecki has in effect argued that the sheer diversity is useful. He argues that foundations not only identify unmet needs and possible solutions but address social emergencies when government is paralyzed by party conflicts or simply too slow to act on a new need.

> In an ideal world, big foundations might be superfluous. But in the real world they are vital because they are adept at targeting problems that both the private sector and the government often neglect.... [P]rivate interests often derail the public interest, and governments are far less effective at tackling global problems.... [Moreover,] eradicating malaria or providing universal Internet access...may not produce results for decades. Politicians...worry about being reelected every few years.[4]

This view harks back in some respects to Tocqueville's argument two centuries earlier that government could not possibly authorize beforehand all the creative initiatives undertaken by individuals free to associate. In the non-profit space alone, the multitude of needs and opportunities as well as possible strategies to meet them is arguably greater than the deliberative processes of democracy and the measured steps of bureaucracies can address even when willing. In the realms of medicine and environmental science, where diseases to be attacked are numerous and concerns ranging from threatened species to global warming are many, the associational world addresses a larger range of issues than governmental structures can readily meet, ideally setting the stage for a reasoned official filtering of large from small societal priorities so that the most important can be addressed.

Regardless of what metaphor we use, space or bazaar or social economy, if one argues (as I do here) that the diversity of emerging causes is better addressed in this apparently chaotic process than in a centralized process, that creativity comes with drawbacks: for one. society may not arrive at the best priorities but only the loudest acclaimed. Furthermore, in nations that have reached a somewhat stable relation of third sector service providers and government providers, the activity of voluntary service organizations has relieved governments of obligation to fully provide needed services, thereby reducing taxes. Achieving this is a conservative political formula that in U.S. history was associated with the Reagan presidency, but in many nations it is now a stable pattern. It is arguably a way of denying social needs or meeting them minimally, as when the burden of meeting family hunger rests on food kitchens. Those who tax themselves by volunteering time or money shoulder an excessive share of the societal burden while others are free to be uninvolved, and national fraternal issues go unaddressed.

What is true of the two great themes of third sector history in the U.S.—that it is much easier to imagine the activation of personal capacity than the organizational net—is especially true in international expressions of fraternity through NGO's and their partnerships with IGOs and governments. With brotherhood more than with other grand ideals it has always been hard to see how local customary civic and familial fraternities relate to the "spirit of brotherhood" with people who are distant in space or who stand across class or cultural divides: that is one of the problems with which this book started. Yet many remarkable moments of popular enthusiasm and compassion reaching across borders have been ignited by stories of need and pictures of those in distress. Connections flowering across geographic and cultural distances are difficult to build on systematically, but one of the remarkable aspects of o ur theme is precisely that in so many famines, disasters and persecutions it has been possible to ignite the imagination of significant publics and the action of networks able to step in.

"Publics" in the "Public Space"

For the purpose of imagining the third sector as a space of fraternity but especially for imagining the international "space," it is useful to distinguish "societies" from "publics," a distinction drawn by historian of international relations Jennifer Mitzen in *Power in Concert: The Nineteenth Century Origins of Global Governance* (2013)[5]. Examining the roots of cooperative action among European states in the nineteenth century and the growth of global governance since, Mintzen argues that when major powers opposed to Napoleon agreed to "act in concert" they not only succeeded in their main goal but carried on the process for several decades, providing a source of stability in Europe and moderating their balance of power competition. She argues that the process of conferral towards concerted action had its own dynamic, as each nation had to prepare to understand the interests of the others and to work toward "concert." Part of the reason for the importance of the process was that it expanded several overlapping "publics" that began to influence international relations. The closest "public" to the process of conferral was the world of diplomats and other concerned governmental leaders and bureaucrats who, as they became professionalized, might have more in common with each other than with their rulers at home. They had to demonstrate skills of interaction with each other and interpret the aims of different partners to the home government, and naturally tended to want a concerted result for their efforts. Less powerful nations were eager for their representatives to take part in conferencing with the great powers, expanding the professionally engaged "public." A second ring of interested and vocal observers had begun to develop with publication of treaties in the eighteenth century: a thin but widely distributed public of intellectuals, journalists, and legal specialists. In the relatively democratic nations, these small but internationally engaged and highly articulate followers soon overlapped with the growing domestic audiences: legislators, voters, and general readers of the world's news. Global governance, says Mitzen, has advanced partly because these overlapping "publics" supported the growth of the current system.

In the contemporary situation, attention to "publics" is useful in conceiving how supportive groupings backstop international NGO's and IGO's as they attempt to extend the pragmatic "spirit of brotherhood" beyond national borders. The IGO's may have policymakers and officials in numerous countries attending to and supportive of their work; the same is true of NGO's, which are extremely numerous and involve multiple small but often dedicated publics. (Mintzen points out that national societies are relatively "thick," with webs of constant interaction and shared culture, whereas international society is "thin.") National societies are the scenes in which we can imagine "social capital" as a fair substitute for *fraternite'*, but international society certainly exists and is dense with relationships in specific spheres, following on uncountably many commercial relations, legal and financial protocols, media interpenetration, and ease of travel.

Mintzen's account of the professional diplomatic "public" and that of intellectuals and political thinkers beyond that specialized sphere reminds us immediately that a wide and influential "public" existed that had shared the ideas of the great *philosophes*, satirists, and artistic dreamers in the generations before the American and French revolutions. Readers of Locke, Voltaire, Rousseau or Paine would lead what Jefferson in the *Declaration* of *Independence* called "the opinion of mankind," a universal public due "decent respect" that would judge the American revolt against England as justified. In some nations, the visionaries and satirists who created the spirit of the Enlightenment were joined by religious figures like Wesley who were more interested in compassion for the poor than in destruction of heresy. The great writers and thinkers who created this public, which was pan-European, did not engage in international diplomacy but often had powerful voices in general policy, providing a broad "public" that the narrower coteries of experts and participants might be forced to heed. Mintzen notes that even at the start of the era of emergent global governance, the overlap with large national "publics" was sometimes important: as her major example, the European great powers would have joined in suppressing the Greek Revolution but that the philhellenic English public, attitudes shaped by artists and thinkers including Byron, led the British government to support the Greeks and refuse action in concert..

In the modern world, complicated "publics" of national officials, diplomats, and IGO staffs attempt to meet global issues from fisheries regulation to global warming to intervention in regional and civil wars. These publics intersect with an international "public" of professionals in comparable fields and state diplomats, but also draw on national organizations that influence national constituencies in almost every nation. This is true across a spectrum from commercial exchanges and shipping rules to fisheries, travel regulation, public health safeguards, and environmental policy. Mintzen notes with respect to NGO's that the realm of non-state actors is so great with respect to some issues that diplomatic professionals dealing with formal relations of nation to nation often find it hard to be sure who must be included or consulted. The ambiguity—the apparent chaos of voices—is familiar to anyone who considers how the third sector, commercial, and governmental actors interact on a politically lively domestic issue in a large democracy. As an example, the issue of global warming attracts great conferences involving large and small nations, international governmental agencies, hundreds of national and international NGO's and hundreds or even thousands of recognized observers from cities and research centers. For many of the thousands of participants their assemblage reflects a conviction that the shared human inheritance is the whole earth and all of earth's species. Participants return home, or track the conferences from afar, then lobby their governments and inform their domestic publics. At the same time, involved national officials try to foster new policies and at the least orient governmental colleagues to issues that are afoot across the globe.

In sum, while the brotherhoods of a global "society" are hard to imagine in terms analogous to traditional notions of the fraternal nation with its thick bonds, a kind of "society" does exist internationally and its common mind, its emerging sense of proper treatment of mankind, is extended in the "publics" that share stories, images and remembered principles. Treaties, declarations, and sustained dialogue among the smaller publics interested in causes or in world affairs express mutual recognition of human needs even as action "in concert" deepens the bonds. Amidst it all, the humanistic empathy with the individual that is the typical focus of arts, media and much of education sometimes operates like a beneficent virus, carrying the grand ideas and the stories of individuals and villages, of human loss and human potential that are the deeper wellspring of the "spirit of brotherhood." None of these factors acts without a context of idealism, and that context—that overarching commitment—is permanently necessary for fraternity to prevail among the inextricably connected nations of a planet growing smaller.

Footnotes

Introduction

[1] T.V.Smith and E.C. Lindemann, *The Democratic Way of Life*, rev. ed.(New York, New American Library, 1951), pp.20-21.

[2] Wilson Carey McWilliams, *The Idea of Fraternity in America* (University of California Press, Berkeley, 1973) p. 8.

[3] Robert D. Putnam, *Bowling Alone: The Collapse and Revival of American Community* (Simon and Shuster, New York 2000), p.351.

[4] See Baggio's summary in Antonio Maria Baggio, "The Forgotten Principle: Fraternity in its Public Dimension," *Claritas, Journal of Dialogue and Culture*, Vol. 2, Article 8, htpps//docs.lib.purdue.edu/claritas/vol2/

[5] For an extensive summary, see Roderigo Mardones, "Fraternity in Politics: New Scholarship and Publications from Latin America," *Claritas, Journal of Tradition and Culture*, Vol 1 No. 2, p.201 at htpps//docs.lib.purdue.edu/claritas/vol 1/iss2/8/.

[6] Jason Horowitz, "Pope Calls for 'Fraternity' this Christmas," *New York Times*, December 26, 2018, p. A6.

[7] Lionel Barber, Henry Foy, and Alex Barker, "Vladimir Putin says liberalism has become obsolete," *Financial Times*, June 27, 2019. Htpps://www.ft.com/content/878d2344-9810-11e9-9573-ee5cbb98ea36.

Chapter 1

[8] The famous text *is I and Thou (1923)*. For the present study, Buber's account of his debt to romantic philosophers in *Between Man and Man* (1936) is even more helpful.

[9] Plato, *Plato: Six Great Dialogue.* (Mineola, New York, Dover, 2007) p. 30.

[10] *Aristotle, The Politics*, trans. Benjamin Jowett. socserv2.socscimcmaster.ca/econ/ugem/3113/Aristotle/Politic s.pdf, *p.6.*

[11] The relevant discussion occurs in the early chapters of Locke's *Two Treatises of Government*.

[12] Discussion of family models (in scripture or fictional prehistory) is found in the early chapters of *The Social Contract.*

6. John Locke, *A Letter Concerning Toleration*, in *Two Treatises of Government and A Letter Concerning Toleration*, ed. Ian Shapiro, Yale, New Haven 2003, p. 224.

[14] Ibid. p. 248

[15] Hannah Arendt, *The Human Condition,* Doubleday Anchor, NY 1959 (1958) p. 232.

[16] Ibid. p. 233.

[17] Smith, T.V. pp.22-23.

[18] Adam Smith, *Theory of Moral Sentiments*, http:/quad.lib.umich.edu/e/ecco. p. 213.

Chapter 2

[1] In John Kekes, *The Enlargement of Life: Moral Imagination at Work* (Ithaca, Cornell U. Press 2010).

[2] A slightly mawkish, staged example relevant to our theme when we come to American fraternity: on the fiftieth anniversary of the Battle of Gettysburg, national reconciliation was exemplified by having the confederate veterans march along the meadow of Pickett's disastrous charge, climbing the ridge that few rebels originally gained, where union veterans met and embraced them. President Wilson offered a speech of enthusiasm for the completion, finally, of reunification of the nation.

[3] Isaiah 45:6 in *New American Bible, World Publishing, 1987, p. 785.*
[4] Harry Orlinsky*, Ancient Israel.* (Ithaca, Cornell University Press) P.144.
[5] This is from the 2013 Easter Sermon, "Apostolic Exhortation"; reprinted in in *C21 Resources*, Fall 2014, p. 6.
[6] Arendt, p. 65 ff.
[7] Faulkner. Nobel Prize Address, 1956.
[8] Rushdie is of course well-known, as is the fatwah against him issued by Ayatollah Komeini. Bao Dai is one of the best known and most available (in English) writers exiled or suppressed after Tianammen Square. Baraheni, the leading Iranian intellectual of his generation, drew world attention when his poetry described imprisonment and torture by the Shah's regime (*God's Shadow: Prison Poems*, 1976): he returned to Iran in 1980 with hopes of democracy and suffered decades of suppression and persecution under Khomeni before escaping to Canada.
[9] "What is better adapted than the festive use of wine, in the first place to test, and in the second place to train the character of a man...?" Plato, T*he Laws,* Book I, classics.mit.edu/Plato/laws.1i/html.
[10] Mark Twain, "The Man That Corrupted Hadleyburg," *The Complete Short Stories* (Alfred Knopf, New York 1957) p.415.

Chapter 3

[1] My description of the needy participant draws heavily on Hoffer's *The True Believer* (Harper, New York 1951) which followed nineteenth century French interpretations of political and religious extremism as psychologically identical.
[2] George Packer, "The Other France: Are the Suburbs of Paris Incubators of Terrorism?" *The New Yorker* August 31, 2015,

p. 69.

[3] Ibid, p. 69.

[4] The American Civil Rights Movement in the South, especially in the late fifties and sixties, the era of sit-downs and protest marches, relied heavily on Negro youth of teen to college years. In many communities the parents would be fired from their jobs as handymen, domestics or low-paid clerks if seen demonstrating, but teenagers were not in that danger and also moved through the community half-observed. They were very brave and very disciplined. I taught a few remarkable young men who had had these teen leadership roles before reaching college age when I taught at Morehouse College in the late 1960's.

[6] Edmund Burke, *Reflections on The French Revolution,* www.constitution.org/eb.rev_fran.htm, p. 58.

[7] See DeTocqueville's *The Revolution of 1848.* Students coming to see the U.S. Senate or House of Representatives in session are often astonished to see only a handful of people there, who are not listening but conferring about their own later speeches or submissions of some document.

[8] Simon Shama, *Citizens: A Chronicle of the French Revolution* (Vintage, New York, 1989).

[9] W. Glenn Gray, *The Warriors: Reflections on Men in Battle* (Harper, Ny. 1970: first published without Arendt's introduction in 1959). Gray's discussion of implied immortality runs through Chapter Two, "The Enduring Appeals of Battle."

[10] Ibid. p.xiii, Arendt's introduction was added for the 1970 paperback edition.

Chapter 4

[1] Plato, *Six Dialogues.* Trans. Benjamin Jowett (Mineola, N.Y. Dover Publications,2007) p. 182.

[2] Ibid. p. 141.
[3] Ibid., p. 144
[4] Shama (*Citizens*) emphasizes the violence of the Revolution from the first, denying the notion that it was joyous and turned cruel.
[5] Plato, p. 162.
[6] "The Gospel According to John," *The New American Bible* (World Publishing,1987) Ch13, V8 ff.
[7] John 13, 31
[8] John 13, 34
[9] John 17,11
[10] John, 16,13
[11] John, 13/21
[12] John, 21/22

Chapter 5
[1] Wordsworth, William, "The French Revolution as it Appeared to Enthusiasts at its Commencement," ll. 3-5 (1805) also appears in Book Eleven of *The Prelude, in Collected Works of Wordsworth*, ed. E. DeSelincourt (London, 1936), p. 746.
[2] Elias Canetti, *Crowds and Power* trans. Carol Stewart (Continuum, NY 1978. Originally published 1960), p. 22.
[3] From "The Second Coming," in *The Collected Poems of W.B. Yeats* (Macmillan, NY 1956), p.185.
[4] From an unpublished poem of mine, "Wise Wolf."
[5] Thomas Rochon, *Culture Moves: Ideas, Activism, and Changing Values* ((Princeton U. Press, 1998) offers a detailed analysis of how small activist groups trigger larger movements.

Chapter 6

[1] Fredrick Engels, *Socialism: Utopian and Scientific* (1880).

Reprinted in
www.marxists.org/archive/marx/works/download/Engels_Soc
ialism_Utopian_and_Scientific.pdf p. 20.
[2]Ibid, p28.
[3] James Russell Lowell, "The Present Crisis," ll. 4-5,
www.poemhunter.com/poem.
[4] See Ischay, P. 189 ff. p. 191.
[5] A remarkable figure of the intersecting and competing
crosscurrents is Sir Roger Casement, knighted for his report
on atrocities in the Belgian Congo. He believed that British
imperialism was different from that of other nations but
concluded that Ireland was oppressed and was hanged for
conspiring with Germany to provide guns for the 1916 Easter
uprising. Possible protests to his sentence were muted by
blackmail as his diaries revealed his homosexuality. The story
is told in Adam Hochschild, *King Leopold's Ghost* (1998).
[6] Ishay, p.236.

Chapter 7
[1] *Collected Works of Wordsworth*, ed. E. DeSelincourt
(London, 1936), p. 746. All subsequent quotations from
Wordsworth are from this edition. *The Prelude* was drafted in
1805 but not published until 1850. The major dialogic work
by which the poet was better known in his lifetime, *The
Excursion*, is even more obviously Shaftesburyan but turns to
religious apologetics. It features dialogues among friends in a
sublime mountain setting that convert a misanthrope—a
victim of excessive optimism about human nature, a former
Revolutionary idealist—to draw on his love of nature and his
empathy with a grieving young boy so that his social instincts
revive. The misanthrope, the character who hates human
nature, is found repeatedly through eighteenth century and
Romantic literature, a problem for the sentimental writer to
account for (and sometimes heal).

2 My thanks to Prof. Antonio DiRenzo for pointing this out.
3 More relevant to our theme than *The Wealth of Nations* is Smith's ethical theory. Smith based his ethics on natural sympathy between humans, developing the Shaftesburyan notion of how the judgments of others regulate extreme passions: "As to love our neighbor as we love ourselves is the great law of Christianity, so it is the great precept of nature to love ourselves only as we love our neighbor, or what comes to the same thing, as our neighbor is capable of loving us." Adam Smith, *The Theory of Moral Sentiments,* http:/quad.lib.umich.edu/e/ecco. p. 24.
4 The relation between the "Soliloquy" and actual creation of literary characters in 18th century fiction is analyzed by Rebecca Tierney-Hynes, "Shaftesbury's *Soliloquy*: Authorship and the Psychology of Romance," *Eighteenth Century Studie.*s Vol. 38, No. 4 (Spring 2005), p. 605-622.
5 See William Robert Scott, *Francis Hutcheson*, and also Peter Kirby, ed. *Francis Hutcheson: an Inquiry Concerning Beauty, Order, Harmony, Design* (The Hague, 1973).
6 "The Privilege of Ourselves: Hannah Arendt on Judgment" in *Hannah Arendt: The Recovery of the Public World*, ed. Melvin A. Hill, (New York, 1979), p. 262'
7 As for MacBeth's "signifying," his successor became the founder of the Stuart line of kings, and *MacBeth* was first staged shortly after James VI of Scotland became James I of England, uniting the kingdoms in a providentially significant historic moment. Modern audiences, of course, don't catch that compliment to the new king.

Chapter 8

1 This essay is a revision of an article, Paul Hamill, "Other People's Faces: English Romantic Poets and the Paradox of Fraternity" published in Studies in Romanticism (Vol. 17, no.

4, 1978)

[2] Arendt's discussion is found in *On Revolution* (New York, Viking Press 1963).

[3] This and other quotations are from *The 1850 Prelude,* in *The Poetical Works of Wordsworth.* Ed. Thomas Hutchinson and Ernest DeSelincourt (London, Oxford University Press). I have placed the chapter and line numbers next to the passages.

[4] "Lines Composed Upon Westminster Bridge, September 3, 1802" http://www.poetryfoundation.org/poem/174783.

[5] Thomas Hutchinson, ed., *The Complete Works of Percy Bysshe Shelley* (Oxford, Oxford University Press, 1921) p. 214.

[6] From Blake's "London" W. H. Stevenson, ed., *The Poems of William Blake* (London, Harlow, Longman, 19710), p.213.

[7] Blake "The Human Abstract, from *Songs of Experience* http://www.poetryloverspage.com/poets/blake/human_abstract.html

[8] *The Confessions of an Opium-Eater*. Ed.Ernest Rhys (London, Everyman's Library, 1907) pp. 239-40.

[9] This is the last line of Coleridge's poem "The Lime-Tree Bower, My Prison."

[10] *The Complete Poems and Plays of T.S. Eliot, 1909-1950* (New York, Harcourt, Brace, and World, 1962) p. 39.

[11] "In a Station of the Metro," http://www.bartleby.com/104/106.html.

Chapter 9

[1] Robert Bellah et al., *Habits of the Heart: Individualism and Commitment un American Life* (Berkeley, U. of California Press, 1985)

[2] *Writings of Washington* Vol 26, "Circular to the States," (1783).

[3] This is an argument made by Jeremy Suri, in *Liberty's*

Surest Guardian: American Nation-building from the Founders to Obama (Simon & Shuster, NY 20011).

[4] Emerson, "Politics" www.emersoncentral.com/texts/essays-secondseries/politics.

[5] John C. Fremont, *Memoirs of My Life* (Cooper Square,New York, 2001 orig.886), p. 280

[6] The "melting pot" image has become less popular as it implies loss of cultural differences: in its time, however, it reflected the charismatic technology of the day, steelmaking. The melting pot in steel production iron, slag, and alloys to create a metal stronger than iron. The implication of the metaphor was not dissolution of traditions, but creation of a populace toughened in the fires of travail and competition, stronger than any of its predecessors.

[7] Longfellow, "The Courtship of Miles Standish" www.hwlongfellow.org/poems *A Searchable Database of Longfellow Poems (*The Maine Historical Society, n.d.)

[8] Walter Scott, "The Lay of the Last Minstrel," www.poets.org/lay-last-minstrel

[9] Citations are from "The Hasty Pudding: A Poem in Three Cantos" http://www.poemhunter.com/poem/the-hasty-pudding/Barlow source

[10] "America the Beautiful" by Katherine Lee Bates underwent several revisions after its first composition in the 1893. The story is told in a Wikipedia article, "America the Beautiful." Lines warning against excessive greed in the early version include: "Til selfish gain no longer stain/The banner of the free!"

[11] Longfellow, "Paul Revere's Ride," www.hwlongfellow.org/poems *A Searchable Database of Longfellow Poems (*The Maine Historical Society, n.d.)

[12] William T. Sherman, *Memoirs* (New York, Barnes and Noble, 2005) p. 777.

[13] Eric Hoffer, *The Ordeal of Change* (Harper and Row, New

York 1963), p. 117.

[14] Evangeline" www.hwlongfellow.org/poems *A Searchable Database of Longfellow Poems* (The Maine Historical Society, n.d.)

[15] "Maud Muller" in http://www.poemhunter.com/john-greenleaf-whittier/ll.105-06.

[16] See David Nasaw, *Andrew Carnegie* (New York, Penguin, 2006) for Carnegie's pride in friendship with Herbert Spencer and Mathew Arnold (p. 240 ff.) and his delight in the New York circle in which he was welcome as a conversationalist (p. 305 et infra).

[17] Thus, the 1888 short story by Sarah Orne Jewett, "Miss Tempy's Watchers," in which two friends of a deceased woman, one poor and one well-off, spend the night watching the bier together and begin to appreciate each other.

[18] Lowell, "The Present Crisis," op. cit.

[19] Ibid.

[20] Harrington, Patrick, *The Other America: Poverty in the United States. (*New York, McMillan, 1962).

[21] Longfellow, "Evangeline", www.hwlongfellow.org/poems *A Searchable Database of Longfellow Poems (*The Maine Historical Society, n.d.), ll. 987-998.

[22] John G Whittier, "Snowbound," http://www.poetryfoundation.org/poem/174758.

[23] Ibid. It is the teacher's initiative and cleverness, not any conflict in status between peddler and teacher, that Whittier notices.

Chapter 10

[1] All citations are from *Leaves of Grass* (New York, Collector's Library Edition, 2004). This is a reprint of the final or "deathbed" edition. In cases where a long poem of many sections is cited, I give the line number as well as the page number.

[2] For a discussion of some of the political implications of Ossian, See Thomas Curley, *Samuel Johnson, the Ossian Fraud, and the Celtic Revival in Great Britain and Ireland* (Cambridge and New York: Cambridge U. Press 2009).
[3] McWillams, *The Idea of Fraternity in America.* (Berkeley, University of California, 1973) p.411.

Chapter 11

[1] Paul Fussell, *The Great War and Modern Memory* (1975), surveys the many disillusioned literary voices concerning the claims of the warring nations to represent civilized values.
[2] Ezra Pound, "E,P. Ode Pour L'Election De Son Sepulchre" Section IV. www.poetryfoundaiton.org/poem/44915.
[3] Ibid., Section V.
[4] T. S. Eliot, "The Wasteland," www.poetryfoundation.org/poem/176735.
[5] A mentor and generous adviser to many writers, Williams continued to work in free or self-invented verse forms but admired other approaches. As an instance of how the plurality of available styles freed up different talents, Williams advised the young Alan Ginsberg to give up writing formal verse because he was not doing it well; Ginsberg turned to the Whitmanesque forms that the San Francisco poets around Ferlinghetti were practicing.
[6] Louis Simpson, "Walt Whitman on Bear Mountain," http://www.poetryfoundation.org/poem/240772.
[7] In 1979, as one of many examples, Baraka, representing an Afrocentric Black Power position, was one of the featured artists at an international literary festival outside of Rome whose major celebrity was Yevgeni Yevtushenko, appearing along with Ginsberg and others. Yevtushenko had published recently "Babi Yar," exposing a slaughter of captured Polish officers by Russian invaders. The poets held an impromptu

press conference on the Spanish Steps, preliminary to the festival. Yevtushenko said to Baraka, "Let us recite some of our poems." Baraka and no book on hand and, like most American poets, had none of his own work by heart. "Then I shall recite some of yours" said Yevtushenko, who then delivered several of Baraka's poems along with his own. I take this as an example of the widespread international awareness of American poetry in the context of defenses of human rights. I hosted Baraka for a reading in the early 1980's and he told me the story.

[8] In addition to P.E.N., Amnesty International advocates for writers jailed for writing against their regimes, "Scholars at Risk" succors academicians who run afoul of their regimes, usually by writing truthfully about corruption, and "Cities of Asylum" supports resettlement and a writing residency to exiled creative writers for a year or more in a friendly city.

Chapter 12

[1] Peter Drucker, "The Third Sector—America's Non-Market Counterculture" in *The Social Contract* Vol 1 #2 (Winter 1990-1992), also www.thesocialcontract.com/artman2/publish/tsc0102/article_16_printer.shtml, p.2..

[2] Arendt's introduces the phrase, now widely used, in *Between Past and Future.*

Chapter 13

[1] Walter Isaacson, *Benjamin Franklin: An American Life* (New York, Simon & Shuster, 2003) p.56.

[2] See Bellah, p. 250 et infra. He quotes Madison: "Is there no virtue among us?...If there be not, no form of government can render us secure."

[3] DeTocqueville, p. 477.

[4] Readers unfamiliar with this patch of history will still recognize a few names associated with its later development. Sylvester Graham devised a cracker, still known by his name, that imitated the wheat-and-honey diet of John the Baptist in the desert (minus the locusts). A prohibition against coffee led C.W. Post to invent an ersatz coffee of parched grain, still sold as Postum; he started the healthy-cereal company that provides your Post Toasties. The most significant successor in preaching bible-conscious health emphasizing grains was popular health lecturer W.K. Kellogg.

[5] Mormonism was eventually an exception due to Joseph Smith's discovery that polygamy was permitted; he was eventually assassinated by a mob in Ohio, and the sect began searching for a more distant spot in which to establish their Zion.

6 Drucker, *The Social Contract*, op. cit.

[7] W.E.B. Dubois, *American Historical Review*, Vol 15, July 1910, pp. 781-99.

[8] "When the Union army and then the Freedmen's Bureau arrived in many parts of the South, black communities were already hard at work educating themselves...." *Liberty's Surest Guardian: Rebuilding Nations after War from the Founders to Obama* (Free Press: New York 2001) p. 76.

[9] An illustration of how the privacy of associations could be manipulated is that in South Carolina in 1948 the Democratic Party attempted to define itself as a private club, excluding blacks from voting in the Democratic primaries. Since the state was entirely controlled by the Democrats, the primary winner would always be assured election and blacks would have effectively no voice in state elections. A courageous federal judge, J. Waites Waring, overturned the arrangement along with many other efforts in succeeding years to sustain segregation; he was so thoroughly ostracized by Charleston

"society," in which he had been prominent, that on retirement from his judgeship he settled in New York City. Partly at the urging of the late Senator Fritz Hollings, he has recently been officially recognized in Charleston as a heroic figure of justice in his era.

[10] See Doris Kearns Goodwin, *No Ordinary Time: Franklin and Eleanor Roosevelt: The Home Front in World War II* (New York, Simon & Shuster, 1994). Many Southern white housewives in the 1940's believed that their black maids belonged to secret "Eleanor Roosevelt Clubs," whose purpose was to teach them to be uppity to their employers. A comparably virulent urban myth—a private truth uniting believers in racial resentment—marked the Obama presidency, when an estimated quarter of whites in Georgia and South Carolina were firmly convinced that Obama was a Muslim born outside the U.S. As with the "Eleanor Clubs" the rumors were encouraged by leaders for whom this secret truth was a bond with their political base.

[11] I am retelling this story as I saw it myself or heard it anecdotally: I was the College of Charleston's grants officer and a member of the group that hoped to save Avery, in part by finding federal planning grants for its museum activity.

[12] For Wilson's policies on segregation in federal employment see A.Scott Berg, *Wilson*, p. 306 ff.

[13] Figures in this chapter are drawn from the annual surveys of *The Chronicle of Philanthropy*.

[14] Andrew Carnegie, *The Gospel of Wealth*, carnegie.org/fileadmin/Media/Publications/PDF/THE_GOSP EL-OF-WEALTH-01.pdf, p.1.

[15] Ibid.

16. See Carol Loomis, "The $600 Billion Challenge" *Fortune* (16 June 2010).

[17] Feeney, a remarkably modest exemplar, is an Irishman who made billions developing the first airport duty-free shops and

then secretly transferred most of his holdings to a charitable foundation chartered in the Bahamas to assure anonymity. His foundation, Atlantic Philanthropies, donated hundreds of millions of dollars anonymously to higher education and medical research until a lawsuit by a partner required divulging the fact that he was no longer one of the world's richest men. Atlantic continues to support education and medical research in Australia, the Pacific rim and the U.S. including especially his alma mater, Cornell University.

Chapter 14

[1] The story of systematically coordinated, multi-centered advances in science as a major innovation is fragmentarily documented in the biographies of scientists involved, including (among others) Norbert Wiener's *I Am a Mathematician* (1956), which describes some of the interdisciplinary dialogue between Harvard and MIT faculty on cybernetics, information science, and neurology that Weaver, an eminent MIT mathematician before assuming foundation leadership, translated into an institutional partnership strategy. Some of the excitement for the scientists involved is expressed in Howard McCulloch, *Embodiments of Mind* (1965).

[2] I heard this anecdote from MIT's Prof. Jerome Lettvin.

4. A fairly stable figure from year to year according to the annual reports of the *Chronicle of Philanthropy*.

5. See Yasuo Takao, "The Rise of the 'Third Sector' in Japan," *Asian Survey* Vol. 41. No.2 (March/April 2001) pp. 290-309.

6. *The Chronicle of Philanthropy*, November 2015, p. 4

Chapter 15

1. Managing the Non-Profit Organization: Principles and

Practices (New York, Harper 1990)

2. Van Til, *Growing Civil Society: From Non-Profit Sector to Third Space* (2006) discusses the problem of mapping and nomenclature in more depth than can be offered here (pp.xii ff.). In other places he is particularly acerbic about the disinclination of charities, many of which are church-based, to challenge systematic causes of poverty and thus of hunger; See pp. 148 et infra.

3 Ibid. p.ix.

4. James Surowiecki, "in Defense of Philanthrocapitalism" *The New Yorker*, Dec 21 & 28, 2015, p. 40.

5. *Power in Concert: The Nineteenth Century Origins of Global Governance* (Chicago, U of Chicago Press 2013).

Works Cited or Referenced

Arendt, Hannah, *The Human Condition.* New York, Doubleday Anchor, 1959.
Aristotle: *The Politics*, trans. Benjamin Jowett. socserv2.socscimcmaster.ca/econ/ugem/3113/Aristotle/Politic s.pdf.
Baggio Antonio Maria, "The Forgotten Principle: Fraternity in its Public Dimension," *Claritas, Journal of Dialogue and Culture*, Vol. 2, Article 8, htpps//docs.lib.purdue.edu/claritas/vol2/
-------------------------- et al, *O Principio Esquesido/1*Sao Paulo, Cidade Nova, 2008. This is the Spanish translation of *Il Principio Dimenticado* (2007),
Balakian, Peter, *The Burning Tigris: The Armenian Genocide and America's Response.* New York, Harper, 2004.
Barlow, Joel "Hasty Pudding: A Poem in Three Cantos," http://www.poemhunter.com/poem/the-hasty-pudding/Barlow
Bates, Katherine Lee, "America the Beautiful" *Wikipedia. https://en.wikipedia.org/wiki/Katharine_Lee_Bates*
Bellah, Robert et al., *Habits of the Heart: Individualism and Commitment in American Life.* New York, Harper and Row,

1986.

Berg, A. Scott, *Wilson.* New York, Berkley Books, 2014.

Blake William, W. H. Stevenson, ed., *The Poems of William Blake* London. Longman, 1910.

Boas, George, *Vox Populi: Essays in the History of an Idea.* Baltimore, Johns Hopkins Press, 1969.

Buber, Martin *Between Man and Man. T*rans. Ronald Gregor-Smith. New York, Rutledge, 2002.

Burke, Edmund, *Reflections on The French Revolution,* www.constiotution.org/eb.rev_fran.htm,

Canetti, Elias, *Crowds and Power*, trans. Carol Stewart. New York, Continuum. 1981.

Carnegie, Andrew, *The Gospel of Wealth.* carnegie.org/fileadmin/Media/Publicaitons/PDG/THEGOSPE L_OF_WEALTH_01.pdf.

Chronicle of Philanthropy, The

Cooper, Anthony Ashley, Third Earl of Shaftesbury, *Characteristics of Men, Manners, Opinions, Times.* Indianapolis, Bobbs-Merrill, 1964.

Curley, Thomas, *Samuel Johnson, the Ossian Fraud, and the Celtic Revival in Great Britain and Ireland* Cambridge and New York: Cambridge U. Press, 2009.

DeQuincey, Thomas, *Confessions of an Opium-Eater,* Ed.Ernest Rhys. London, Everyman's Library, 1907.

DeTocqueville, Alexis, *Democracy in America.* Trans. Henry reeves. New York, Barnes and Noble, 2003.

Drago, Edmund Lee. *Initiative, Paternalism, and Race Relations: Charleston's Avery Normal Institute.* Athens, U. of Georgia Press. 1960.

Drucker, Peter, "The Third Sector: America's Non-Market Counter-Culture." *The Social Contract.* http://www.thesocialcontract.com/artman2/publish/tsc0102/art icle_16.shtml.

----------------, *Managing the Non-Profit Sector: Principles and Practices*. New York, Harper, 1995.

DuBois, W.E.B., "Reconstruction and its Benefits," *American Historical Review*, Vol. 15, July 1910, pp. 781-99.

Eliot, T.S. "The Wasteland", in *The Complete Poems and Plays of T.S. Eliot, 1909-1950*. New York, Harcourt, Brace, and World, 1962.

Engels, Fredrick , *Socialism: Utopian and Scientific* (1880) . Reprinted in www.marxists.org/archive/marx/works/download/Engels_Soc ialism_Utopian_and_Scientific.pdf

Erikson, Erik, *Childhood and Society*. New York, WW. Norton, 1963.

Faulkner, William, "Nobel Banquet Address" www.nobelprizes.org/nobel_prizes/literature/laureate/1949/fa ulkner-speech

Fielden, Jay, "Philanthropy Issue," *Town and Country*. New York, Hearst Magazines, May 2015.

Foner, Eric, *Reconstruction: America's Unfinished Revolution 1863-1877*. New York, Harper & Row, 1988.

Francis I, "Apostolic Exhortation," 2013 Easter Sermon, reprinted in in *C21 Resources*, Fall 2014, p. 6.

Fremont, John C., *Memoirs of My Life*. New York, Copper Square Press, 2001.

Friedman, Lawrence J. and McGarvie, Mark D., eds. *Charity, Philanthropy and Civility in American History*. Cambridge, U.K., Cambridge University Press, 2004.

Fussell, Paul, *The Great War and Modern Memory*. Oxford University Press, 1975.

Goodwin, Doris Kearns, *No Ordinary Time: Franklin and Eleanor Roosevelt: The Home Front in World War II*. New York, Simon & Shuster, 1994.

Gray, Glenn, *The Warriors: Reflections on Men in Battle*.New York , Harper and Row Torchbook, 1970.

Hammack, David C., ed., *Making the Nonprofit Sector in the*

United States: A Reader. Bloomington, Indiana University Press, 1998.

Hill, Melvin A. ed., *Hannah Arendt: The Recovery of the Public World.* New York, St. Martin's Press, 1979.

Hill, Melvin, ed., *Hannah Arendt: The Recovery of the Public World.* New York ,St. Martin's Press, 1979.

Hoffer, Eric, *The True Believer.* New York, Harper and Row, 1966.

--------------, *The Ordeal of Change.* New York, Harper and Row, 1967.

Holmes. O.W. *Over the Teacups.* Cambridge, Mass., Riverside Press, 1891.

Holmes. O.W., *The Autocrat of the Breakfast Table.* Cambridge, Mass., Riverside Press, 1891.

Hutcheson, Frances *Francis Hutcheson: An Inquiry Concerning Beauty, Order, Harmony, Design.* Ed Peter Kirby. The Hague, 1973.

Isaacson, Walter, *Benjamin Franklin: An American Life.* New York, Simon & Shuster 2003.

Isaiah, "The Book of Isaiah," in *The New American Bible.* World Publishing, 1969.

Ischay, Micheline, *The History of Human Rights: From Ancient Times to the Globalization Era.* Berkeley, University of California Press, 2004.

Israel, Jonathan, *Revolutionary Ideas: An Intellectual History of the French Revolution from The Rights of Man to Robespierre.* Oxford and Princeton. Princeton U. Press, 2014.

John, "The Gospel According to John," *The New American Bible.* World Publishing, 1957.

Kekes, John, *The Enlargement of Life: Moral Imagination at Work.* Ithaca, Cornell U. Press 2010.

Layton, Daphne Niobe, *Philanthropy and Voluntarism: An Annotated Bibliography.* New York, The Foundation Center, 1987.

Locke, John, *Two Treatises of Government and A Letter Concerning Toleration*. New Haven, Yale University Press, 2003.

Longfellow, Henry Wadsworth. "Evangeline," "The Courtship of Miles Standish," "The Hanging of the Crane," in www.hwlongfellow.org/poems (*A Searchable Database of Longfellow Poems*, the Maine Historical Society).

Loomis, Carol, "The $600 Billion Challenge," *Fortune* (16 June 2010).

Lowell, James Russell, *Project Gutenberg's Poems of James Russell Lowell*. www.gutenberg.org/files/38520.

Lukacs, John, *Budapest 1900: A Historical Portrait of a City and its Culture*. New York, Grove Press, 1988.

Luke, "The Acts of the Apostles" in *The New American Bible*. World Publishing, 1969.

MacMillan, Margaret, *Paris 1919: Six Months that Changed the World*. New York, Random House, 2003.

Mardones, Roderigo, "Fraternity in Politics: New Scholarship and Publications from Latin America," *Claritas, Journal of Tradition and Culture*, Vol 1 No. 2, p.201 at htpps//docs.lib.purdue.edu/claritas/vol 1/iss2/8/.

McCulloch, Howard, *Embodiments of Mind*. Cambridge, Ma. MIT Press, 1965.

McWilliams, Wilson Carey, *The Idea of Fraternity in America*. Berkeley, University of California Press, 1973.

Nasaw, David, *Andrew Carnegie*. New York, Penguin Books, 2007.

Okrent, David, *Last Call: The Rise and Fall of Prohibition*. New York,Scribner's, 2011.

Orlinsky, Harry M., *Ancient Israel*, second edition. Ithaca, New York, Cornell University Press, 1985.

Ortega y Gasset, Jose, *The Revolt of the Masse*. New York, W.W. Norton, 1957.

Pabst, Adrian "Liberty, Equality and Fraternity? On the

Legacy and Enduring Significance of the French Revolution." *The Rhodes Forum* 2/26/15. http://wpfdc.org/liberty-equality-and-fraternity-on-the-legacy-and-enduring-significance-of-the-french-revolution.

Packer, George, "The Other France: Are the Suburbs of Paris Incubators of Terrorism?" *The New Yorker*, August 31, 2015, p. 69.

Pelikan, Jaroslav "The Vindication of Tradition: The 1983 Jefferson Lecture on the Humanities."

Plato, "The Symposium," trans. Benjamin Jowett, in Tom Crawford, ed., *Plato: Six Great Dialogues* Mineola, N.Y., Dover Publications, 1957.

Pound, Ezra, "E.P. Ode Pour L'Election De Son Sepulchre" www.poetryfoundaiton.org/poem/44915.

Riesman, David and Nathan Glazer and Reuel Denny. *The Lonely Crowd: A Study of the Changing American Character. Revised edition. New Have, Yale University press, 2001.*

Rochon, Thomas, *Culture Moves: Ideas, Activism, and Changing Values*. Princeton, Princeton University Press, 1998.

Rousseau, Jean-Jacques, *The Social Contract and Discourses*. New York, Dutton, 1950.

Schiller, Friedrich, *On the Aesthetic Education of Man: A Series of Letter*. Trans. Reginald Snell. New York, Frederick Ungar, 1965.

Scott, Walter, "The Lay of the Last Minstrel," www.poets.org/lay-last-minstrel

Scott, William Robert, *Francis Hutcheson: his life, teaching and position in the history of philosophy*. Cambridge, University Press, 1900.

Shama, Simon, *Citizens: A Chronicle of the French Revolution*. New York, Alfred A. Knopf, 1989.

Sherman, William Tecumseh, *Memoirs*. New York, Barnes and Noble, 2005.

Simpson, Louis, "Walt Whitman on Bear Mountain"
/www.poetryfoundation.org/poem/240772
Smith, Adam, *The Theory of Moral Sentiments,*
http:/quad.lib.umich.edu/e/ecco.
Smith, T.V. and Lindemann, E.C., *The Democratic Way of Life: An American Interpretation.* New York, New American Library, 1951.
Surowiecki, James. "In Defense of Philanthrocapitalism, *The New Yorker*, Dec 21 & 28, 2015, p. 40.
Tackett, Timothy, *The Coming of the Terror in the French Revolution.* Cambridge. Mass. and London, Harvard U. Press 2015.
Tierney-Hynes, Rebecca, "Shaftesbury's *Soliloquy*: Authorship and the Psychology of Romance," *Eighteenth Century Studie*s Vol. 38, No. 4 (Spring 2005), p. 605-622.
Trachtenberg, Alan, *Shades of Hiawatha: Staging Indians, Making Americans 1880-1930.* New York, Hill and Wang, 2005.
Trachtenburg, Alan, *The Shades of Hiawatha: Staging Indians, Making Americans.* New York, Hill and Wang, 2004.
Twain, Mark (pseud.) "The Man Who Corrupted Hadleyburg" in *Mark Twain: The Complete Short Stories.* New York, Alfred A. Knopf, 2012.
Van Til, Jon, *Growing Civil Society: From Non-Profit Sector to Third Space.* Bloomington, Indiana U.Press, 2008.
Whitman, Walt, *Leaves of Grass.* New York, Collector's Library Edition, 2004.
Whittier, John Greenleaf, *Poems of Whittier.*
http://www.poemhunter.com/john-greenleaf-whittier/poems/
Wilson, Woodrow, *Division and Re-union.*
ttps://archive.org/details/divisionandreun00wilsgoog.
Woodruff, Nan Elizabeth, *As Rare as Rain: Federal Relief in the Great Southern Drought of 1930-31.* Urbana and Chicago,

University of Illinois Press, 1985.
Wordsworth, William, The Poetical Works of Wordsworth. Ed. Thomas Hutchinson. Revised E. De Selincourt .London, Oxford University Press, 1964.
Yeats, William Butler *The Collected Poems of W.B. Yeats. New York,* (Macmillan, 1956.

Made in the USA
Columbia, SC
21 September 2019